# Applied Deep Learning with Python

Use scikit-learn, TensorFlow, and Keras to create intelligent
systems and machine learning solutions

**Alex Galea**
**Luis Capelo**

BIRMINGHAM - MUMBAI

# Applied Deep Learning with Python

Acquisitions Editors:  Aditya Date, Koushik Sen
Content Development Editors: Tanmayee Patil, Rina Yadav
Production Coordinator: Ratan Pote


First published: August 2018

Production reference: 2260719

Published by Packt Publishing Ltd.
Livery Place
35 Livery Street
Birmingham
B3 2PB, UK.


ISBN 978-1-78980-474-4

www.packtpub.com

`mapt.io`

Mapt is an online digital library that gives you full access to over 5,000 books and videos, as well as industry leading tools to help you plan your personal development and advance your career. For more information, please visit our website.

# Why subscribe?

- Spend less time learning and more time coding with practical eBooks and Videos from over 4,000 industry professionals

- Improve your learning with Skill Plans built especially for you

- Get a free eBook or video every month

- Mapt is fully searchable

- Copy and paste, print, and bookmark content

# Packt.com

Did you know that Packt offers eBook versions of every book published, with PDF and ePub files available? You can upgrade to the eBook version at `www.Packt.com` and as a print book customer, you are entitled to a discount on the eBook copy. Get in touch with us at `service@packt.com` for more details.

At `www.PacktPub.com`, you can also read a collection of free technical articles, sign up for a range of free newsletters, and receive exclusive discounts and offers on Packt books and eBooks.

# Contributors

## About the authors

**Alex Galea** has been professionally practicing data analytics since graduating with a Master's degree in Physics from the University of Guelph, Canada. He developed a keen interest in Python while researching quantum gases as part of his graduate studies. Alex is currently doing web data analytics, where Python continues to play a key role in his work. He is a frequent blogger about data-centric projects that involve Python and Jupyter Notebooks.

**Luis Capelo** is a Harvard-trained analyst and programmer who specializes in the design and development of data science products. He is based in the great New York City, USA.

He is the head of the Data Products team at Forbes, where they both investigate new techniques for optimizing article performance and create clever bots that help them distribute their content. Previously, he led a team of world-class scientists at the Flowminder Foundation, where we developed predictive models for assisting the humanitarian community. Prior to that, he worked for the United Nations as part of the Humanitarian Data Exchange team (founders of the Center for Humanitarian Data).

He is a native of Havana, Cuba, and the founder and owner of a small consultancy firm dedicated to supporting the nascent Cuban private sector.

# About the reviewers

**Elie Kawerk** likes to solve problems using the analytical skills he has accumulated over the years. He uses the data science process, including statistical methods and machine learning, to extract insights from data and get value out of it.

His formal training is in computational physics. He used to simulate atomic and molecular physics phenomena with the help of supercomputers using the good old FORTRAN language; this involved a lot of linear algebra and quantum physics equations.

**Manoj Pandey** is a Python programmer and the founder and organizer of PyData Delhi. He works on research and development from time to time, and is currently working with RaRe Technologies on their incubator program for a computational linear algebra project. Prior to this, he has worked with Indian startups and small design/development agencies, and teaches Python/JavaScript to many on Codementor.

# Packt is searching for authors like you

If you're interested in becoming an author for Packt, please visit `authors.packtpub.com` and apply today. We have worked with thousands of developers and tech professionals, just like you, to help them share their insight with the global tech community. You can make a general application, apply for a specific hot topic that we are recruiting an author for, or submit your own idea.

# Table of Contents

# Preface

This Learning Path takes a step-by-step approach to teach you how to get started with data science, machine learning, and deep learning. Each module is designed to build on the learning of the previous chapter. The book contains multiple demos that use real-life business scenarios for you to practice and apply your new skills in a highly relevant context.

In the first part of this Learning Path, you will learn entry-level data science. You'll learn about commonly used libraries that are part of the Anaconda distribution, and then explore machine learning models with real datasets to give you the skills and exposure you need for the real world.

In the second part, you'll be introduced to neural networks and deep learning. You will then learn how to train, evaluate, and deploy Tensorflow and Keras models as real-world web applications. By the time you are done reading, you will have the knowledge to build applications in the deep learning environment and create elaborate data visualizations and predictions.

## Who this book is for

If you're a Python programmer stepping out into the world of data science, this is the right-way to get started. It is also ideal for experienced developers, analysts, or data scientists, who want to work with TensorFlow and Keras. We assume that you are familiar with Python, web application development, Docker commands, and concepts of linear algebra, probability, and statistics.

# What this book covers

*Chapter 1, Jupyter Fundamentals,* covers the fundamentals of data analysis in Jupyter. We will start with usage instructions and features of Jupyter such as magic functions and tab completion. We will then transition to data science specific material. We will run an exploratory analysis in a live Jupyter Notebook. We will use visual assists such as scatter plots, histograms, and violin plots to deepen our understanding of the data. We will also perform simple predictive modeling.,

*Chapter 2, Data Cleaning and Advanced Machine Learning,* shows how predictive models can be trained in Jupyter Notebooks. We will talk about how to plan a machine learning strategy. This chapter also explains the machine learning terminology such as supervised learning, unsupervised learning, classification, and regression. We will discuss methods for preprocessing data using scikit-learn and pandas.,

*Chapter 3, Web Scraping and Interactive Visualizations,* explains how to scrap web page tables and then use interactive visualizations to study the data. We will start by looking at how HTTP requests work, focusing on GET requests and their response status codes. Then, we will go into the Jupyter Notebook and make HTTP requests with Python using the Requests library. We will see how Jupyter can be used to render HTML in the notebook, along with actual web pages that can be interacted with. After making requests, we will see how Beautiful Soup can be used to parse text from the HTML, and used this library to scrape tabular data.

*Chapter 4, Introduction to Neural Networks and Deep Learning,* helps you set up and configure deep learning environment and start looking at individual models and case studies. It also discusses neural networks and its idea along with their origins and explores their power.

*Chapter 5, Model Architecture,* shows how to predict Bitcoin prices using deep learning model.

*Chapter 6, Model Evaluation and Optimization,* shows how to evaluate a neural network model. We will modify the network's hyper parameters to improve its performance.

*Chapter 7, Productization,* explains how to create a working application from a deep learning model. We will deploy our Bitcoin prediction model as an application that is capable of handling new data by creating a new models.

# To get the most out of this book

This book will be most applicable to professionals and students interested in data analysis and want to enhance their knowledge in the field of developing applications using TensorFlow and Keras. For the best experience, you should have knowledge of programming fundamentals and some experience with Python. In particular, having some familiarity with Python libraries such as Pandas, matplotlib, and scikit-learn will be useful.

# Download the example code files

You can download the example code files for this book from your account at www.packtpub.com. If you purchased this book elsewhere, you can visit www.packtpub.com/support and register to have the files emailed directly to you.

You can download the code files by following these steps:

1. Log in or register at www.packtpub.com.
2. Select the **SUPPORT** tab.
3. Click on **Code Downloads & Errata**.
4. Enter the name of the book in the **Search** box and follow the onscreen instructions.

Once the file is downloaded, please make sure that you unzip or extract the folder using the latest version of:

- WinRAR/7-Zip for Windows
- Zipeg/iZip/UnRarX for Mac
- 7-Zip/PeaZip for Linux

The code bundle for the book is also hosted on GitHub at https://github.com/TrainingByPackt/Applied-Deep-Learning-with-Python. In case there's an update to the code, it will be updated on the existing GitHub repository.

We also have other code bundles from our rich catalog of books and videos available at https://github.com/TrainingByPackt/Applied-Deep-Learning-with-Python. Check them out!

# Conventions used

There are a number of text conventions used throughout this book.

`CodeInText`: Indicates code words in text, database table names, folder names, filenames, file extensions, pathnames, dummy URLs, user input, and Twitter handles. Here is an example: "We can see the `NotebookApp` being run on a local server."

A block of code is set as follows:

```
fig, ax = plt.subplots(1, 2)
sns.regplot('RM', 'MEDV', df, ax=ax[0],
scatter_kws={'alpha': 0.4}))
sns.regplot('LSTAT', 'MEDV', df, ax=ax[1],
scatter_kws={'alpha': 0.4}))
```

When we wish to draw your attention to a particular part of a code block, the relevant lines or items are set in bold:

```
cat chapter-1/requirements.txt
matplotlib==2.0.2
numpy==1.13.1
pandas==0.20.3
requests==2.18.4
```

Any command-line input or output is written as follows:

```
pip install version_information
pip install ipython-sql
```

**Bold**: Indicates a new term, an important word, or words that you see onscreen. For example, words in menus or dialog boxes appear in the text like this. Here is an example: "Notice how the **white dress** price was used to pad the **missing values**."

 Warnings or important notes appear like this.

 Tips and tricks appear like this.

# Get in touch

Feedback from our readers is always welcome.

**General feedback**: Email feedback@packtpub.com and mention the book title in the subject of your message. If you have questions about any aspect of this book, please email us at questions@packtpub.com.

**Errata**: Although we have taken every care to ensure the accuracy of our content, mistakes do happen. If you have found a mistake in this book, we would be grateful if you would report this to us. Please visit www.packtpub.com/submit-errata, selecting your book, clicking on the Errata Submission Form link, and entering the details.

**Piracy**: If you come across any illegal copies of our works in any form on the Internet, we would be grateful if you would provide us with the location address or website name. Please contact us at copyright@packtpub.com with a link to the material.

**If you are interested in becoming an author**: If there is a topic that you have expertise in and you are interested in either writing or contributing to a book, please visit authors.packtpub.com.

# Reviews

Please leave a review. Once you have read and used this book, why not leave a review on the site that you purchased it from? Potential readers can then see and use your unbiased opinion to make purchase decisions, we at Packt can understand what you think about our products, and our authors can see your feedback on their book. Thank you!

For more information about Packt, please visit packtpub.com.

# 1
# Jupyter Fundamentals

Jupyter Notebooks are one of the most important tools for data scientists using Python. This is because they're an ideal environment for developing reproducible data analysis pipelines. Data can be loaded, transformed, and modeled all inside a single Notebook, where it's quick and easy to test out code and explore ideas along the way. Furthermore, all of this can be documented "**inline**" using formatted text, so you can make notes for yourself or even produce a structured report. Other comparable platforms - for example, RStudio or Spyder - present the user with multiple windows, which promote arduous tasks such as copy and pasting code around and rerunning code that has already been executed. These tools also tend to involve **Read Eval Prompt Loops (REPLs)** where code is run in a terminal session that has saved memory. This type of development environment is bad for reproducibility and not ideal for development either. Jupyter Notebooks solve all these issues by giving the user a single window where code snippets are executed and outputs are displayed inline. This lets users develop code efficiently and allows them to look back at previous work for reference, or even to make alterations.

We'll start the chapter by explaining exactly what Jupyter Notebooks are and continue to discuss why they are so popular among data scientists. Then, we'll open a Notebook together and go through some exercises to learn how the platform is used. Finally, we'll dive into our first analysis and perform an exploratory analysis in the section *Basic Functionality and Features*.

By the end of this chapter, you will be able to:

- Learn what a Jupyter Notebook is and why it's useful for data analysis
- Use Jupyter Notebook features
- Study Python data science libraries
- Perform simple exploratory data analysis

 All the codes from this book are available as chapter-specific IPython notebooks in the code bundle. All color plots from this book are also available in the code bundle.

# Basic Functionality and Features

In this section, we first demonstrate the usefulness of Jupyter Notebooks with examples and through discussion. Then, in order to cover the fundamentals of Jupyter Notebooks for beginners, we'll see the basic usage of them in terms of launching and interacting with the platform. For those who have used Jupyter Notebooks before, this will be mostly a review; however, you will certainly see new things in this topic as well.

## What is a Jupyter Notebook and Why is it Useful?

Jupyter Notebooks are locally run web applications which contain live code, equations, figures, interactive apps, and Markdown text. The standard language is Python, and that's what we'll be using for this book; however, note that a variety of alternatives are supported. This includes the other dominant data science language, R:

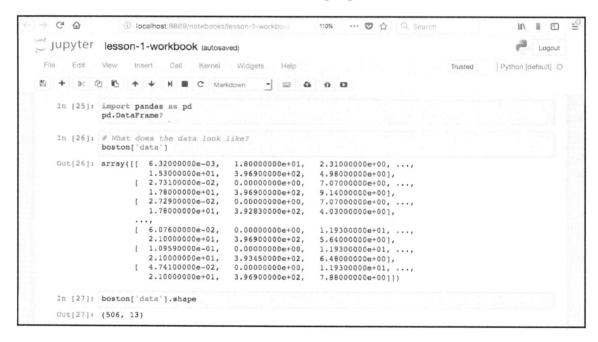

Those familiar with R will know about R Markdown. Markdown documents allow for Markdown-formatted text to be combined with executable code. Markdown is a simple language used for styling text on the web. For example, most GitHub repositories have a README.md Markdown file. This format is useful for basic text formatting. It's comparable to HTML but allows for much less customization.

Commonly used symbols in Markdown include hashes (#) to make text into a heading, square and round brackets to insert hyperlinks, and stars to create italicized or bold text:

```
# Markdown!

This is a basic [Markdown]
(https://en.wikipedia.org/wiki/Markdown) document.

### Sub heading

It's *simple*, but **powerful**.
```

# Markdown!

This is a basic Markdown document.

## Sub heading

It's *simple*, but **powerful**.

Having seen the basics of Markdown, let's come back to R Markdown, where Markdown text can be written alongside executable code. Jupyter Notebooks offer the equivalent functionality for Python, although, as we'll see, they function quite differently than R Markdown documents. For example, R Markdown assumes you are writing Markdown unless otherwise specified, whereas Jupyter Notebooks assume you are inputting code. This makes it more appealing to use Jupyter Notebooks for rapid development and testing.

From a data science perspective, there are two primary types for a Jupyter Notebook depending on how they are used: lab-style and deliverable.

Lab-style Notebooks are meant to serve as the programming analog of research journals. These should contain all the work you've done to load, process, analyze, and model the data. The idea here is to document everything you've done for future reference, so it's usually not advisable to delete or alter previous lab-style Notebooks. It's also a good idea to accumulate multiple date-stamped versions of the Notebook as you progress through the analysis, in case you want to look back at previous states.

Deliverable Notebooks are intended to be presentable and should contain only select parts of the lab-style Notebooks. For example, this could be an interesting discovery to share with your colleagues, an in-depth report of your analysis for a manager, or a summary of the key findings for stakeholders.

In either case, an important concept is reproducibility. If you've been diligent in documenting your software versions, anyone receiving the reports will be able to rerun the Notebook and compute the same results as you did. In the scientific community, where reproducibility is becoming increasingly difficult, this is a breath of fresh air.

# Navigating the Platform

Now, we are going to open up a Jupyter Notebook and start to learn the interface. Here, we will assume you have no prior knowledge of the platform and go over the basic usage.

## Introducing Jupyter Notebooks

1. Navigate to the companion material directory in the terminal.

 On Unix machines such as Mac or Linux, command-line navigation can be done using ls to display directory contents and cd to change directories. On Windows machines, use dir to display directory contents and use cd to change directories instead. If, for example, you want to change the drive from C: to D:, you should execute d: to change drives.

2. Start a new local Notebook server here by typing the following into the terminal: jupyter notebook.
   A new window or tab of your default browser will open the Notebook Dashboard to the working directory. Here, you will see a list of folders and files contained therein.

3. Click on a folder to navigate to that particular path and open a file by clicking on it. Although its main use is editing IPYNB Notebook files, Jupyter functions as a standard text editor as well.

4. Reopen the terminal window used to launch the app. We can see the NotebookApp being run on a local server. In particular, you should see a line like this:

```
[I 20:03:01.045 NotebookApp] The Jupyter Notebook is running
at:
http:// localhost:8888/?token=e915bb06866f19ce462d959a9193a94c7
c088e81765f9d8a
```

Going to that HTTP address will load the app in your browser window, as was done automatically when starting the app. Closing the window does not stop the app; this should be done from the terminal by typing *Ctrl + C*.

5. Close the app by typing *Ctrl + C* in the terminal. You may also have to confirm by entering y. Close the web browser window as well.

6. When loading the NotebookApp, there are various options available to you. In the terminal, see the list of available options by running the following:
   jupyter notebook --help.

---

7. One such option is to specify a specific port. Open a NotebookApp at `local port 9000` by running the following:
```
jupyter notebook --port 9000
```

8. The primary way to create a new Jupyter Notebook is from the Jupyter Dashboard. Click **New** in the upper-right corner and select a kernel from the drop-down menu (that is, select something in the Notebooks section):

Kernels provide programming language support for the Notebook. If you have installed Python with Anaconda, that version should be the default kernel. Conda virtual environments will also be available here.

Virtual environments are a great tool for managing multiple projects on the same machine. Each virtual environment may contain a different version of Python and external libraries. Python has built-in virtual environments; however, the Conda virtual environment integrates better with Jupyter Notebooks and boasts other nice features. The documentation is available at `https://conda.io/docs/user-guide/tasks/manage-environments.html`.

9. With the newly created blank Notebook, click on the top cell and type `print('hello world')`, or any other code snippet that writes to the screen. Execute it by clicking on the cell and pressing *Shift + Enter*, or by selecting **Run Cell** in the **Cell menu**.

Any `stdout` or `stderr` output from the code will be displayed beneath as the cell runs. Furthermore, the string representation of the object written in the final line will be displayed as well. This is very handy, especially for displaying tables, but sometimes we don't want the final object to be displayed. In such cases, a semicolon (; ) can be added to the end of the line to suppress the display.

New cells expect and run code input by default; however, they can be changed to render Markdown instead.

10. Click into an empty cell and change it to accept Markdown-formatted text. This can be done from the drop-down menu icon in the toolbar or by selecting **Markdown** from the **Cell** menu. Write some text in here (any text will do), making sure to utilize Markdown formatting symbols such as #.

11. Focus on the toolbar at the top of the Notebook:

There is a Play icon in the toolbar, which can be used to run cells. As we'll see later, however, it's handier to use the keyboard shortcut *Shift + Enter* to run cells. Right next to this is a Stop icon, which can be used to stop cells from running. This is useful, for example, if a cell is taking too long to run:

New cells can be manually added from the Insert menu:

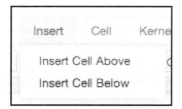

Cells can be copied, pasted, and deleted using icons or by selecting options from the Edit menu:

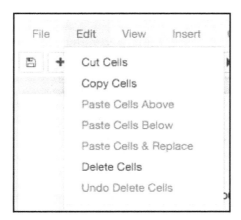

Cells can also be moved up and down this way:

There are useful options under the Cell menu to run a group of cells or the entire Notebook:

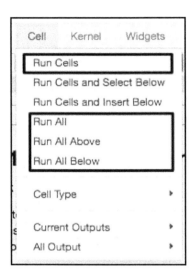

12. Experiment with the toolbar options to move cells up and down, insert new cells, and delete cells.

    An important thing to understand about these Notebooks is the shared memory between cells. It's quite simple: every cell existing on the sheet has access to the global set of variables. So, for example, a function defined in one cell could be called from any other, and the same applies to variables. As one would expect, anything within the scope of a function will not be a global variable and can only be accessed from within that specific function.

13. Open the Kernel menu to see the selections. The Kernel menu is useful for stopping script executions and restarting the Notebook if the kernel dies. Kernels can also be swapped here at any time, but it is unadvisable to use multiple kernels for a single Notebook due to reproducibility concerns.

14. Open the **File** menu to see the selections. The **File** menu contains options for downloading the Notebook in various formats. In particular, it's recommended to save an HTML version of your Notebook, where the content is rendered statically and can be opened and viewed "as you would expect" in web browsers.

    The Notebook name will be displayed in the upper-left corner. New Notebooks will automatically be named **Untitled**.

15. Change the name of your IPYNB `Notebook` file by clicking on the current name in the upper-left corner and typing the new name. Then, save the file.

16. Close the current tab in your web browser (exiting the Notebook) and go to the Jupyter Dashboard tab, which should still be open. (If it's not open, then reload it by copy and pasting the HTTP link from the terminal.)

    Since we didn't shut down the Notebook, we just saved and exited, it will have a green book symbol next to its name in the Files section of the Jupyter Dashboard and will be listed as Running on the right side next to the last modified date. Notebooks can be shut down from here.

17. Quit the Notebook you have been working on by selecting it (checkbox to the left of the name) and clicking the orange Shutdown button:

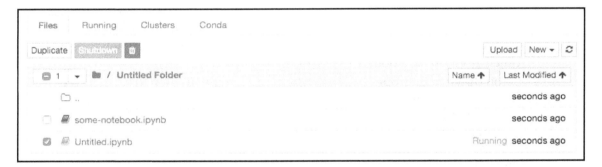

 If you plan to spend a lot of time working with Jupyter Notebooks, it's worthwhile to learn the keyboard shortcuts. This will speed up your workflow considerably. Particularly useful commands to learn are the shortcuts for manually adding new cells and converting cells from code to Markdown formatting. Click on **Keyboard Shortcuts** from the **Help menu** to see how.

# Jupyter Features

Jupyter has many appealing features that make for efficient Python programming. These include an assortment of things, from methods for viewing docstrings to executing Bash commands. Let's explore some of these features together in this section.

 The official IPython documentation can be found here: `http://ipython.readthedocs.io/en/stable/`. It has details on the features we will discuss here and others.

## Exploring some of Jupyter's most useful features

1. From the Jupyter Dashboard, navigate to the `chapter-1` directory and open the `chapter-1-workbook.ipynb` file by selecting it. The standard file extension for Jupyter Notebooks is `.ipynb`, which was introduced back when they were called IPython Notebooks.

2. Scroll down to Subtopic `Jupyter Features` in the Jupyter Notebook. We start by reviewing the basic keyboard shortcuts. These are especially helpful to avoid having to use the mouse so often, which will greatly speed up the workflow. Here are the most useful keyboard shortcuts. Learning to use these will greatly improve your experience with Jupyter Notebooks as well as your own efficiency:
   - *Shift + Enter* is used to run a cell
   - The *Esc key* is used to leave a cell
   - The *M* key is used to change a cell to Markdown (after pressing Esc)
   - The *Y* key is used to change a cell to code (after pressing Esc)
   - *Arrow keys* move cells (after pressing Esc)
   - The *Enter key* is used to enter a cell

Moving on from shortcuts, the help option is useful for beginners and experienced coders alike. It can help provide guidance at each uncertain step.

Users can get help by adding a question mark to the end of any object and running the cell. Jupyter finds the docstring for that object and returns it in a pop-out window at the bottom of the app.

3. Run the **Getting Help** section cells and check out how Jupyter displays the docstrings at the bottom of the Notebook. Add a cell in this section and get help on the object of your choice:

```
Getting Help

    • add question mark to end of object


In [3]:  # Get the numpy arange docstring
         import numpy as np
         np.arange?


Docstring:
arange([start,] stop[, step,], dtype=None)

Return evenly spaced values within a given interval.

Values are generated within the half-open interval ``[start, stop)``
(in other words, the interval including `start` but excluding `stop`).
For integer arguments the function is equivalent to the Python built-in
`range <http://docs.python.org/lib/built-in-funcs.html>`_ function,
but returns an ndarray rather than a list.
```

Tab completion can be used to do the following:

- List available modules when importing external libraries
- List available modules of imported external libraries
- Function and variable completion

This can be especially useful when you need to know the available input arguments for a module, when exploring a new library, to discover new modules, or simply to speed up workflow. They will save time writing out variable names or functions and reduce bugs from typos. The tab completion works so well that you may have difficulty coding Python in other editors after today!

4. Click into an empty code cell in the Tab Completion section and try using tab completion in the ways suggested immediately above. For example, the first suggestion can be done by typing import (including the space after) and then pressing the Tab key:

> **Tab Completion**
>
> Example of Jupyter tab completion include:
>
> - listing available modules on import
>   ```
>   import <tab>
>   from numpy import <tab>
>   ```
> - listing available modules after import
>   ```
>   np.<tab>
>   ```

5. Last but not least of the basic Jupyter Notebook features are **magic** commands. These consist of one or two percent signs followed by the command. Magics starting with %% will apply to the entire cell, and magics starting with % will only apply to that line. This will make sense when seen in an example.

Scroll to the **Jupyter Magic Functions** section and run the cells containing %lsmagic and %matplotlib inline:

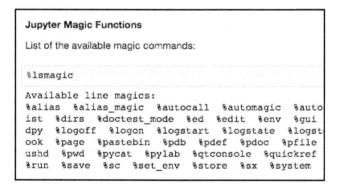

%lsmagic lists the available options. We will discuss and show examples of some of the most useful ones. The most common magic command you will probably see is %matplotlib inline, which allows matplotlib figures to be displayed in the Notebook without having to explicitly use plt.show().

The timing functions are very handy and come in two varieties: a standard timer (`%time` or `%%time`) and a timer that measures the average runtime of many iterations (`%timeit` and `%%timeit`).

6. Run the cells in the Timers section. Note the difference between using one and two percent signs.

   Even by using a Python kernel (as you are currently doing), other languages can be invoked using magic commands. The built-in options include JavaScript, R, Pearl, Ruby, and Bash. Bash is particularly useful, as you can use Unix commands to find out where you are currently (`pwd`), what's in the directory (`ls`), make new folders (`mkdir`), and write file contents (`cat / head / tail`).

7. Run the first cell in the **Using bash in the notebook section**. This cell writes some text to a file in the working directory, prints the directory contents, prints an empty line, and then writes back the contents of the newly created file before removing it:

```
Using bash in the notebook

In [9]:   %%bash

          echo "using bash from inside Jupyter!" > test-file.txt
          ls
          echo ""
          cat test-file.txt
          rm test-file.txt

          Lesson 1
          Lesson 1.docx
          Lesson 1.pptx
          lesson-1-workbook.html
          lesson-1-workbook.ipynb
          test-file.txt
          ~$sson 1.docx

          using bash from inside Jupyter!
```

8. Run the following cells containing only `ls` and `pwd`. Note how we did not have to explicitly use the Bash magic command for these to work.

   There are plenty of external magic commands that can be installed. A popular one is `ipython-sql`, which allows for SQL code to be executed in cells.

9. If you've not already done so, install `ipython-sql` now. Open a new terminal window and execute the following code:

```
pip install ipython-sql
```

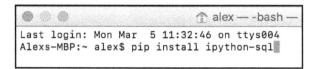

10. Run the `%load_ext sql` cell to load the external command into the Notebook:

```
# Source: https://github.com/catherinedevlin/ipython-sql
# do pip install ipython-sql in the terminal
%load_ext sql
```

This allows for connections to remote databases so that queries can be executed (and thereby documented) right inside the Notebook.

11. Run the cell containing the SQL sample query:

```
%%sql sqlite://

SELECT *
FROM (
    SELECT 'Hello' as msg_1
) A JOIN (
    SELECT 'World!' as msg_2
) B;

Done.

msg_1   msg_2

Hello   World!
```

Here, we first connect to the local sqlite source; however, this line could instead point to a specific database on a local or remote server. Then, we execute a simple SELECT to show how the cell has been converted to run SQL code instead of Python.

12. Moving on to other useful magic functions, we'll briefly discuss one that helps with documentation. The command is `%version_information`, but it does not come as standard with Jupyter. Like the SQL one we just saw, it can be installed from the command line with pip.

    If not already done, install the version documentation tool now from the terminal using `pip`. Open up a new window and run the following code:

    ```
    pip install version_information
    ```

    Once installed, it can then be imported into any Notebook using `%load_ext version_information`. Finally, once loaded, it can be used to display the versions of each piece of software in the Notebook.

13. Run the cell that loads and calls the version_information command:

```
%load_ext version_information
%version_information requests, numpy, pandas, matplotlib, seaborn, sklearn
```

| Software | Version |
|---|---|
| Python | 3.5.4 64bit [GCC 4.2.1 Compatible Clang 4.0.1 (tags/RELEASE_401/final)] |
| IPython | 6.1.0 |
| OS | Darwin 16.5.0 x86_64 i386 64bit |
| requests | 2.18.4 |
| numpy | 1.13.1 |
| pandas | 0.20.3 |
| matplotlib | 2.0.2 |
| seaborn | 0.8.0 |
| sklearn | 0.19.0 |
| Wed Oct 11 19:46:08 2017 PDT | |

# Converting a Jupyter Notebook to a Python Script

You can convert a Jupyter Notebook to a Python script. This is equivalent to copying and pasting the contents of each code cell into a single .py file. The Markdown sections are also included as comments.

The conversion can be done from the NotebookApp or in the command line as follows:

```
jupyter nbconvert --to=python chapter-1-notebook.ipynb
```

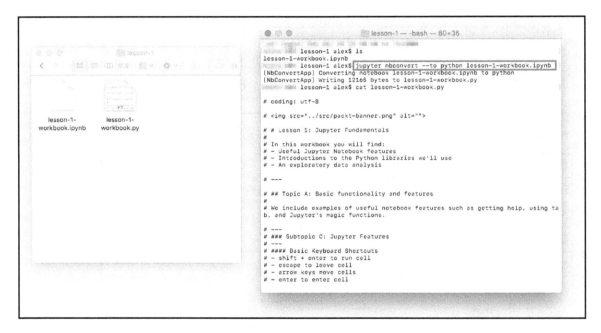

This is useful, for example, when you want to determine the library requirements for a Notebook using a tool such as pipreqs. This tool determines the libraries used in a project and exports them into a requirements.txt file (and it can be installed by running pip install pipreqs).

The command is called from outside the folder containing your `.py` files. For example, if the `.py` files are inside a folder called `chapter-1`, you could do the following:

```
pipreqs chapter-1/
```

The resulting `requirements.txt` file for `chapter-1-workbook.ipynb` looks like this:

```
cat chapter-1/requirements.txt
matplotlib==2.0.2
numpy==1.13.1
pandas==0.20.3
requests==2.18.4
seaborn==0.8
beautifulsoup4==4.6.0
scikit_learn==0.19.0
```

# Python Libraries

Having now seen all the basics of Jupyter Notebooks, and even some more advanced features, we'll shift our attention to the Python libraries we'll be using in this book. Libraries, in general, extend the default set of Python functions. Examples of commonly used standard libraries are `datetime`, `time`, and `os`. These are called standard libraries because they come standard with every installation of Python.

For data science with Python, the most important libraries are external, which means they do not come standard with Python.

The external data science libraries we'll be using in this book are `NumPy`, `Pandas`, `Seaborn`, `matplotlib`, `scikit-learn`, `Requests`, and `Bokeh`. Let's briefly introduce each.

 It's a good idea to import libraries using industry standards, for example, `import numpy as np`; this way, your code is more readable. Try to avoid doing things such as from `numpy import *`, as you may unwittingly overwrite functions. Furthermore, it's often nice to have modules linked to the library via a dot (. ) for code readability.

- **NumPy** offers multi-dimensional data structures (arrays) on which operations can be performed far quicker than standard Python data structures (for example, lists). This is done in part by performing operations in the background using C. NumPy also offers various mathematical and data manipulation functions.

- **Pandas** is Python's answer to the R DataFrame. It stores data in 2-D tabular structures where columns represent different variables and rows correspond to samples. Pandas provides many handy tools for data wrangling such as filling in `NaN` entries and computing statistical descriptions of the data. Working with Pandas DataFrames will be a big focus of this book.

- **Matplotlib** is a plotting tool inspired by the MATLAB platform. Those familiar with R can think of it as Python's version of ggplot. It's the most popular Python library for plotting figures and allows for a high level of customization.

- **Seaborn** works as an extension to matplotlib, where various plotting tools useful for data science are included. Generally speaking, this allows for analysis to be done much faster than if you were to create the same things manually with libraries such as matplotlib and scikit-learn.

- **Scikit-learn** is the most commonly used machine learning library. It offers top-of-the-line algorithms and a very elegant API where models are instantiated and then fit with data. It also provides data processing modules and other tools useful for predictive analytics.

- **Requests** is the go-to library for making HTTP requests. It makes it straightforward to get HTML from web pages and interface with APIs. For parsing the HTML, many choose `BeautifulSoup4`, which we will also cover in this book.
- **Bokeh** is an interactive visualization library. It functions similar to matplotlib, but allows us to add hover, zoom, click, and use other interactive tools to our plots. It also allows us to render and play with the plots inside our Jupyter Notebook.

Having introduced these libraries, let's go back to our Notebook and load them, by running the import statements. This will lead us into our first analysis, where we finally start working with a dataset.

# Import the external libraries and set up the plotting environment

1. Open up the `chapter 1` Jupyter Notebook and scroll to the `Python Libraries section`.

   Just like for regular Python scripts, libraries can be imported into the Notebook at any time. It's best practice to put the majority of the packages you use at the top of the file. Sometimes it makes sense to load things midway through the Notebook and that is completely OK.

2. Run the cells to import the external libraries and set the plotting options:

```
# Common standard libraries

import datetime
import time
import os

# Common external libraries

import pandas as pd
import numpy as np
import sklearn # scikit-learn
import requests
from bs4 import BeautifulSoup
```

For a nice Notebook setup, it's often useful to set various options along with the imports at the top. For example, the following can be run to change the figure's appearance to something more aesthetically pleasing than the `matplotlib` and Seaborn defaults:

```
import matplotlib.pyplot as plt
%matplotlib inline
import seaborn as sns
# See here for more options:
https://matplotlib.org/users/customizing.html
%config InlineBackend.figure_format='retina'
sns.set() # Revert to matplotlib defaults
plt.rcParams['figure.figsize'] = (9, 6)
plt.rcParams['axes.labelpad'] = 10
sns.set_style("darkgrid")
```

So far in this book, we've gone over the basics of using Jupyter Notebooks for data science. We started by exploring the platform and finding our way around the interface. Then, we discussed the most useful features, which include tab completion and magic functions. Finally, we introduced the Python libraries we'll be using in this book.

The next section will be very interactive as we perform our first analysis together using the Jupyter Notebook.

# Our First Analysis - The Boston Housing Dataset

So far, this chapter has focused on the features and basic usage of Jupyter. Now, we'll put this into practice and do some data exploration and analysis.

The dataset we'll look at in this section is the so-called *Boston housing dataset*. It contains US census data concerning houses in various areas around the city of Boston. Each sample corresponds to a unique area and has about a dozen measures. We should think of samples as rows and measures as columns. The data was first published in 1978 and is quite small, containing only about 500 samples.

Now that we know something about the context of the dataset, let's decide on a rough plan for the exploration and analysis. If applicable, this plan would accommodate the relevant question(s) under study. In this case, the goal is not to answer a question but to instead show Jupyter in action and illustrate some basic data analysis methods.

Our general approach to this analysis will be to do the following:

- Load the data into Jupyter using a Pandas DataFrame
- Quantitatively understand the features
- Look for patterns and generate questions
- Answer the questions to the problems

# Loading the Data into Jupyter Using a Pandas DataFrame

Oftentimes, data is stored in tables, which means it can be saved as a `comma-separated variable (CSV)` file. This format, and many others, can be read into Python as a DataFrame object, using the Pandas library. Other common formats include `tab-separated variable (TSV)`, SQL tables, and JSON data structures. Indeed, Pandas has support for all of these. In this example, however, we are not going to load the data this way because the dataset is available directly through scikit-learn.

 An important part after loading data for analysis is ensuring that it's clean. For example, we would generally need to deal with missing data and ensure that all columns have the correct datatypes. The dataset we use in this section has already been cleaned, so we will not need to worry about this. However, we'll see messier data in the second chapter and explore techniques for dealing with it.

## Load the Boston housing dataset

1. In the chapter 1 Jupyter Notebook, scroll to subtopic `Loading the Data into Jupyter Using a Pandas DataFrame` of `Our First Analysis: The Boston Housing Dataset`. The Boston housing dataset can be accessed from the `sklearn.datasets` module using the `load_boston` method.

2. Run the first two cells in this section to load the Boston dataset and see the data structures type:

```
from sklearn import datasets
boston = datasets.load_boston()

type(boston)

sklearn.utils.Bunch
```

The output of the second cell tells us that it's a scikit-learn Bunch object. Let's get some more information about that to understand what we are dealing with.

3. Run the next cell to import the base object from scikit-learn utils and print the docstring in our Notebook:

```
In [4]:  from sklearn.utils import Bunch
         Bunch?

Init signature: Bunch(**kwargs)
Docstring:
Container object for datasets

Dictionary-like object that exposes its keys as attributes.

>>> b = Bunch(a=1, b=2)
>>> b['b']
2
```

Reading the resulting docstring suggests that it's basically a dictionary, and can essentially be treated as such.

4. Print the field names (that is, the keys to the dictionary) by running the next cell. We find these fields to be self-explanatory: ['DESCR', 'target', 'data', 'feature_names'].

5.  Run the next cell to print the dataset description contained in
    `boston['DESCR']`. Note that in this call, we explicitly want to print the field
    value so that the Notebook renders the content in a more readable format than
    the string representation (that is, if we just type boston['DESCR'] without
    wrapping it in a print statement). We then see the dataset information as we've
    previously summarized:

```
Boston House Prices dataset
===========================
Notes
------
Data Set Characteristics:
:Number of Instances: 506
:Number of Attributes: 13 numeric/categorical predictive
:Median Value (attribute 14) is usually the target
:Attribute Information (in order):
- CRIM per capita crime rate by town
...
- MEDV Median value of owner-occupied homes in $1000's
:Missing Attribute Values: None
```

Of particular importance here are the feature descriptions (under
`Attribute Information`). We will use this as reference during our analysis.

Now, we are going to create a Pandas DataFrame that contains the data. This is
beneficial for a few reasons: all of our data will be contained in one object, there
are useful and computationally efficient DataFrame methods we can use, and
other libraries such as Seaborn have tools that integrate nicely with DataFrames.

In this case, we will create our DataFrame with the standard constructor method.

6. Run the cell where Pandas is imported and the docstring is retrieved for `pd.DataFrame`:

```
In [5]:   import pandas as pd
          pd.DataFrame?

Init signature: pd.DataFrame(data=None, index=None, columns=None, dtype=None, copy=False)
Docstring:
Two-dimensional size-mutable, potentially heterogeneous tabular data
structure with labeled axes (rows and columns). Arithmetic operations
align on both row and column labels. Can be thought of as a dict-like
container for Series objects. The primary pandas data structure

Parameters
----------
data : numpy ndarray (structured or homogeneous), dict, or DataFrame
    Dict can contain Series, arrays, constants, or list-like objects
index : Index or array-like
    Index to use for resulting frame. Will default to np.arange(n) if
    no indexing information part of input data and no index provided
columns : Index or array-like
    Column labels to use for resulting frame. Will default to
    np.arange(n) if no column labels are provided
```

The docstring reveals the DataFrame input parameters. We want to feed in boston['data'] for the data and use boston['feature_names'] for the headers.

7. Run the next few cells to print the data, its shape, and the feature names:

```
# What does the data look like?
boston['data']

array([[  6.32000000e-03,   1.80000000e+01,   2.31000000e+00, ...,
          1.53000000e+01,   3.96900000e+02,   4.98000000e+00],
       [  2.73100000e-02,   0.00000000e+00,   7.07000000e+00, ...,
          1.78000000e+01,   3.96900000e+02,   9.14000000e+00],
       [  2.72900000e-02,   0.00000000e+00,   7.07000000e+00, ...,
          1.78000000e+01,   3.92830000e+02,   4.03000000e+00],
       ...,
       [  6.07600000e-02,   0.00000000e+00,   1.19300000e+01, ...,
          2.10000000e+01,   3.96900000e+02,   5.64000000e+00],
       [  1.09590000e-01,   0.00000000e+00,   1.19300000e+01, ...,
          2.10000000e+01,   3.93450000e+02,   6.48000000e+00],
       [  4.74100000e-02,   0.00000000e+00,   1.19300000e+01, ...,
          2.10000000e+01,   3.96900000e+02,   7.88000000e+00]])

boston['data'].shape

(506, 13)

boston['feature_names']

array(['CRIM', 'ZN', 'INDUS', 'CHAS', 'NOX', 'RM', 'AGE', 'DIS', 'RAD',
       'TAX', 'PTRATIO', 'B', 'LSTAT'],
      dtype='<U7')
```

Looking at the output, we see that our data is in a 2D NumPy array. Running the command boston['data'].shape returns the length (number of samples) and the number of features as the first and second outputs, respectively

8. Load the data into a Pandas DataFrame df by running the following:

```
df = pd.DataFrame(data=boston['data'],
columns=boston['feature_names'])
```

In machine learning, the variable that is being modeled is called the target variable; it's what you are trying to predict given the features. For this dataset, the suggested target is MEDV, the median house value in 1,000s of dollars

9. Run the next cell to see the shape of the target:

```
# Still need to add the target variable
boston['target'].shape

(506,)
```

We see that it has the same length as the features, which is what we expect. It can, therefore, be added as a new column to the DataFrame.

10. Add the target variable to `df` by running the cell with the following:

```
df['MEDV'] = boston['target']
```

11. To distinguish the target from our features, it can be helpful to store it at the front of our DataFrame.
Move the target variable to the front of df by running the cell with the following:

```
y = df['MEDV'].copy()
del df['MEDV']
df = pd.concat((y, df), axis=1)
```

Here, we introduce a dummy variable y to hold a copy of the target column before removing it from the DataFrame. We then use the Pandas concatenation function to combine it with the remaining DataFrame along the 1st axis (as opposed to the 0th axis, which combines rows).

You will often see dot notation used to reference DataFrame columns. For example, previously we could have done `y = df.MEDV.copy()`. This does not work for deleting columns, however; `del df.MEDV` would raise an error.

12. Now that the data has been loaded in its entirety, let's take a look at the DataFrame.

We can do `df.head()` or `df.tail()` to see a glimpse of the data and `len(df)` to make sure the number of samples is what we expect. Run the next few cells to see the head, tail, and length of `df`:

```
df.head()
```

| | MEDV | CRIM | ZN | INDUS | CHAS | NOX | RM | AGE | DIS | RAD | TAX | PTRATIO | B |
|---|---|---|---|---|---|---|---|---|---|---|---|---|---|
| 0 | 24.0 | 0.00632 | 18.0 | 2.31 | 0.0 | 0.538 | 6.575 | 65.2 | 4.0900 | 1.0 | 296.0 | 15.3 | 396.90 |
| 1 | 21.6 | 0.02731 | 0.0 | 7.07 | 0.0 | 0.469 | 6.421 | 78.9 | 4.9671 | 2.0 | 242.0 | 17.8 | 396.90 |
| 2 | 34.7 | 0.02729 | 0.0 | 7.07 | 0.0 | 0.469 | 7.185 | 61.1 | 4.9671 | 2.0 | 242.0 | 17.8 | 392.83 |
| 3 | 33.4 | 0.03237 | 0.0 | 2.18 | 0.0 | 0.458 | 6.998 | 45.8 | 6.0622 | 3.0 | 222.0 | 18.7 | 394.63 |
| 4 | 36.2 | 0.06905 | 0.0 | 2.18 | 0.0 | 0.458 | 7.147 | 54.2 | 6.0622 | 3.0 | 222.0 | 18.7 | 396.90 |

```
df.tail()
```

| | MEDV | CRIM | ZN | INDUS | CHAS | NOX | RM | AGE | DIS | RAD | TAX | PTRATIO | B |
|---|---|---|---|---|---|---|---|---|---|---|---|---|---|
| 501 | 22.4 | 0.06263 | 0.0 | 11.93 | 0.0 | 0.573 | 6.593 | 69.1 | 2.4786 | 1.0 | 273.0 | 21.0 | 391.99 |
| 502 | 20.6 | 0.04527 | 0.0 | 11.93 | 0.0 | 0.573 | 6.120 | 76.7 | 2.2875 | 1.0 | 273.0 | 21.0 | 396.90 |
| 503 | 23.9 | 0.06076 | 0.0 | 11.93 | 0.0 | 0.573 | 6.976 | 91.0 | 2.1675 | 1.0 | 273.0 | 21.0 | 396.90 |
| 504 | 22.0 | 0.10959 | 0.0 | 11.93 | 0.0 | 0.573 | 6.794 | 89.3 | 2.3889 | 1.0 | 273.0 | 21.0 | 393.45 |
| 505 | 11.9 | 0.04741 | 0.0 | 11.93 | 0.0 | 0.573 | 6.030 | 80.8 | 2.5050 | 1.0 | 273.0 | 21.0 | 396.90 |

```
len(df)
```

```
506
```

Each row is labeled with an index value, as seen in bold on the left side of the table. By default, these are a set of integers starting at 0 and incrementing by one for each row.

13. Printing `df.dtypes` will show the datatype contained within each column.

    Run the next cell to see the datatypes of each column.

    For this dataset, we see that every field is a float and therefore most likely a continuous variable, including the target. This means that predicting the target variable is a regression problem.

14. The next thing we need to do is clean the data by dealing with any missing data, which Pandas automatically sets as NaN values. These can be identified by running `df.isnull()`, which returns a Boolean DataFrame of the same shape as `df`. To get the number of NaN's per column, we can do `df.isnull().sum()`. Run the next cell to calculate the number of NaN values in each column:

```
# Identify and NaNs
df.isnull().sum()

MEDV        0
CRIM        0
ZN          0
INDUS       0
CHAS        0
NOX         0
RM          0
AGE         0
DIS         0
RAD         0
TAX         0
PTRATIO     0
B           0
LSTAT       0
dtype: int64
```

For this dataset, we see there are no NaN's, which means we have no immediate work to do in cleaning the data and can move on.

15. To simplify the analysis, the final thing we'll do before exploration is remove some of the columns. We won't bother looking at these, and instead focus on the remainder in more detail.

Remove some columns by running the cell that contains the following code:

```
for col in ['ZN', 'NOX', 'RAD', 'PTRATIO', 'B']:
    del df[col]
```

# Data Exploration

Since this is an entirely new dataset that we've never seen before, the first goal here is to understand the data. We've already seen the textual description of the data, which is important for qualitative understanding. We'll now compute a quantitative description.

## Explore the Boston housing dataset

1. Navigate to Subtopic *Data exploration in the Jupyter Notebook* and run the cell containing `df.describe()`:

```
df.describe().T
```

|  | count | mean | std | min | 25% | 50% | 75% | max |
|---|---|---|---|---|---|---|---|---|
| **MEDV** | 506.0 | 22.532806 | 9.197104 | 5.00000 | 17.025000 | 21.20000 | 25.000000 | 50.0000 |
| **CRIM** | 506.0 | 3.593761 | 8.596783 | 0.00632 | 0.082045 | 0.25651 | 3.647423 | 88.9762 |
| **INDUS** | 506.0 | 11.136779 | 6.860353 | 0.46000 | 5.190000 | 9.69000 | 18.100000 | 27.7400 |
| **CHAS** | 506.0 | 0.069170 | 0.253994 | 0.00000 | 0.000000 | 0.00000 | 0.000000 | 1.0000 |
| **RM** | 506.0 | 6.284634 | 0.702617 | 3.56100 | 5.885500 | 6.20850 | 6.623500 | 8.7800 |
| **AGE** | 506.0 | 68.574901 | 28.148861 | 2.90000 | 45.025000 | 77.50000 | 94.075000 | 100.0000 |
| **DIS** | 506.0 | 3.795043 | 2.105710 | 1.12960 | 2.100175 | 3.20745 | 5.188425 | 12.1265 |
| **TAX** | 506.0 | 408.237154 | 168.537116 | 187.00000 | 279.000000 | 330.00000 | 666.000000 | 711.0000 |
| **LSTAT** | 506.0 | 12.653063 | 7.141062 | 1.73000 | 6.950000 | 11.36000 | 16.955000 | 37.9700 |

This computes various properties including the mean, standard deviation, minimum, and maximum for each column. This table gives a high-level idea of how everything is distributed. Note that we have taken the transform of the result by adding a .T to the output; this swaps the rows and columns. Going forward with the analysis, we will specify a set of columns to focus on.

2. Run the cell where these "focus columns" are defined:

```
cols = ['RM', 'AGE', 'TAX', 'LSTAT', 'MEDV']
```

3. This subset of columns can be selected from `df` using square brackets. Display this subset of the DataFrame by running `df[cols].head()`:

```
df[cols].head()
```

|   | RM | AGE | TAX | LSTAT | MEDV |
|---|------|------|-------|-------|------|
| 0 | 6.575 | 65.2 | 296.0 | 4.98 | 24.0 |
| 1 | 6.421 | 78.9 | 242.0 | 9.14 | 21.6 |
| 2 | 7.185 | 61.1 | 242.0 | 4.03 | 34.7 |
| 3 | 6.998 | 45.8 | 222.0 | 2.94 | 33.4 |
| 4 | 7.147 | 54.2 | 222.0 | 5.33 | 36.2 |

As a reminder, let's recall what each of these columns is. From the dataset documentation, we have the following:

- RM average number of rooms per dwelling
- AGE proportion of owner-occupied units built prior to 1940
- TAX full-value property-tax rate per $10,000
- LSTAT % lower status of the population
- MEDV Median value of owner-occupied homes in $1000's

To look for patterns in this data, we can start by calculating the pairwise correlations using `pd.DataFrame.corr`.

4. Calculate the pairwise correlations for our selected columns by running the cell containing the following code:

```
df[cols].corr()
```

|       | RM        | AGE       | TAX       | LSTAT     | MEDV      |
|-------|-----------|-----------|-----------|-----------|-----------|
| RM    | 1.000000  | -0.240265 | -0.292048 | -0.613808 | 0.695360  |
| AGE   | -0.240265 | 1.000000  | 0.506456  | 0.602339  | -0.376955 |
| TAX   | -0.292048 | 0.506456  | 1.000000  | 0.543993  | -0.468536 |
| LSTAT | -0.613808 | 0.602339  | 0.543993  | 1.000000  | -0.737663 |
| MEDV  | 0.695360  | -0.376955 | -0.468536 | -0.737663 | 1.000000  |

This resulting table shows the correlation score between each set of values. Large positive scores indicate a strong positive (that is, in the same direction) correlation. As expected, we see maximum values of 1 on the diagonal.

Pearson coefficient is defined as the co-variance between two variables, divided by the product of their standard deviations:

$$\rho_{X,Y} = \frac{cov(X,Y)}{\sigma_X \sigma_Y}$$

The co-variance, in turn, is defined as follows:

$$cov(X,Y) = \frac{1}{n} \sum_{i=0}^{n} (x_i - \bar{X})(y_i - \bar{Y})$$

Here, n is the number of samples, $x_i$ and $y_i$ are the individual samples being summed over, and $\bar{X}$ and $\bar{Y}$ are the means of each set.

Instead of straining our eyes to look at the preceding table, it's nicer to visualize it with a heatmap. This can be done easily with Seaborn.

5. Run the next cell to initialize the plotting environment, as discussed earlier in the chapter. Then, to create the heatmap, run the cell containing the following code:

```
import matplotlib.pyplot as plt
import seaborn as sns
%matplotlib inline

ax = sns.heatmap(df[cols].corr(),
cmap=sns.cubehelix_palette(20, light=0.95, dark=0.15))
ax.xaxis.tick_top() # move labels to the top
plt.savefig('../figures/chapter-1-boston-housing-corr.png',
bbox_inches='tight', dpi=300)
```

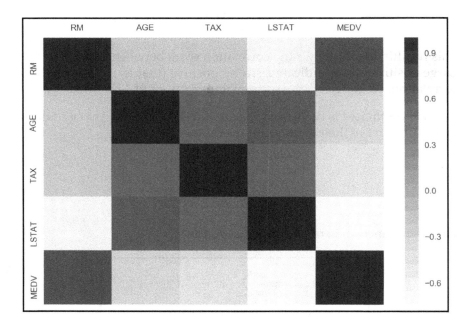

We call `sns.heatmap` and pass the pairwise correlation matrix as input. We use a custom color palette here to override the Seaborn default. The function returns a `matplotlib.axes` object which is referenced by the variable `ax`. The final figure is then saved as a high-resolution PNG to the `figures` folder.

6. For the final step in our dataset exploration exercise, we'll visualize our data using Seaborn's `pairplot` function.

7. Visualize the DataFrame using Seaborn's pairplot function. Run the cell containing the following code:

```
sns.pairplot(df[cols],
plot_kws={'alpha': 0.6},
diag_kws={'bins': 30})
```

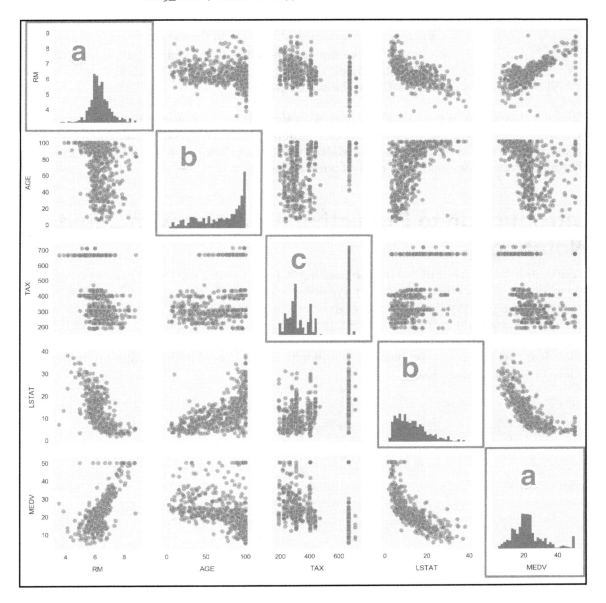

Having previously used a heatmap to visualize a simple overview of the correlations, this plot allows us to see the relationships in far more detail. Looking at the histograms on the diagonal, we see the following:

- a: RM and MEDV have the closest shape to normal distributions.
- b: AGE is skewed to the left and LSTAT is skewed to the right (this may seem counter intuitive but skew is defined in terms of where the mean is positioned in relation to the max).
- c: For TAX, we find a large amount of the distribution is around 700. This is also evident from the scatter plots

Taking a closer look at the **MEDV** histogram in the bottom right, we actually see something similar to **TAX** where there is a large upper-limit bin around $50,000. Recall when we did `df.describe()`, the min and max of **MDEV** was 5k and 50k, respectively. This suggests that median house values in the dataset were capped at 50k.

# Introduction to Predictive Analytics with Jupyter Notebooks

Continuing our analysis of the Boston housing dataset, we can see that it presents us with a regression problem where we predict a continuous target variable given a set of features. In particular, we'll be predicting the median house value (**MEDV**). We'll train models that take only one feature as input to make this prediction. This way, the models will be conceptually simple to understand and we can focus more on the technical details of the scikit-learn API. Then, in the next chapter, you'll be more comfortable dealing with the relatively complicated models.

# Linear models with Seaborn and scikit-learn

1. Scroll to Subtopic`Introduction to predictive analytics` in the Jupyter Notebook and look just above at the pairplot we created in the previous section. In particular, look at the scatter plots in the bottom-left corner:

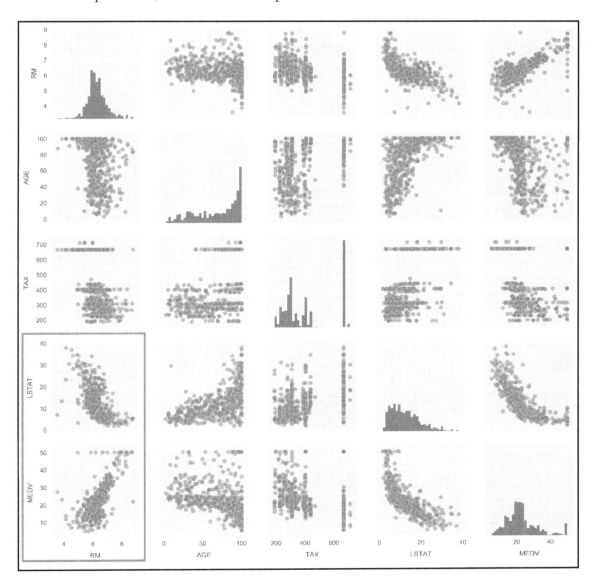

Note how the number of rooms per house (**RM**) and the % of the population that is lower class (**LSTAT**) are highly correlated with the median house value (**MDEV**). Let's pose the following question: how well can we predict **MDEV** given these variables?

To help answer this, let's first visualize the relationships using Seaborn. We will draw the scatter plots along with the line of best fit linear models.

2. Draw scatter plots along with the linear models by running the cell that contains the following:

```
fig, ax = plt.subplots(1, 2)
sns.regplot('RM', 'MEDV', df, ax=ax[0],
scatter_kws={'alpha': 0.4}))
sns.regplot('LSTAT', 'MEDV', df, ax=ax[1],
scatter_kws={'alpha': 0.4}))
```

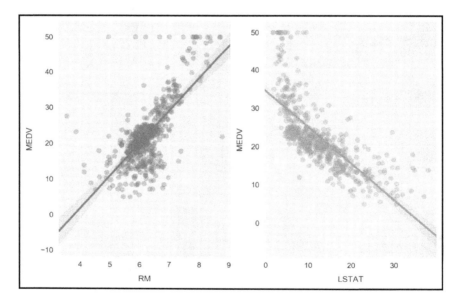

The line of best fit is calculated by minimizing the ordinary least squares error function, something Seaborn does automatically when we call the `regplot` function. Also note the shaded areas around the lines, which represent 95% confidence intervals.

These 95% confidence intervals are calculated by taking the standard deviation of data in bins perpendicular to the line of best fit, effectively determining the confidence intervals at each point along the line of best fit. In practice, this involves Seaborn bootstrapping the data, a process where new data is created through random sampling with replacement. The number of bootstrapped samples is automatically determined based on the size of the dataset, but can be manually set as well by passing the `n_boot` argument.

3. Seaborn can also be used to plot the residuals for these relationships. Plot the residuals by running the cell containing the following:

```
fig, ax = plt.subplots(1, 2)
ax[0] = sns.residplot('RM', 'MEDV', df, ax=ax[0],
                scatter_kws={'alpha': 0.4})
ax[0].set_ylabel('MDEV residuals $(y-\hat{y})$')
ax[1] = sns.residplot('LSTAT', 'MEDV', df, ax=ax[1],
                scatter_kws={'alpha': 0.4})
ax[1].set_ylabel('')
```

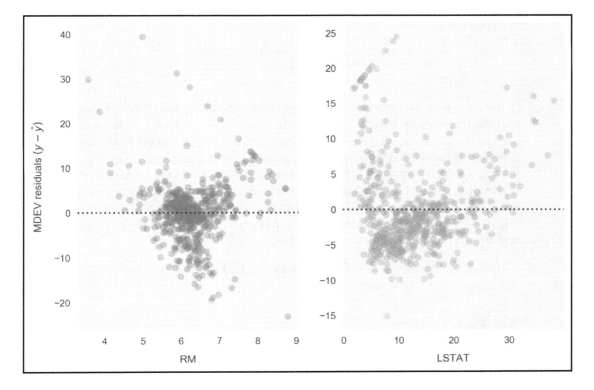

Each point on these residual plots is the difference between that sample (y) and the linear model prediction ( ŷ). Residuals greater than zero are data points that would be underestimated by the model. Likewise, residuals less than zero are data points that would be overestimated by the model.

Patterns in these plots can indicate sub-optimal modeling. In each preceding case, we see diagonally arranged scatter points in the positive region. These are caused by the $50,000 cap on MEDV. The RM data is clustered nicely around 0, which indicates a good fit. On the other hand, LSTAT appears to be clustered lower than 0.

4. Moving on from visualizations, the fits can be quantified by calculating the mean squared error. We'll do this now using scikit-learn. Defile a function that calculates the line of best fit and mean squared error, by running the cell that contains the following:

```
def get_mse(df, feature, target='MEDV'):
# Get x, y to model
y = df[target].values
x = df[feature].values.reshape(-1,1)
...
...
error = mean_squared_error(y, y_pred)
print('mse = {:.2f}'.format(error))
print()
```

In the get_mse function, we first assign the variables y and x to the target **MDEV** and the dependent feature, respectively. These are cast as NumPy arrays by calling the values attribute. The dependent features array is reshaped to the format expected by scikit-learn; this is only necessary when modeling a one-dimensional feature space. The model is then instantiated and fitted on the data. For linear regression, the fitting consists of computing the model parameters using the ordinary least squares method (minimizing the sum of squared errors for each sample). Finally, after determining the parameters, we predict the target variable and use the results to calculate the MSE.

5. Call the get_mse function for both RM and LSTAT, by running the cell containing the following:

```
get_mse(df, 'RM')
get_mse(df, 'LSTAT')
```

```
get_mse(df, 'RM')
get_mse df, 'LSTAT'

MEDV ~ RM
model: y = -34.671 + 9.102x
mse = 43.60

MEDV ~ LSTAT
model: y = 34.554 + -0.950x
mse = 38.48
```

Comparing the **MSE**, it turns out the error is slightly lower for **LSTAT**. Looking back to the scatter plots, however, it appears that we might have even better success using a polynomial model for LSTAT. In the next activity, we will test this by computing a third-order polynomial model with scikit-learn.

Forgetting about our Boston housing dataset for a minute, consider another real-world situation where you might employ polynomial regression. The following example is modeling weather data. In the following plot, we see temperatures (lines) and precipitations (bars) for Vancouver, BC, Canada:

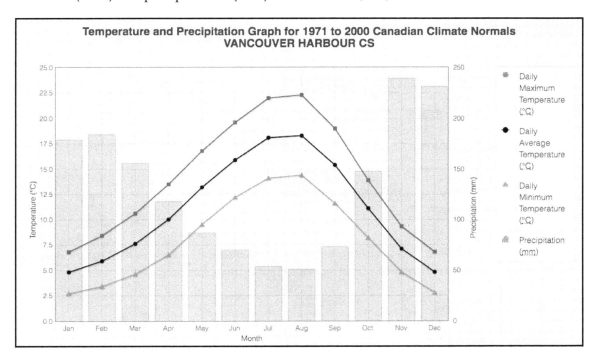

Any of these fields are likely to be fit quite well by a fourth-order polynomial. This would be a very valuable model to have, for example, if you were interested in predicting the temperature or precipitation for a continuous range of dates.

You can find the data source for this here:

```
http://climate.weather.gc.ca/climate_normals/results_e.html?stnID=888.
```

# Activity: Building a Third-Order Polynomial Model

Shifting our attention back to the Boston housing dataset, we would like to build a third-order polynomial model to compare against the linear one. Recall the actual problem we are trying to solve: predicting the median house value, given the lower class population percentage. This model could benefit a prospective Boston house purchaser who cares about how much of their community would be lower class.

Use scikit-learn to fit a polynomial regression model to predict the median house value (MEDV), given the LSTAT values. We are hoping to build a model that has a lower mean squared error (MSE).

## Linear models with Seaborn and scikit-learn

1. Scroll to the empty cells at the bottom of Subtopic Introduction to Predictive Analysis in your Jupyter Notebook. These will be found beneath the linear-model MSE calculation cell under the Activity heading.

 You should fill these empty cells in with code as we complete the activity. You may need to insert new cells as these become filled up; please do so as needed!

2. Given that our data is contained in the DataFrame df, we will first pull out our dependent feature and target variable using the following:

```
y = df['MEDV'].values
x = df['LSTAT'].values.reshape(-1,1)
```

This is identical to what we did earlier for the linear model.

3. Check out what x looks like by printing the first few samples with print(x[:3]) :

```
print('x =')
print(x[:3], '...etc')

x =
[[ 4.98]
 [ 9.14]
 [ 4.03]] ...etc
```

Notice how each element in the array is itself an array with length 1. This is what `reshape(-1,1)` does, and it is the form expected by scikit-learn.

4. Next, we are going to transform x into "polynomial features". The rationale for this may not be immediately obvious but will be explained shortly. Import the appropriate transformation tool from scikit-learn and instantiate the third-degree polynomial feature transformer:

```
from sklearn.preprocessing import PolynomialFeatures
poly = PolynomialFeatures(degree=3)
```

5. At this point, we simply have an instance of our feature transformer. Now, let's use it to transform the LSTAT feature (as stored in the variable x) by running the `fit_transform` method.

Build the polynomial feature set by running the following code:

```
x_poly = poly.fit_transform(x)
```

6. Check out what `x_poly` looks like by printing the first few samples with print(x_poly[:3]).

```
print('x_poly =')
print(x_poly[:3], '...etc')

x_poly =
[[   1.         4.98      24.8004    123.505992]
 [   1.         9.14      83.5396    763.551944]
 [   1.         4.03      16.2409     65.450827]] ...etc
```

Unlike x, the arrays in each row now have length 4, where the values have been calculated as $x^0$, $x^1$, $x^2$, and $x^3$.

We are now going to use this data to fit a linear model. Labeling the features as a, b, c, and d, we will calculate the coefficients $\alpha_0$, $\alpha_1$, $\alpha_2$, and $\alpha_3$ and of the linear model:

$$y = \alpha_0 a + \alpha_1 b + \alpha_2 c + \alpha_3 d$$

We can plug in the definitions of a, b, c, and d, to get the following polynomial model, where the coefficients are the same as the previous ones:

$$y = \alpha_0 + \alpha_1 x + \alpha_2 x^2 + \alpha_3 x^3$$

7. We'll import the Linear Regression class and build our linear classification model the same way as before, when we calculated the **MSE**. Run the following:

```
from sklearn.linear_model import LinearRegression
clf = LinearRegression()
clf.fit(x_poly, y)
```

8. Extract the coefficients and print the polynomial model using the following code:

```
a_0 = clf.intercept_ + clf.coef_[0]      #intercept
a_1, a_2, a_3 = clf.coef_[1:]            #other coefficients
msg = 'model: y = {:.3f} + {:.3f}x +
{:.3f}x^2 + {:.3f}x^3'\.format(a_0, a_1,  a_2, a_3)
print(msg)
```

```
msg = 'model: y = {:.3f} + {:.3f}x + {:.3f}x^2 + {:.3f}x^3'\
          .format(x_0, x_1, x_2, x_3)
print(msg)

model: y = 48.650 + -3.866x + 0.149x^2 + -0.002x^3
```

To get the actual model intercept, we have to add the `intercept_` and `coef_[0]` attributes. The higher-order coefficients are then given by the remaining values of `coef_`.

9. Determine the predicted values for each sample and calculate the residuals by running the following code:

```
y_pred = clf.predict(x_poly)
resid_MEDV = y - y_pred
```

10. Print some of the residual values by running `print(resid_MEDV[:10])`:

```
print('residuals =')
print(resid_MEDV[:10], '...etc')

residuals =
[ -8.84025736  -2.61360313  -0.65577837  -5.11949581   4.23191217
   -3.56387056   3.16728909  12.00336372   4.03348935   2.87915437] ...etc
```

We'll plot these soon to compare with the linear model residuals, but first we will calculate the **MSE**.

11. Run the following code to print the MSE for the third-order polynomial model:

```
from sklearn.metrics import mean_squared_error
error = mean_squared_error(y, y_pred)
print('mse = {:.2f}'.format(error))
```

```
error = mean_squared_error(y, y_pred)
print('mse = {:.2f}'.format(error))

mse = 28.88
```

As can be seen, the **MSE** is significantly less for the polynomial model compared to the linear model (which was 38.5). This error metric can be converted to an average error in dollars by taking the square root. Doing this for the polynomial model, we find the average error for the median house value is only $5,300.

Now, we'll visualize the model by plotting the polynomial line of best fit along with the data.

12. Plot the polynomial model along with the samples by running the following:

```
fig, ax = plt.subplots()
# Plot the samples
ax.scatter(x.flatten(), y, alpha=0.6)
# Plot the polynomial model
x_ = np.linspace(2, 38, 50).reshape(-1, 1)
x_poly = poly.fit_transform(x_)
y_ = clf.predict(x_poly)
ax.plot(x_, y_, color='red', alpha=0.8)
ax.set_xlabel('LSTAT'); ax.set_ylabel('MEDV');
```

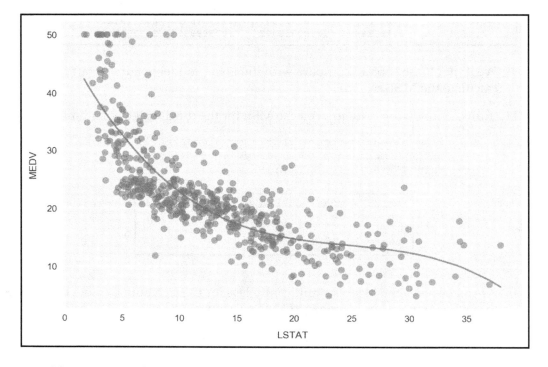

Here, we are plotting the red curve by calculating the polynomial model predictions on an array of x values. The array of x values was created using np.linspace, resulting in 50 values arranged evenly between 2 and 38.

Now, we'll plot the corresponding residuals. Whereas we used Seaborn for this earlier, we'll have to do it manually to show results for a scikit-learn model. Since we already calculated the residuals earlier, as reference by the resid_MEDV variable, we simply need to plot this list of values on a scatter chart.

13. Plot the residuals by running the following:

```
fig, ax = plt.subplots(figsize=(5, 7))
ax.scatter(x, resid_MEDV, alpha=0.6)
ax.set_xlabel('LSTAT')
ax.set_ylabel('MEDV Residual $(y-\hat{y})$')
plt.axhline(0, color='black', ls='dotted');
```

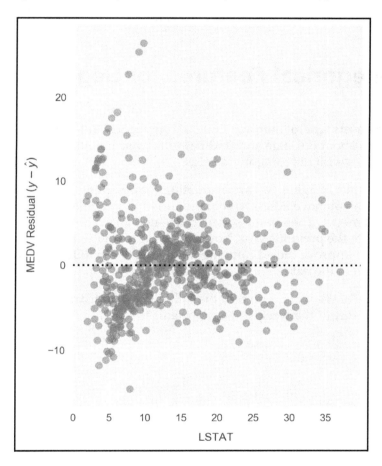

Compared to the linear model LSTAT residual plot, the polynomial model residuals appear to be more closely clustered around y - ŷ = 0. Note that y is the sample MEDV and ŷ is the predicted value. There are still clear patterns, such as the cluster near x = 7 and y = -7 that indicates suboptimal modeling.

Having successfully modeled the data using a polynomial model, let's finish up this chapter by looking at categorical features. In particular, we are going to build a set of categorical features and use them to explore the dataset in more detail.

# Using Categorical Features for Segmentation Analysis

Often, we find datasets where there are a mix of continuous and categorical fields. In such cases, we can learn about our data and find patterns by segmenting the continuous variables with the categorical fields.

As a specific example, imagine you are evaluating the return on investment from an ad campaign. The data you have access to contain measures of some calculated **return on investment (ROI)** metric. These values were calculated and recorded daily and you are analyzing data from the previous year. You have been tasked with finding data-driven insights on ways to improve the ad campaign. Looking at the ROI daily time series, you see a weekly oscillation in the data.

Segmenting by day of the week, you find the following ROI distributions (where 0 represents the first day of the week and 6 represents the last).

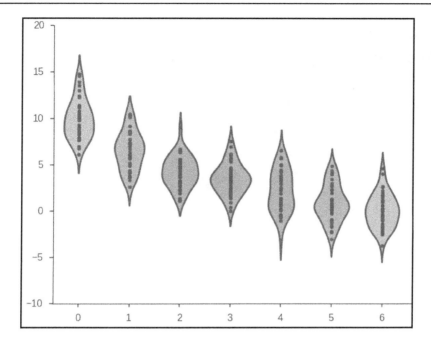

As a specific example, imagine you are evaluating the return on investment from an ad campaign. The data you have access to contain measures of some calculated return on investment (**ROI**) metric. These values were calculated and recorded daily and you are analyzing data from the previous year. You have been tasked with finding data-driven insights on ways to improve the ad campaign. Looking at the ROI daily time series, you see a weekly oscillation in the data. Segmenting by day of the week, you find the following ROI distributions (where 0 represents the first day of the week and 6 represents the last).

Since we don't have any categorical fields in the Boston housing dataset we are working with, we'll create one by effectively discretizing a continuous field. In our case, this will involve binning the data into "low", "medium", and "high" categories. It's important to note that we are not simply creating a categorical data field to illustrate the data analysis concepts in this section. As will be seen, doing this can reveal insights from the data that would otherwise be difficult to notice or altogether unavailable.

# Create categorical fields from continuous variables and make segmented visualizations

1. Scroll up to the pair plot in the Jupyter Notebook where we compared MEDV, LSTAT, TAX, AGE, and RM:

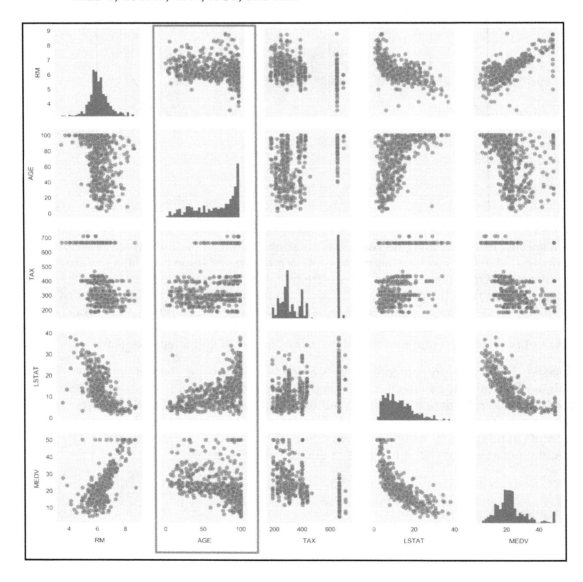

Take a look at the panels containing AGE. As a reminder, this feature is defined as the *proportion of owner-occupied units built prior to 1940*. We are going to convert this feature to a categorical variable. Once it's been converted, we'll be able to replot this figure with each panel segmented by color according to the age category.

2. Scroll down to Subtopic `Building and exploring categorical features` and click into the first cell. Type and execute the following to plot the AGE cumulative distribution:

```
sns.distplot(df.AGE.values, bins=100,
hist_kws={'cumulative': True},
kde_kws={'lw': 0})
plt.xlabel('AGE')
plt.ylabel('CDF')
plt.axhline(0.33, color='red')
plt.axhline(0.66, color='red')
plt.xlim(0, df.AGE.max());
```

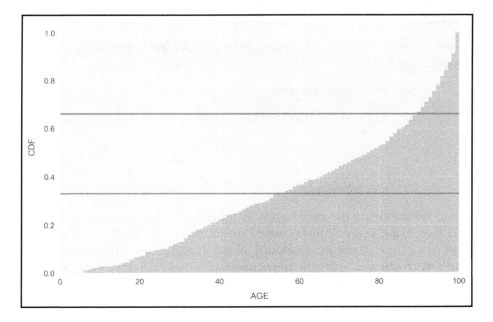

Note that we set `kde_kws={'lw': 0}` in order to bypass plotting the kernel density estimate in the preceding figure.

Looking at the plot, there are very few samples with low AGE, whereas there are far more with a very large AGE. This is indicated by the steepness of the distribution on the far right-hand side.

3. The red lines indicate 1/3 and 2/3 points in the distribution. Looking at the places where our distribution intercepts these horizontal lines, we can see that only about 33% of the samples have AGE less than 55 and 33% of the samples have AGE greater than 90! In other words, a third of the housing communities have less than 55% of homes built prior to 1940. These would be considered relatively new communities. On the other end of the spectrum, another third of the housing communities have over 90% of homes built prior to 1940. These would be considered very old.

We'll use the places where the red horizontal lines intercept the distribution as a guide to split the feature into categories: **Relatively New**, **Relatively Old**, and **Very Old**.

4. Setting the segmentation points as 50 and 85, create a new categorical feature by running the following code:

```
def get_age_category(x):
    if x < 50:
        return 'Relatively New'
    elif 50 <= x < 85:
        return 'Relatively Old'
    else:
        return 'Very Old'
df['AGE_category'] = df.AGE.apply(get_age_category)
```

Here, we are using the very handy Pandas method apply, which applies a function to a given column or set of columns. The function being applied, in this case `get_ age_category`, should take one argument representing a row of data and return one value for the new column. In this case, the row of data being passed is just a single value, the AGE of the sample.

The apply method is great because it can solve a variety of problems and allows for easily readable code. Often though, vectorized methods such as `pd.Series.str` can accomplish the same thing much faster. Therefore, it's advised to avoid using it if possible, especially when working with large datasets. We'll see some examples of vectorized methods in the upcoming chapters.

5. Check on how many samples we've grouped into each age category by typing `df.groupby('AGE_category').size()` into a new cell and running

```
# Check the segmented counts
df.groupby('AGE_category').size()

AGE_category
Relatively New    147
Relatively Old    149
Very Old          210
dtype: int64
```

Looking at the result, it can be seen that two class sizes are fairly equal, and the Very Old group is about 40% larger. We are interested in keeping the classes comparable in size, so that each is well-represented and it's straightforward to make inferences from the analysis.

 It may not always be possible to assign samples into classes evenly, and in real-world situations, it's very common to find highly imbalanced classes. In such cases, it's important to keep in mind that it will be difficult to make statistically significant claims with respect to the under-represented class. Predictive analytics with imbalanced classes can be particularly difficult. The following blog post offers an excellent summary of methods for handling imbalanced classes when doing machine learning: https://svds.com/learning-imbalanced-classes/.

Let's see how the target variable is distributed when segmented by our new feature AGE_category.

6. Make a violin plot by running the following code:

```
sns.violinplot(x='MEDV', y='AGE_category', data=df,
order=['Relatively New', 'Relatively Old', 'Very Old']);
```

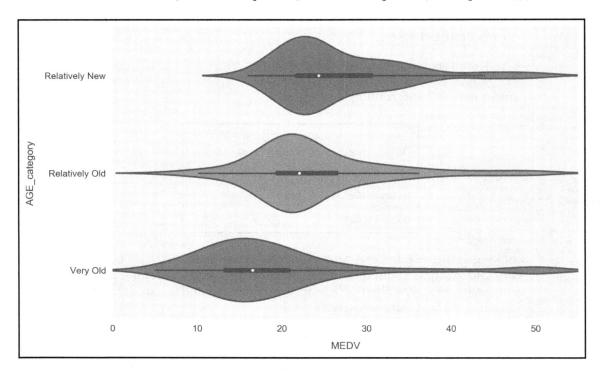

The violin plot shows a kernel density estimate of the median house value distribution for each age category. We see that they all resemble a normal distribution. The Very Old group contains the lowest median house value samples and has a relatively large width, whereas the other groups are more tightly centered around their average. The young group is skewed to the high end, which is evident from the enlarged right half and position of the white dot in the thick black line within the body of the distribution.

This white dot represents the mean and the thick black line spans roughly 50% of the population (it fills to the first quantile on either side of the white dot). The thin black line represents boxplot whiskers and spans 95% of the population. This inner visualization can be modified to show the individual data points instead, by passing `inner='point'` to `sns.violinplot()`. Let's do that now.

7. Redo the violin plot adding the inner='point' argument to the sns.violinplot call:

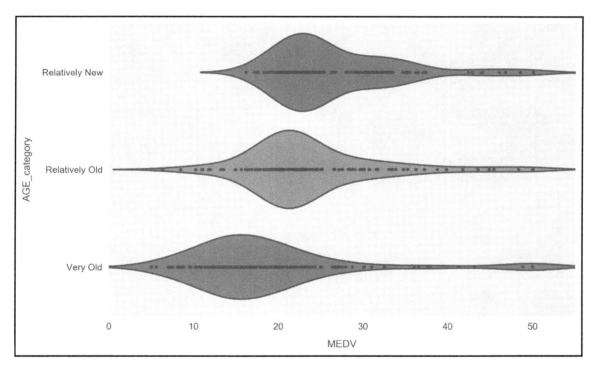

It's good to make plots like this for test purposes in order to see how the underlying data connects to the visual. We can see, for example, how there are no median house values lower than roughly $16,000 for the Relatively New segment, and therefore the distribution tail actually contains no data. Due to the small size of our dataset (only about 500 rows), we can see this is the case for each segment.

8. Re-do the pairplot from earlier, but now include color labels for each AGE category. This is done by simply passing the hue argument, as follows:

```
cols = ['RM', 'AGE', 'TAX', 'LSTAT', 'MEDV', 'AGE_category']
sns.pairplot(df[cols], hue='AGE_category',
hue_order=['Relatively New', 'Relatively Old', 'Very Old'],
plot_kws={'alpha': 0.5}, diag_kws={'bins': 30});
```

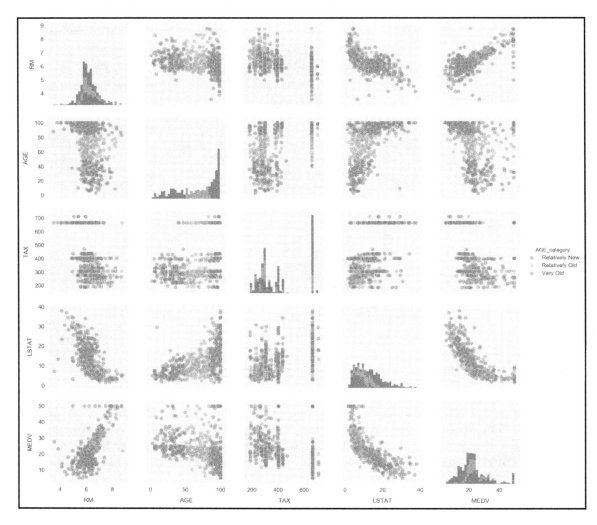

Looking at the histograms, the underlying distributions of each segment appear similar for **RM** and **TAX**. The **LSTAT** distributions, on the other hand, look more distinct. We can focus on them in more detail by again using a violin plot.

9. Make a violin plot comparing the LSTAT distributions for each `AGE_category` segment:

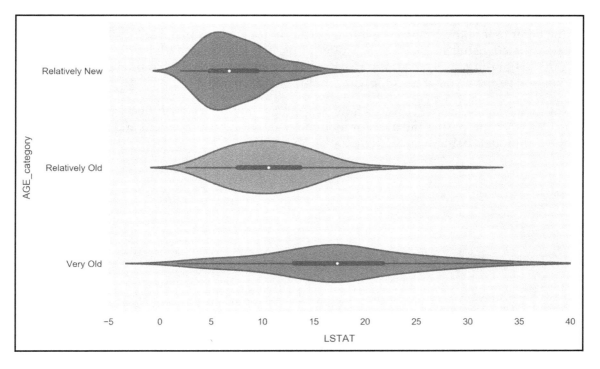

Unlike the **MEDV** violin plot, where each distribution had roughly the same width, here we see the width increasing along with **AGE**. Communities with primarily old houses (the Very Old segment) contain anywhere from very few to many lower class residents, whereas Relatively New communities are much more likely to be predominantly higher class, with over 95% of samples having less lower class percentages than the Very Old communities. This makes sense, because Relatively New neighborhoods would be more expensive.

# Summary

In this chapter, you have seen the fundamentals of data analysis in Jupyter.

We began with usage instructions and features of Jupyter such as magic functions and tab completion. Then, transitioning to data-science-specific material, we introduced the most important libraries for data science with Python.

In the latter half of the chapter, we ran an exploratory analysis in a live Jupyter Notebook. Here, we used visual assists such as scatter plots, histograms, and violin plots to deepen our understanding of the data. We also performed simple predictive modeling, a topic which will be the focus of the following chapter in this book.

In the next chapter, we will discuss how to approach predictive analytics, what things to consider when preparing the data for modeling, and how to implement and compare a variety of models using Jupyter Notebooks.

# Data Cleaning and Advanced Machine Learning 2

The goal of data analytics, in general, is to uncover actionable insights that result in positive business outcomes. In the case of predictive analytics, the aim is to do this by determining the most likely future outcome of a target, based on previous trends and patterns.

The benefits of predictive analytics are not restricted to big technology companies. Any business can find ways to benefit from machine learning, given the right data.

Companies all around the world are collecting massive amounts of data and using predictive analytics to cut costs and increase profits. Some of the most prevalent examples of this are from the technology giants Google, Facebook, and Amazon, who utilize big data on a huge scale. For example, Google and Facebook serve you personalized ads based on predictive algorithms that guess what you are most likely to click on. Similarly, Amazon recommends personalized products that you are most likely to buy, given your previous purchases.

Modern predictive analytics is done with machine learning, where computer models are trained to learn patterns from data. As we saw briefly in the previous chapter, software such as scikit-learn can be used with Jupyter Notebooks to efficiently build and test machine learning models. As we will continue to see, Jupyter Notebooks are an ideal environment for doing this type of work, as we can perform ad-hoc testing and analysis, and easily save the results for reference later.

In this chapter, we will again take a hands-on approach by running through various examples and activities in a Jupyter Notebook. Where we saw a couple of examples of machine learning in the previous chapter, here we'll take a much slower and more thoughtful approach. Using an employee retention problem as our overarching example for the chapter, we will discuss how to approach predictive analytics, what things to consider when preparing the data for modeling, and how to implement and compare a variety of models using Jupyter Notebooks.

By the end of this chapter, you will be able to:

- Plan a machine learning classification strategy
- Preprocess data to prepare it for machine learning
- Train classification models
- Use validation curves to tune model parameters
- Use dimensionality reduction to enhance model performance

# Preparing to Train a Predictive Model

Here, we will cover the preparation required to train a predictive model. Although not as technically glamorous as training the models themselves, this step should not be taken lightly. It's very important to ensure you have a good plan before proceeding with the details of building and training a reliable model. Furthermore, once you've decided on the right plan, there are technical steps in preparing the data for modeling that should not be overlooked.

 We must be careful not to go so deep into the weeds of technical tasks that we lose sight of the goal. Technical tasks include things that require programming skills, for example, constructing visualizations, querying databases, and validating predictive models. It's easy to spend hours trying to implement a specific feature or get the plots looking just right. Doing this sort of thing is certainly beneficial to our programming skills, but we should not forget to ask ourselves if it's really worth our time with respect to the current project.

Also, keep in mind that Jupyter Notebooks are particularly well-suited for this step, as we can use them to document our plan, for example, by writing rough notes about the data or a list of models we are interested in training. Before starting to train models, it's good practice to even take this a step further and write out a well-structured plan to follow. Not only will this help you stay on track as you build and test the models, but it will allow others to understand what you're doing when they see your work.

After discussing the preparation, we will also cover another step in preparing to train the predictive model, which is cleaning the dataset. This is another thing that Jupyter Notebooks are well-suited for, as they offer an ideal testing ground for performing dataset transformations and keeping track of the exact changes. The data transformations required for cleaning raw data can quickly become intricate and convoluted; therefore, it's important to keep track of your work. As discussed in the first chapter, tools other than Jupyter Notebooks just don't offer very good options for doing this efficiently.

# Determining a Plan for Predictive Analytics

When formulating a plan for doing predictive modeling, one should start by considering stakeholder needs. A perfect model will be useless if it doesn't solve a relevant problem. Planning a strategy around business needs ensures that a successful model will lead to actionable insights.

Although it may be possible in principle to solve many business problems, the ability to deliver the solution will always depend on the availability of the necessary data. Therefore, it's important to consider the business needs in the context of the available data sources. When data is plentiful, this will have little effect, but as the amount of available data becomes smaller, so too does the scope of problems that can be solved.

These ideas can be formed into a standard process for determining a predictive analytics plan, which goes as follows:

1. Look at the available data to understand the range of realistically solvable business problems. At this stage, it might be too early to think about the exact problems that can be solved. Make sure you understand the data fields available and the
   time frames they apply to.
2. Determine the business needs by speaking with key stakeholders. Seek out a problem where the solution will lead to actionable business decisions.
3. Assess the data for suitability by considering the availability of sufficiently diverse and large feature space. Also, take into account the condition of the data: are there large chunks of missing values for certain variables or time ranges?

Steps 2 and 3 should be repeated until a realistic plan has taken shape. At this point, you will already have a good idea of what the model input will be and what you might expect as output.

Once we've identified a problem that can be solved with machine learning, along with the appropriate data sources, we should answer the following questions to lay a framework for the project. Doing this will help us determine which types of machine learning models we can use to solve the problem:

- Is the training data labeled with the target variable we want to predict?

  If the answer is yes, then we will be doing supervised machine learning. Supervised learning has many real-world use cases, whereas it's much rarer to find business cases for doing predictive analytics on unlabeled data.

If the answer is no, then you are using unlabeled data and hence doing unsupervised machine learning. An example of an unsupervised learning method is cluster analysis, where labels are assigned to the nearest cluster for each sample.

- If the data is labeled, then are we solving a regression or classification problem?

In a regression problem, the target variable is continuous, for example, predicting the amount of rain tomorrow in centimeters. In a classification problem, the target variable is discrete and we are predicting class labels. The simplest type of classification problem is binary, where each sample is grouped into one of two classes. For example, will it rain tomorrow or not?

- What does the data look like? How many distinct sources?

Consider the size of the data in terms of width and height, where width refers to the number of columns (features) and height refers to the number of rows. Certain algorithms are more effective at handling large numbers of features than others. Generally, the bigger the dataset, the better in terms of accuracy. However, training can be very slow and memory intensive for large datasets. This can always be reduced by performing aggregations on the data or using dimensionality reduction techniques.

If there are different data sources, can they be merged into a single table? If not, then we may want to train models for each and take an ensemble average for the final prediction model. An example where we may want to do this is with various sets of times series data on different scales. Consider we have the following data sources: a table with the AAPL stock closing prices on a daily time scale and iPhone sales data on a monthly time scale.

We could merge the data by adding the monthly sales data to each sample in the daily time scale table or grouping the daily data by month, but it might be better to build two models, one for each dataset, and use a combination of the results from each in the final prediction model.

# Preprocessing Data for Machine Learning

Data preprocessing has a huge impact on machine learning. Like the saying "you are what you eat," the model's performance is a direct reflection of the data it's trained on. Many models depend on the data being transformed so that the continuous feature values have comparable limits. Similarly, categorical features should be encoded into numerical values. Although important, these steps are relatively simple and do not take very long.

The aspect of preprocessing that usually takes the longest is cleaning up messy data. Just take a look at this pie plot showing what data scientists from a particular survey spent most of their time doing.

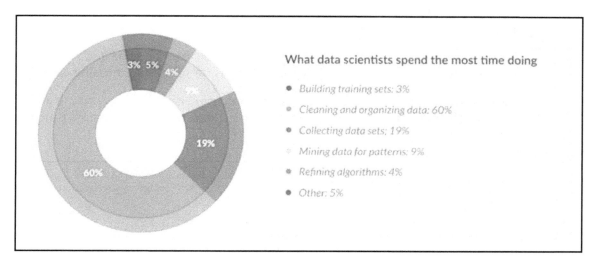

What data scientists spend the most time doing

- Building training sets: 3%
- Cleaning and organizing data: 60%
- Collecting data sets: 19%
- Mining data for patterns: 9%
- Refining algorithms: 4%
- Other: 5%

Another thing to consider is the size of the datasets being used by many data scientists. As the dataset size increases, the prevalence of messy data increases as well, along with the difficulty in cleaning it.

Simply dropping the missing data is usually not the best option, because it's hard to justify throwing away samples where most of the fields have values. In doing so, we could lose valuable information that may hurt final model performance.

The steps involved in data preprocessing can be grouped as follows:

- Merging data sets on common fields to bring all data into a single table
- Feature engineering to improve the quality of data, for example, the use of dimensionality reduction techniques to build new features
- Cleaning the data by dealing with duplicate rows, incorrect or missing values, and other issues that arise
- Building the training data sets by standardizing or normalizing the required data and splitting it into training and testing sets

Let's explore some of the tools and methods for doing the preprocessing.

# Exploring data preprocessing tools and methods

1. Start the `NotebookApp` from the project directory by executing `jupyter notebook`. Navigate to the `chapter-2` directory and open up the `chapter-2-workbook.ipynb` file. Find the cell near the top where the packages are loaded, and run it.

   We are going to start by showing off some basic tools from Pandas and scikit-learn. Then, we'll take a deeper dive into methods for rebuilding missing data.

2. Scroll down to Subtopic `Preprocessing data for machine learning` and run the cell containing `pd.merge?` to display the docstring for the merge function in the notebook:

```
Signature: pd.merge(left, right, how='inner', on=None, left_on=None, right_on=None, left_
index=False, right_index=False, sort=False, suffixes=('_x', '_y'), copy=True, indicator=F
alse)
Docstring:
Merge DataFrame objects by performing a database-style join operation by
columns or indexes.

If joining columns on columns, the DataFrame indexes *will be
ignored*. Otherwise if joining indexes on indexes or indexes on a column or
columns, the index will be passed on.

Parameters
----------
left : DataFrame
right : DataFrame
how : {'left', 'right', 'outer', 'inner'}, default 'inner'
    * left: use only keys from left frame, similar to a SQL left outer join;
      preserve key order
    * right: use only keys from right frame, similar to a SQL right outer join;
      preserve key order
    * outer: use union of keys from both frames, similar to a SQL full outer
      join; sort keys lexicographically
    * inner: use intersection of keys from both frames, similar to a SQL inner
      join; preserve the order of the left keys
on : label or list
    Field names to join on. Must be found in both DataFrames. If on is
    None and not merging on indexes, then it merges on the intersection of
    the columns by default.
left_on : label or list, or array-like
    Field names to join on in left DataFrame. Can be a vector or list of
    vectors of the length of the DataFrame to use a particular vector as
    the join key instead of columns
```

As we can see, the function accepts left and right DataFrame to merge. You can specify one or more columns to group on as well as how they are grouped, that is, to use the left, right, outer, or inner sets of values. Let's see an example of this in use.

3. Exit the help popup and run the cell containing the following sample DataFrames:

```
df_1 = pd.DataFrame({'product': ['red shirt', 'red shirt', 'red shirt',
                                 'white dress'],
                     'price': [49.33, 49.33, 32.49, 199.99]}),
df_2 = pd.DataFrame({'product': ['red shirt', 'blue pants',
                                 'white tuxedo', 'white dress'],
                     'in_stock': [True, True, False, False]})
```

Here, we will build two simple DataFrames from scratch. As can be seen, they contain a `product` column with some shared entries.

Now, we are going to perform an inner merge on the `product` shared column and print the result.

4. Run the next cell to perform the inner merge:

```
# Inner merge

df = pd.merge(left=df_1, right=df_2, on='product', how='inner')
df
```

|   | price  | product     | in_stock |
|---|--------|-------------|----------|
| 0 | 49.33  | red shirt   | True     |
| 1 | 49.33  | red shirt   | True     |
| 2 | 32.49  | red shirt   | True     |
| 3 | 199.99 | white dress | False    |

Note how only the shared items, **red shirt,** and white dress, are included. To include all entries from both tables, we can do an outer merge instead. Let's do this now.

5. Run the next cell to perform an outer merge:

```
# Outer merge
df = pd.merge(left=df_1, right=df_2, on='product', how='outer')
df
```

|   | price | product | in_stock |
|---|-------|---------|----------|
| 0 | 49.33 | red shirt | True |
| 1 | 49.33 | red shirt | True |
| 2 | 32.49 | red shirt | True |
| 3 | 199.99 | white dress | False |
| 4 | NaN | blue pants | True |
| 5 | NaN | white tuxedo | False |

This returns all of the data from each table where missing values have been labeled with NaN.

6. Run the next cell to perform an outer merge:

```
# Outer merge
df = pd.merge(left=df_1, right=df_2, on='product', how='outer')
df
```

|   | price | product | in_stock |
|---|-------|---------|----------|
| 0 | 49.33 | red shirt | True |
| 1 | 49.33 | red shirt | True |
| 2 | 32.49 | red shirt | True |
| 3 | 199.99 | white dress | False |
| 4 | NaN | blue pants | True |
| 5 | NaN | white tuxedo | False |

This returns all of the data from each table where missing values have been labeled with NaN.

Since this is our first time encountering an NaN value in this book, now is a good time to discuss how these work in Python.

First of all, you can define an NaN variable by doing, for example, a = float('nan').

However, if you want to test for equality, you cannot simply use standard comparison methods.

It's best to do this instead with a high-level function from a library such as NumPy. This is illustrated with the following code:

```
a = float('nan')

bool(a)
True

a == float('nan')
False

a is float('nan')
False

np.isnan(a)
True
```

Some of these results may seem counter-intuitive. There is a logic behind this behavior, however, and for a deeper understanding of the fundamental reasons for standard comparisons returning False, check out this excellent Stack Overflow thread: https://stackoverflow.com/questions/1565164/what-is-the-rationale-for-all-comparisons-returning-false-for-ieee754-nan-values.

1. You may have noticed that our most recently merged table has duplicated data in the first few rows. Let's see how to handle this.

   Run the cell containing df.drop_duplicates() to return a version of the DataFrame with no duplicate rows:

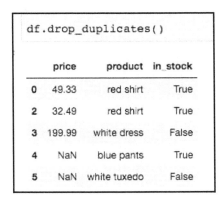

   This is the easiest and "standard" way to drop duplicate rows. To apply these changes to df, we can either set inplace=True or do something like df = df.drop_duplicated(). Let's see another method, which uses masking to select or drop duplicate rows.

2. Run the cell containing df.duplicated() to print the True/False series, marking duplicate rows:

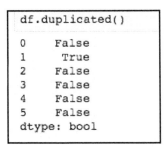

We can take the sum of this result to determine how many rows have duplicates, or it can be used as a mask to select the duplicated rows.

3. Do this by running the next two cells:

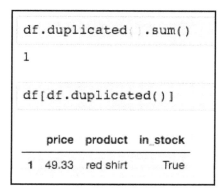

4. We can compute the opposite of the mask with a simple tilde (~) to extract the deduplicated DataFrame. Run the following code and convince yourself the output is the same as that from `df.drop_duplicates()`:

```
df[~df.duplicated()]
```

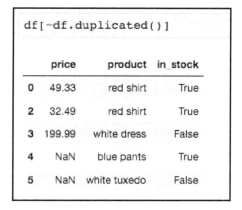

5. This can also be used to drop duplicates from a subset of the full DataFrame. For example, run the cell containing the following code:

```
df[~df['product'].duplicated()]
```

```
df[~df['product'].duplicated()]
```

|   | price  | product      | in_stock |
|---|--------|--------------|----------|
| 0 | 49.33  | red shirt    | True     |
| 3 | 199.99 | white dress  | False    |
| 4 | NaN    | blue pants   | True     |
| 5 | NaN    | white tuxedo | False    |

Here, we are doing the following things:

- Creating a mask (a `True/False` series) for the product row, where duplicates are marked with e
- Using the tilde (~) to take the opposite of that mask, so that duplicates are instead marked with False and everything else is `True`
- Using that mask to filter out the `False` rows of df, which correspond to the duplicated products

As expected, we now see that only the first red shirt row remains, as the duplicate product rows have been removed.

In order to proceed with the steps, let's replace df with a deduplicated version of itself. This can be done by running `drop_duplicates` and passing the parameter `inplace=True`.

6. Deduplicate the DataFrame and save the result by running the cell containing the following code:
```
df.drop_duplicates(inplace=True)
```

Continuing on to other preprocessing methods, let's ignore the duplicated rows and first deal with the missing data. This is necessary because models cannot be trained on incomplete samples. Using the missing price data for blue pants and white tuxedo as an example, let's show some different options for handling NaN values.

7. One option is to drop the rows, which might be a good idea if your NaN samples are missing the majority of their values. Do this by running the cell containing `df.dropna()`:

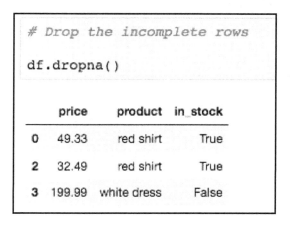

8. If most of the values are missing for a feature, it may be best to drop that column entirely. Do this by running the cell containing the same method as before, but this time with the axes parameter passed to indicate columns instead of rows:

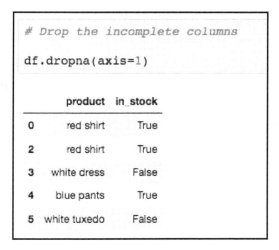

Simply dropping the NaN values is usually not the best option, because losing data is never good, especially if only a small fraction of the sample values is missing. Pandas offers a method for filling in NaN entries in a variety of different ways, some of which we'll illustrate now.

9. Run the cell containing df.fillna? to print the docstring for the Pandas NaN-fill method:

```
Signature: df.fillna(value=None, method=None, axis=None, inplace=False, limit=None, downc
ast=None, **kwargs)
Docstring:
Fill NA/NaN values using the specified method

Parameters
----------
value : scalar, dict, Series, or DataFrame
    Value to use to fill holes (e.g. 0), alternately a
    dict/Series/DataFrame of values specifying which value to use for
    each index (for a Series) or column (for a DataFrame). (values not
    in the dict/Series/DataFrame will not be filled). This value cannot
    be a list.
method : {'backfill', 'bfill', 'pad', 'ffill', None}, default None
    Method to use for filling holes in reindexed Series
    pad / ffill: propagate last valid observation forward to next valid
    backfill / bfill: use NEXT valid observation to fill gap
axis : {0 or 'index', 1 or 'columns'}
inplace : boolean, default False
    If True, fill in place. Note: this will modify any
    other views on this object, (e.g. a no-copy slice for a column in a
    DataFrame).
```

Note the options for the value parameter; this could be, for example, a single value or a dictionary/series type map based on index. Alternatively, we can leave the value as None and pass a fill method instead. We'll see examples of each in this chapter.

10. Fill in the missing data with the average product price by running the cell containing the following code:
```
df.fillna(value=df.price.mean())
```

```
# Fill with the average

df.fillna(value=df.price.mean())
```

|   | price      | product     | in_stock |
|---|------------|-------------|----------|
| 0 | 49.330000  | red shirt   | True     |
| 2 | 32.490000  | red shirt   | True     |
| 3 | 199.990000 | white dress | False    |
| 4 | 93.936667  | blue pants  | True     |
| 5 | 93.936667  | white tuxedo| False    |

11. Now, fill in the missing data using the pad method by running the cell containing the following code instead:

```
df.fillna(method='pad')
```

```
# Fill with the previous value in that column

df.fillna(method='pad')
```

|   | price  | product     | in_stock |
|---|--------|-------------|----------|
| 0 | 49.33  | red shirt   | True     |
| 2 | 32.49  | red shirt   | True     |
| 3 | 199.99 | white dress | False    |
| 4 | 199.99 | blue pants  | True     |
| 5 | 199.99 | white tuxedo| False    |

Notice how the **white dress** price was used to pad the missing values below it.

To conclude this section, we will prepare our simple table to be used for training a machine learning algorithm. Don't worry, we won't actually try to train any models on such a small dataset! We start this process by encoding the class labels for the categorical data.

12. Before encoding the labels, run the first cell in the `Building training data sets` section to add another column of data representing the average product ratings:

```
df = df.fillna(value=df.price.mean())
ratings = ['low', 'medium', 'high']
np.random.seed(2)
df['rating'] = np.random.choice(ratings, len(df))
df
```

| | price | product | in_stock | rating |
|---|---|---|---|---|
| 0 | 49.330000 | red shirt | True | low |
| 2 | 32.490000 | red shirt | True | medium |
| 3 | 199.990000 | white dress | False | low |
| 4 | 93.936667 | blue pants | True | high |
| 5 | 93.936667 | white tuxedo | False | high |

Imagining we want to use this table to train a predictive model, we should first think about changing all the variables to numeric types.

13. The simplest column to handle is the Boolean list:`in_stock`. This should be changed to numeric values, for example, 0 and 1, before using it to train a predictive model. This can be done in many ways, for example, by running the cell containing the following code: `df.in_stock = df.in_stock.map({False: 0, True: 1})`

```
# Convert in_stock to binary

df.in_stock = df.in_stock.map({False: 0, True: 1})
df
```

| | price | product | in_stock | rating |
|---|---|---|---|---|
| 0 | 49.330000 | red shirt | 1 | low |
| 2 | 32.490000 | red shirt | 1 | medium |
| 3 | 199.990000 | white dress | 0 | low |
| 4 | 93.936667 | blue pants | 1 | high |
| 5 | 93.936667 | white tuxedo | 0 | high |

14. Another option for encoding features is scikit-learn's LabelEncoder, which can be used to map the class labels to integers at a higher level. Let's test this by running the cell containing the following code:

```
from sklearn.preprocessing import LabelEncoder
rating_encoder = LabelEncoder()
_df = df.copy()
_df.rating = rating_encoder.fit_transform(df.rating)
_df
```

```
# Encode labels

from sklearn.preprocessing import LabelEncoder
rating_encoder = LabelEncoder()
_df = df.copy()
_df.rating = rating_encoder.fit_transform(df.rating)
_df
```

|   | price | product | in_stock | rating |
|---|---|---|---|---|
| 0 | 49.330000 | red shirt | 1 | 1 |
| 2 | 32.490000 | red shirt | 1 | 2 |
| 3 | 199.990000 | white dress | 0 | 1 |
| 4 | 93.936667 | blue pants | 1 | 0 |
| 5 | 93.936667 | white tuxedo | 0 | 0 |

This might bring to mind the preprocessing we did in the previous chapter when building the polynomial model. Here, we instantiate a label encoder and then "train" it and "transform" our data using the `fit_transform` method. We apply the result to a copy of our DataFrame, `_df`.

15. The features can then be converted back using the class we reference with the variable `rating_encoder,` by running `rating_encoder.inverse_transform(df.rating)`:

```
# Convert back if needed

rating_encoder.inverse_transform(_df.rating)

array(['low', 'medium', 'low', 'high', 'high'], dtype=object)
```

You may notice a problem here. We are working with a so-called "ordinal" feature, where there's an inherent order to the labels. In this case, we should expect that a rating of "low" would be encoded with a 0 and a rating of "high" would be encoded with a 2. However, this is not the result we see. In order to achieve proper ordinal label encoding, we should again use the map, and build the dictionary ourselves.

16. Encode the ordinal labels properly by running the cell containing the following code:

```
ordinal_map = {rating: index for index, rating in enumerate
(['low','medium', 'high'])}
print(ordinal_map)
df.rating = df.rating.map(ordinal_map)
```

```
# Encode ordinal labels
ordinal_map = {rating: index for index, rating in enumerate(['low', 'medium', 'high'])}
print(ordinal_map)

df.rating = df.rating.map(ordinal_map)
df
```

```
{'low': 0, 'high': 2, 'medium': 1}
```

|   | price | product | in_stock | rating |
|---|---|---|---|---|
| 0 | 49.330000 | red shirt | 1 | 0 |
| 2 | 32.490000 | red shirt | 1 | 1 |
| 3 | 199.990000 | white dress | 0 | 0 |
| 4 | 93.936667 | blue pants | 1 | 2 |
| 5 | 93.936667 | white tuxedo | 0 | 2 |

We first create the mapping dictionary. This is done using a dictionary comprehension and enumeration, but looking at the result, we see that it could just as easily be defined *manually* instead. Then, as done earlier for the in_stock column, we apply the dictionary mapping to the feature. Looking at the result, we see that rating now makes more sense than before, where low is labeled with 0, medium with 1, and high with 2.

Now that we've discussed ordinal features, let's touch on another type called nominal features. These are fields with no inherent order, and in our case, we see that product is a perfect example.

Most scikit-learn models can be trained on data like this, where we have strings instead of integer-encoded labels. In this situation, the necessary conversions are done under the hood. However, this may not be the case for all models in scikit learn, or other machine learning and deep learning libraries. Therefore, it's good practice to encode these ourselves during preprocessing

17. A commonly used technique to convert class labels from strings to numerical values is called one-hot encoding. This splits the distinct classes out into separate features. It can be accomplished elegantly with `pd.get_dummies()`. Do this by running the cell containing the following code: `df = pd.get_dummies(df)`

The final DataFrame then looks as follows:

| | price | in_stock | rating | product_blue pants | product_red shirt | product_white dress | product_white tuxedo |
|---|---|---|---|---|---|---|---|
| 0 | 49.330 | 1 | 1 | 0 | 1 | 0 | 0 |
| 1 | 49.330 | 1 | 2 | 0 | 1 | 0 | 0 |
| 2 | 32.490 | 1 | 1 | 0 | 1 | 0 | 0 |
| 3 | 199.990 | 0 | 0 | 0 | 0 | 1 | 0 |
| 4 | 82.785 | 1 | 0 | 1 | 0 | 0 | 0 |
| 5 | 82.785 | 0 | 1 | 0 | 0 | 0 | 1 |

Here, we see the result of one-hot encoding: the product column has been split into 4, one for each unique value. Within each column, we find either a 1 or 0 representing whether that row contains the particular value or product.

Moving on and ignoring any data scaling (which should usually be done), the final step is to split the data into training and test sets to use for machine learning. This can be done using scikit-learn's train_test_split. Let's assume we are going to try to predict whether an item is in stock, given the other feature values.

18. Split the data into training and test sets by running the cell containing the following code:

```
features = ['price', 'rating', 'product_blue pants',
'product_red shirt', 'product_white dress',
'product_white tuxedo']
X = df[features].values
target = 'in_stock'
y = df[target].values
```

```
from sklearn.model_selection import train_test_split
X_train, X_test, y_train, y_test = \
train_test_split(X, y, test_size=0.3)
```

```
print('              shape')
print('---------------')
print('X_train', X_train.shape)
print('X_test ', X_test.shape)
print('y_train', y_train.shape)
print('y_test ', y_test.shape)
```

```
              shape
---------------
X_train (3, 6)
X_test  (2, 6)
y_train (3,)
y_test  (2,)
```

Here, we are selecting subsets of the data and feeding them into the `train_test_ split` function. This function has four outputs, which are unpacked into the training and testing splits for features (X) and the target (y).

Observe the shape of the output data, where the test set has roughly 30% of the samples and the training set has roughly 70%.

We'll see similar code blocks later when preparing real data to use for training predictive models.

This concludes the section on cleaning data for use in machine learning applications. Let's take a minute to note how effective our Jupyter Notebook was for testing various methods of transforming the data, and ultimately documenting the pipeline we decided upon. This could easily be applied to an updated version of the data by altering only specific cells of code, prior to processing. Also, should we desire any changes to the processing, these can easily be tested in the notebook, and specific cells may be changed to accommodate the alterations. The best way to achieve this would probably be to copy the notebook over to a new file so that we can always keep a copy of the original analysis for reference.

Moving on to an activity, we'll now apply the concepts from this section to a large dataset as we prepare it for use in training predictive models.

# Activity: Preparing to Train a Predictive Model for the Employee-Retention Problem

Suppose you are hired to do freelance work for a company who wants to find insights into why their employees are leaving. They have compiled a set of data they think will be helpful in this respect. It includes details on employee satisfaction levels, evaluations, time spent at work, department, and salary.

The company shares its data with you by sending you a file called `hr_data.csv` and asking what you think can be done to help stop employees from leaving. To apply the concepts we've learned thus far to a real-life problem. In particular, we seek to:

- Determine a plan for using predictive analytics to provide impactful business insights, given the available data.
- Prepare the data for use in machine learning models.

 Starting with this activity and continuing through the remainder of this chapter, we'll be using *Human Resources Analytics*, which is a Kaggle dataset. There is a small difference between the dataset we use in this book and the online version. Our human resource analytics data contains some `NaN` values. These were manually removed from the online version of the dataset, for the purposes of illustrating data cleaning techniques. We have also added a column of data called `is_smoker`, for the same purposes.

1. With the `chapter-2-workbook.ipynb` notebook file open, scroll to the Activity section.
2. Check the head of the table by running the following code:

```
%%bash
head ../data/hr-analytics/hr_data.csv
```

Judging by the output, convince yourself that it looks to be in standard CSV format. For CSV files, we should be able to simply load the data with `pd.read_csv`.

3. Load the data with Pandas by running `df = pd.read_csv('../data/hranalytics/hr_data.csv')`. Use tab completion to help type the file path.

4. Inspect the columns by printing df.columns and make sure the data has loaded as expected by printing the DataFrame head and tail with `df.head()` and `df.tail()`:

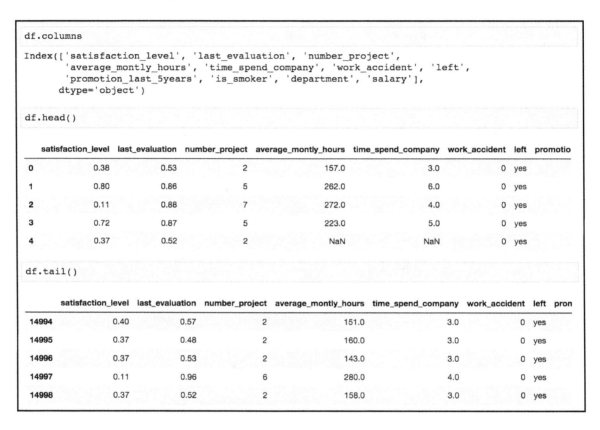

```
df.columns
Index(['satisfaction_level', 'last_evaluation', 'number_project',
       'average_montly_hours', 'time_spend_company', 'work_accident', 'left',
       'promotion_last_5years', 'is_smoker', 'department', 'salary'],
      dtype='object')

df.head()
```

| | satisfaction_level | last_evaluation | number_project | average_montly_hours | time_spend_company | work_accident | left | promotio |
|---|---|---|---|---|---|---|---|---|
| 0 | 0.38 | 0.53 | 2 | 157.0 | 3.0 | 0 | yes | |
| 1 | 0.80 | 0.86 | 5 | 262.0 | 6.0 | 0 | yes | |
| 2 | 0.11 | 0.88 | 7 | 272.0 | 4.0 | 0 | yes | |
| 3 | 0.72 | 0.87 | 5 | 223.0 | 5.0 | 0 | yes | |
| 4 | 0.37 | 0.52 | 2 | NaN | NaN | 0 | yes | |

```
df.tail()
```

| | satisfaction_level | last_evaluation | number_project | average_montly_hours | time_spend_company | work_accident | left | pron |
|---|---|---|---|---|---|---|---|---|
| 14994 | 0.40 | 0.57 | 2 | 151.0 | 3.0 | 0 | yes | |
| 14995 | 0.37 | 0.48 | 2 | 160.0 | 3.0 | 0 | yes | |
| 14996 | 0.37 | 0.53 | 2 | 143.0 | 3.0 | 0 | yes | |
| 14997 | 0.11 | 0.96 | 6 | 280.0 | 4.0 | 0 | yes | |
| 14998 | 0.37 | 0.52 | 2 | 158.0 | 3.0 | 0 | yes | |

We can see that it appears to have loaded correctly. Based on the tail index values, there are nearly 15,000 rows; let's make sure we didn't miss any.

5. Check the number of rows (including the header) in the `CSV file` with the following code:

```
with open('../data/hr-analytics/hr_data.csv') as f:
print(len(f.read().splitlines()))
```

```
# How many lines in the CSV (including header)

with open('../data/hr-analytics/hr_data.csv') as f:
    print(len(f.read().splitlines()))
```
```
15000
```

6. Compare this result to `len(df)` to make sure we've loaded all the data:

```
# How many samples did we load into Python?

len(df)
```
```
14999
```

Now that our client's data has been properly loaded, let's think about how we can use predictive analytics to find insights into why their employees are leaving.

Let's run through the first steps for creating a predictive analytics plan:

- **Look at the available data**: We've already done this by looking at the columns, data types, and the number of samples
- **Determine the business needs**: The client has clearly expressed their needs: reduce the number of employees who leave
- **Assess the data for suitability**: Let's try to determine a plan that can help satisfy the client's needs, given the provided data

Recall, as mentioned earlier, that effective analytics techniques lead to impactful business decisions. With that in mind, if we were able to predict how likely an employee is to quit, the business could selectively target those employees for special treatment. For example, their salary could be raised or their number of projects reduced. Furthermore, the impact of these changes could be estimated using the model!

To assess the validity of this plan, let's think about our data. Each row represents an employee who either works for the company or has **left**, as labeled by the column named left. We can, therefore, train a model to predict this target, given a set of features.

Assess the target variable. Check the distribution and number of missing entries by running the following code:

```
df.left.value_counts().plot('barh')
print(df.left.isnull().sum())
```

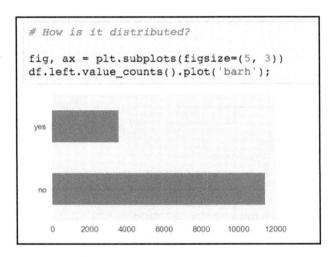

Here's the output of the second code line:

```
# How much missing data?

df.left.isnull().sum()

0
```

About three-quarters of the samples are employees who have not left. The group who has left makes up the other quarter of the samples. This tells us we are dealing with an imbalanced classification problem, which means we'll have to take special measures to account for each class when calculating accuracies. We also see that none of the target variables are missing (no NaN values).

Now, we'll assess the features:

1. Print the data type of each by executing `df.dtypes`. Observe how we have a mix of continuous and discrete features:

```
# Print datatypes

df.dtypes

satisfaction_level      float64
last_evaluation         float64
number_project            int64
average_montly_hours    float64
time_spend_company      float64
work_accident             int64
left                     object
promotion_last_5years     int64
is_smoker                object
department               object
salary                   object
dtype: object
```

2. Display the feature distributions by running the following code:

```
for f in df.columns:
try:
fig = plt.figure()
...
print('-'*30)
```

This code snippet is a little complicated, but it's very useful for showing an overview of both the continuous and discrete features in our dataset. Essentially, it assumes each feature is continuous and attempts to plot its distribution, and reverts to simply plotting the value counts if the feature turns out to be discrete.

The result is as follows:

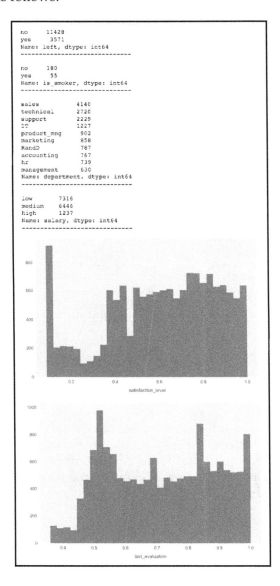

```
no      11428
yes      3571
Name: left, dtype: int64
-------------------------------

no       180
yes       55
Name: is_smoker, dtype: int64
-------------------------------

sales        4140
technical    2720
support      2229
IT           1227
product_mng   902
marketing     858
RandD         787
accounting    767
hr            739
management    630
Name: department, dtype: int64
-------------------------------

low      7316
medium   6446
high     1237
Name: salary, dtype: int64
-------------------------------
```

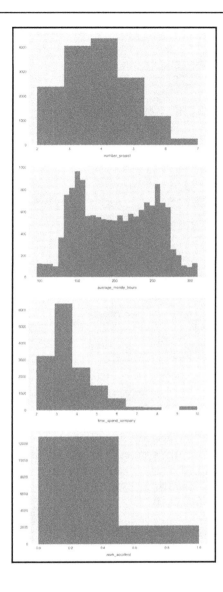

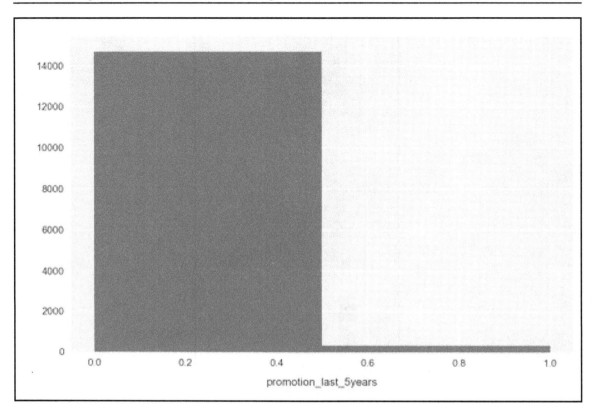

For many features, we see a wide distribution over the possible values, indicating a good variety in the feature spaces. This is encouraging; features that are strongly grouped around a small range of values may not be very informative for the model. This is the case for `promotion_last_5years`, where we see that the vast majority of samples are 0.

The next thing we need to do is remove any `NaN` values from the dataset.

1. Check how many `NaN` values are in each column by running the following code:
   `df.isnull().sum() / len(df) * 100`

```
# How many NaNs?

df.isnull().sum() / len(df) * 100
satisfaction_level      0.000000
last_evaluation         0.000000
number_project          0.000000
average_montly_hours    2.453497
time_spend_company      1.006734
work_accident           0.000000
left                    0.000000
promotion_last_5years   0.000000
is_smoker              98.433229
department              0.000000
salary                  0.000000
dtype: float64
```

We can see there are about 2.5% missing for `average_montly_hours`, 1% missing for `time_spend_company`, and 98% missing for `is_smoker`! Let's use a couple of different strategies that we've learned about to handle these.

2. Since there is barely any information in the `is_smoker` metric, let's drop this column. Do this by running: `del df['is_smoker']`.

3. Since time_spend_company is an integer field, we'll use the median value to fill the NaN values in this column. This can be done with the following code:

```
fill_value = df.time_spend_company.median()
df.time_spend_company =
df.time_spend_company.fillna(fill_value)
```

The final column to deal with is `average_montly_hours`. We could do something similar and use the median or rounded mean as the integer fill value. Instead, let's try to take advantage of its relationship with another variable. This may allow us to fill the missing data more accurately.

4. Make a boxplot of `average_montly_hours` segmented by `number_project`. This can be done by running the following code:

```
sns.boxplot(x='number_project', y='average_montly_hours',
data=df)
```

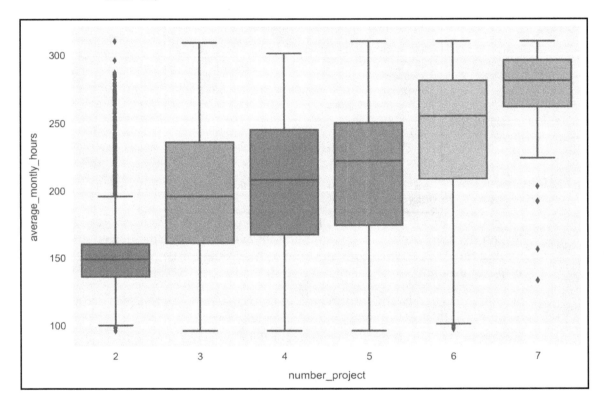

We can see how the number of projects is correlated with `average_monthly_hours`, a result that is hardly surprising. We'll exploit this relationship by filling in the `NaN` values of `average_montly_hours` differently, depending on the number of projects for that sample. Specifically, we'll use the mean of each group.

5. Calculate the mean of each group by running the following code:

```
mean_per_project = df.groupby('number_project')\.
average_montly_hours.mean()
mean_per_project = dict(mean_per_project)
print(mean_per_project)
```

```
# Calculate fill values for average_montly_hours

mean_per_project = df.groupby('number_project')\
                     .average_montly_hours.mean()
mean_per_project = dict(mean_per_project)
mean_per_project

{2: 160.16353543979506,
 3: 197.47882323104236,
 4: 205.07858315740089,
 5: 211.99962839093274,
 6: 238.73947368421054,
 7: 276.01587301587301}
```

We can then map this onto the `number_project` column and pass the resulting series object as the argument to `fillna`.

6. Fill the NaN values in `average_montly_hours` by executing the following code:

```
fill_values = df.number_project.map(mean_per_project)
df.average_montly_hours = df.average_montly_hours.fillna(fill_values)
```

7. Confirm that `df` has no more NaN values by running the following assertion test. If it does not raise an error, then you have successfully removed the NaNs from the table:

```
assert df.isnull().sum().sum() == 0
```

8. Finally, we will transform the string and Boolean fields into integer representations. In particular, we'll manually convert the target variable `left` from yes and no to 1 and 0 and build the one-hot encoded features. Do this by running the following code:

```
df.left = df.left.map({'no': 0, 'yes': 1})
df = pd.get_dummies(df)
```

9. Print `df.columns` to show the fields:

```
df.columns
Index(['satisfaction_level', 'last_evaluation', 'number_project',
       'average_montly_hours', 'time_spend_company', 'work_accident', 'left',
       'promotion_last_5years', 'department_IT', 'department_RandD',
       'department_accounting', 'department_hr', 'department_management',
       'department_marketing', 'department_product_mng', 'department_sales',
       'department_support', 'department_technical', 'salary_high',
       'salary_low', 'salary_medium'],
      dtype='object')
```

We can see that `department` and `salary` have been split into various binary features.

The final step to prepare our data for machine learning is scaling the features, but for various reasons (for example, some models do not require scaling), we'll do it as part of the model-training workflow in the next activity.

10. We have completed the data preprocessing and are ready to move on to training models! Let's save our preprocessed data by running the following code:

```
df.to_csv('../data/hr-analytics/hr_data_processed.csv',
index=False)
```

Again, we pause here to note how well the Jupyter Notebook suited our needs when performing this initial data analysis and clean-up. Imagine, for example, we left this project in its current state for a few months. Upon returning to it, we would probably not remember what exactly was going on when we left it. Referring back to this notebook though, we would be able to retrace our steps and quickly recall what we previously learned about the data. Furthermore, we could update the data source with any new data and re-run the notebook to prepare the new set of data for use in our machine learning algorithms. Recall that in this situation, it would be best to make a copy of the notebook first, so as not to lose the initial analysis.

To summarize, we've learned and applied methods for preparing to train a machine learning model. We started by discussing steps for identifying a problem that can be solved with predictive analytics. This consisted of:

- Looking at the available data
- Determining the business needs
- Assessing the data for suitability

We also discussed how to identify supervised versus unsupervised and regression versus classification problems.

After identifying our problem, we learned techniques for using Jupyter Notebooks to build and test a data transformation pipeline. These techniques included methods and best practices for filling missing data, transforming categorical features, and building train/test data sets.

In the remainder of this chapter, we will use this preprocessed data to train a variety of classification models. To avoid blindly applying algorithms we don't understand, we start by introducing them and overviewing how they work. Then, we use Jupyter to train and compare their predictive capabilities. Here, we have the opportunity to discuss more advanced topics in machine learning like overfitting, k-fold cross-validation, and validation curves.

# Training Classification Models

As we've already seen in the previous chapter, using libraries such as scikit-learn and platforms such as Jupyter, predictive models can be trained in just a few lines of code. This is possible by abstracting away the difficult computations involved with optimizing model parameters. In other words, we deal with a black box where the internal operations are hidden instead. With this simplicity also comes the danger of misusing algorithms, for example, by overfitting during training or failing to properly test on unseen data. We'll show how to avoid these pitfalls while training classification models and produce trustworthy results with the use of k-fold cross-validation and validation curves.

# Introduction to Classification Algorithms

Recall the two types of supervised machine learning: regression and classification. In regression, we predict a continuous target variable. For example, recall the linear and polynomial models from the first chapter. In this chapter, we focus on the other type of supervised machine learning: classification. Here, the goal is to predict the class of a sample using the available metrics.

In the simplest case, there are only two possible classes, which means we are doing binary classification. This is the case for the example problem in this chapter, where we try to predict whether an employee has left or not. If we have more than two class labels instead, we are doing multi-class classification.

Although there is little difference between binary and multi-class classification when training models with scikit-learn, what's done inside the "black box" is notably different. In particular, multi-class classification models often use the one-versus-rest method. This works as follows for a case with three class labels. When the model is "fit" with the data, three models are trained, and each model predicts whether the sample is part of an individual class or part of some other class. This might bring to mind the one-hot encoding for features that we did earlier. When a prediction is made for a sample, the class label with the highest confidence level is returned.

In this chapter, we'll train three types of classification models: Support Vector Machines, Random Forests, and k-Nearest Neighbors classifiers. Each of these algorithms is quite different. As we will see, however, they are quite similar to train and use for predictions thanks to scikit-learn. Before swapping over to the Jupyter Notebook and implementing these, we'll briefly see how they work. SVM's attempt to find the best hyperplane to divide classes by. This is done by maximizing the distance between the hyperplane and the closest samples of each class, which are called support vectors.

This linear method can also be used to model nonlinear classes using the kernel trick. This method maps the features into a higher-dimensional space in which the hyper plane is determined. This hyperplane we've been talking about is also referred to as the decision surface, and we'll visualize it when training our models.

k-Nearest Neighbors classification algorithms memorize the training data and make predictions depending on the K nearest samples in the feature space. With three features, this can be visualized as a sphere surrounding the prediction sample. Often, however, we are dealing with more than three features and therefore hyperspheres are drawn to find the closest K samples.

Random Forests are an ensemble of decision trees, where each has been trained on different subsets of the training data.

A decision tree algorithm classifies a sample based on a series of decisions. For example, the first decision might be "if feature $x_1$ is less than or greater than 0." The data would then be split on this condition and fed into descending branches of the tree. Each step in the decision tree is decided based on the feature split that maximizes the information gain.

Essentially, this term describes the mathematics that attempts to pick the best possible split of the target variable.

Training a Random Forest consists of creating bootstrapped (that is, randomly sampled data with replacement) datasets for a set of decision trees. Predictions are then made based on the majority vote. These have the benefit of less overfitting and better generalizability.

 Decision trees can be used to model a mix of continuous and categorical data, which makes them very useful. Furthermore, as we will see later in this chapter, the tree depth can be limited to reduce overfitting. For a detailed (but brief) look into the decision tree algorithm, check out this popular Stack Overflow answer: `https://stackoverflow. com/a/ 1859910/3511819`. There, the author shows a simple example and discusses concepts such as node purity, information gain, and entropy.

# Training two-feature classification models with scikit-learn

We'll continue working on the employee retention problem that we introduced in the first topic. We previously prepared a dataset for training a classification model, in which we predicted whether an employee has left or not. Now, we'll take that data and use it to train classification models:

1. If you have not already done so, start the `NotebookApp` and open the `chapter-2-workbook.ipynb` file. Scroll down to `Topic Training classification models`. Run the first couple of cells to set the default figure size and load the processed data that we previously saved to a `CSV file`.

   For this example, we'll be training classification models on two continuous features:

   `satisfaction_level` and `last_evaluation`.

2. Draw the bivariate and univariate graphs of the continuous target variables by running the cell with the following code:

```
sns.jointplot('satisfaction_level',
'last_evaluation', data=df, kind='hex')
```

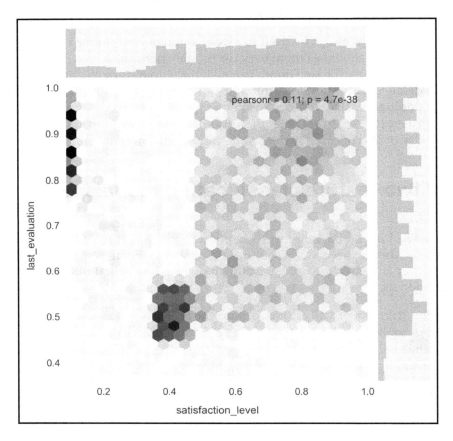

As you can see in the preceding image, there are some very distinct patterns in the data.

3. Re-plot the bivariate distribution, segmenting on the target variable, by running the cell containing the following code:

```
plot_args = dict(shade=True, shade_lowest=False)
for i, c in zip((0, 1), ('Reds', 'Blues')):
    sns.kdeplot(df.loc[df.left==i, 'satisfaction_level'],
        df.loc[df.left==i, 'last_evaluation'],
        cmap=c, **plot_args)
```

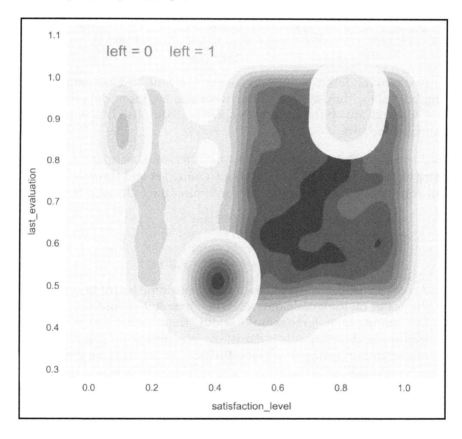

Now, we can see how the patterns are related to the target variable. For the remainder of this section, we'll try to exploit these patterns to train effective classification models.

4. Split the data into training and test sets by running the cell containing the following code:

```
from sklearn.model_selection import train_test_split
features = ['satisfaction_level', 'last_evaluation']
    X_train, X_test, y_train, y_test =
    train_test_split(df[features].values, df['left'].values,
    test_size=0.3, random_state=1)
```

Our first two models, the Support Vector Machine and k-Nearest Neighbors algorithm, are most effective when the input data is scaled so that all of the features are on the same order. We'll accomplish this with scikit-learn's `StandardScaler`.

5. Load `StandardScaler` and create a new instance, as referenced by the scaler variable. Fit the `scaler` on the training set and transform it. Then, transform the test set. Run the cell containing the following code:

```
from sklearn.preprocessing import StandardScaler
scaler = StandardScaler()
X_train_std = scaler.fit_transform(X_train)
X_test_std = scaler.transform(X_test)
```

An easy mistake to make when doing machine learning is to "fit" the scaler on the whole dataset, when in fact it should only be "fit" to the training data. For example, scaling the data before splitting into training and testing sets is a mistake We don't want this because the model training should not be influenced in any way by the test data.

6. Import the scikit-learn support vector machine class and fit the model on the training data by running the cell containing the following code:

```
from sklearn.svm import
SVC svm = SVC(kernel='linear', C=1, random_state=1)
svm.fit(X_train_std, y_train)
```

Then, we train a linear SVM classification model. The C parameter controls the penalty for misclassification, allowing the variance and bias of the model to be controlled.

7. Compute the accuracy of this model on unseen data by running the cell containing the following code:

```
from sklearn.metrics import accuracy_score
y_pred = svm.predict(X_test_std)
acc = accuracy_score(y_test, y_pred)
print('accuracy = {:.1f}%'.format(acc*100))
>> accuracy = 75.9%
```

We predict the targets for our test samples and then use scikit-learn's `accuracy_score` function to determine the accuracy. The result looks promising at ~75%! Not bad for our first model. Recall, though, the target is imbalanced. Let's see how accurate the predictions are for each class.

8. Calculate the confusion matrix and then determine the accuracy within each class by running the cell containing the following code:

```
from sklearn.metrics import confusion_matrix
cmat = confusion_matrix(y_test, y_pred)
scores = cmat.diagonal() / cmat.sum(axis=1) * 100
print('left = 0 : {:.2f}%'.format(scores[0]))
print('left = 1 : {:.2f}%'.format(scores[1]))
>> left = 0 : 100.00%
>> left = 1 : 0.00%
```

It looks like the model is simply classifying every sample as 0, which is clearly not helpful at all. Let's use a contour plot to show the predicted class at each point in the feature space. This is commonly known as the decision-regions plot.

9. Plot the decision regions using a helpful function from the `mlxtend` library. Run the cell containing the following code:

```
from mlxtend.plotting import plot_decision_regions
N_samples = 200
X, y = X_train_std[:N_samples], y_train[:N_samples]
plot_decision_regions(X, y, clf=svm)
```

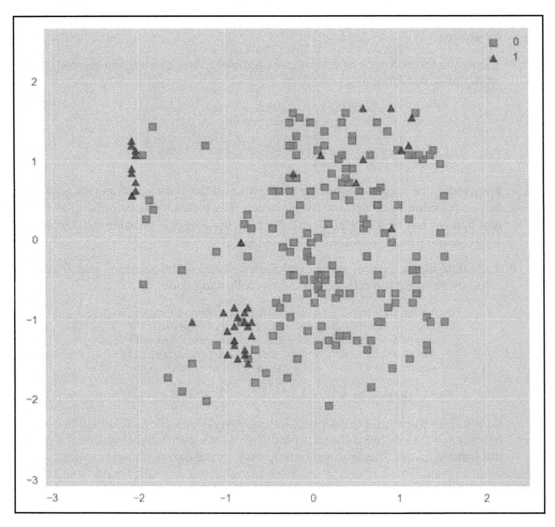

The function plots decision regions along with a set of samples passed as arguments. In order to see the decision regions properly without too many samples obstructing our view, we pass only a 200-sample subset of the test data to the `plot_ decision_regions` function. In this case, of course, it does not matter. We see the result is entirely red, indicating every point in the feature space would be classified as 0.

It shouldn't be surprising that a linear model can't do a good job of describing these nonlinear patterns. Recall earlier we mentioned the kernel trick for using SVM's to classify nonlinear problems. Let's see if doing this can improve the result.

10. Print the docstring for scikit-learn's SVM by running the cell containing SVC. Scroll down and check out the parameter descriptions. Notice the `kernel` option, which is actually enabled by default as `rbf`. Use this kernel option to train a new SVM by running the cell containing the following code:

    ```
    svm = SVC(kernel='rbf', C=1, random_state=1)
    svm.fit(X_train_std, y_train)
    ```

11. In order to assess this and future model performance more easily, let's define a function called `check_model_fit`, which computes various metrics that we can use to compare the models. Run the cell where this function is defied.

    Each computation done in this function has already been seen in this example; it simply calculates accuracies and plots the decision regions.

12. Show the newly trained kernel-SVM results on the training data by running the cell containing the following code:

```
check_model_fit(svm, X_test_std, y_test)
```

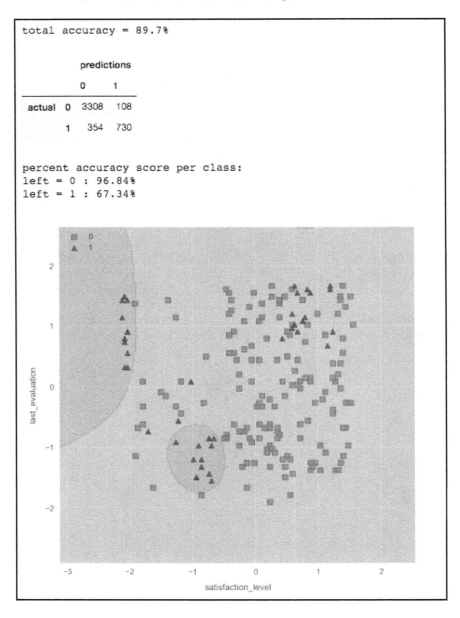

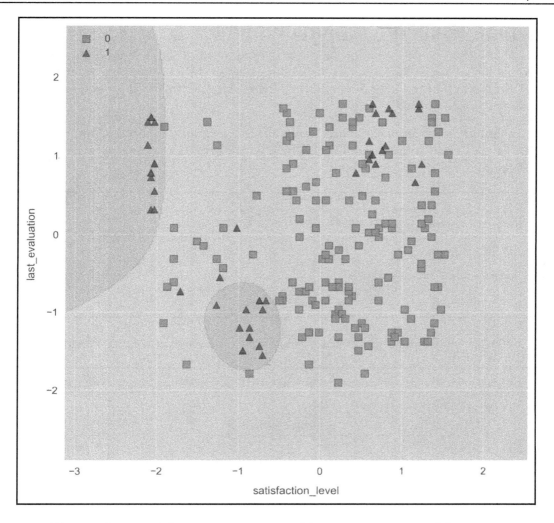

The result is much better. Now, we are able to capture some of the non-linear patterns in the data and correctly classify the majority of the employees who have left.

# The plot_decision_regions Function

The `plot_decision_regions` function is provided by `mlxtend`, a Python library developed by Sebastian *Raschka*. It's worth taking a peek at the source code (which is of course written in Python) to understand how these plots are drawn. It's really not too complicated.

In a Jupyter Notebook, import the function with from `mlxtend.plotting` import `plot_decision_regions`, and then pull up the help with `plot_decision_regions?` and scroll to the bottom to see the local file path:

```
In [152]:  from mlxtend.plotting import plot_decision_regions
           plot_decision_regions?

Returns
---------
ax : matplotlib.axes.Axes object
File:       ~/anaconda/lib/python3.5/site-packages/mlxtend/plotting/decision_regions.py
Type:       function
```

Then, open up the file and check it out! For example, you could run cat in the notebook:

```
In [153]:  cat ~/anaconda/lib/python3.5/site-packages/mlxtend/plotting/decision_regions.py

           def plot_decision_regions(X, y, clf,
                                     feature_index=None,
                                     filler_feature_values=None,
                                     filler_feature_ranges=None,
                                     ax=None,
                                     X_highlight=None,
                                     res=0.02, legend=1,
                                     hide_spines=True,
                                     markers='s^oxv<>',
                                     colors='red,blue,limegreen,gray,cyan'):
               """Plot decision regions of a classifier.

               Please note that this functions assumes that class labels are
               labeled consecutively, e.g,. 0, 1, 2, 3, 4, and 5. If you have class
               labels with integer labels > 4, you may want to provide additional colors
               and/or markers as `colors` and `markers` arguments.
               See http://matplotlib.org/examples/color/named_colors.html for more
               information.
```

This is okay, but not ideal as there's no color markup for the code. It's better to copy it (so you don't accidentally alter the original) and open it with your favorite text editor.

When drawing attention to the code responsible for mapping the decision regions, we see a contour plot of predictions Z over an array X_predict that spans the feature space.

```python
xx, yy = np.meshgrid(np.arange(x_min, x_max, xres),
                     np.arange(y_min, y_max, yres))

if dim == 1:
    X_predict = np.array([xx.ravel()]).T
else:
    X_grid = np.array([xx.ravel(), yy.ravel()]).T
    X_predict = np.zeros((X_grid.shape[0], dim))
    X_predict[:, x_index] = X_grid[:, 0]
    X_predict[:, y_index] = X_grid[:, 1]
    if dim > 2:
        for feature_idx in filler_feature_values:
            X_predict[:, feature_idx] = filler_feature_values[feature_idx]
Z = clf.predict(X_predict)
Z = Z.reshape(xx.shape)
# Plot decisoin region
ax.contourf(xx, yy, Z,
            alpha=0.3,
            colors=colors,
            levels=np.arange(Z.max() + 2) - 0.5)
```

Let's move on to the next model: k-Nearest Neighbors.

# Training k-nearest neighbors for our model

1. Load the scikit-learn KNN classification model and print the docstring by running the cell containing the following code:

```python
from sklearn.neighbors import KNeighborsClassifier
KNeighborsClassifier?
```

The n_neighbors parameter decides how many samples to use when making a classification. If the weights parameter is set to uniform, then class labels are decided by majority vote. Another useful choice for the weights is distance, where closer samples have a higher weight in the voting. Like most model parameters, the best choice for this depends on the particular dataset.

2. Train the KNN classifier with `n_neighbors=3`, and then compute the accuracy and decision regions. Run the cell containing the following code:

```
knn = KNeighborsClassifier(n_neighbors=3)
knn.fit(X_train_std, y_train)

check_model_fit(knn, X_test_std, y_test)
```

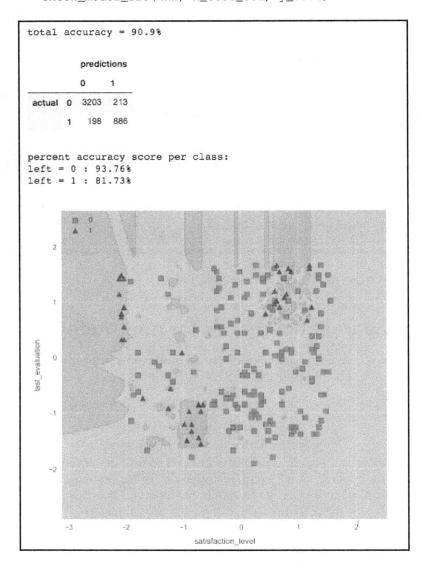

total accuracy = 90.9%

|  |  | predictions | |
|---|---|---|---|
|  |  | 0 | 1 |
| actual | 0 | 3203 | 213 |
|  | 1 | 198 | 886 |

percent accuracy score per class:
left = 0 : 93.76%
left = 1 : 81.73%

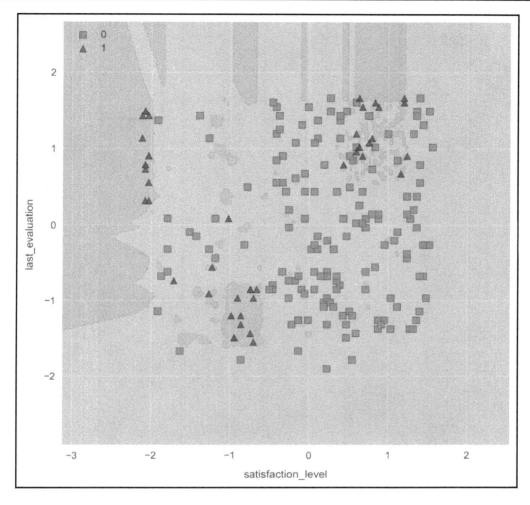

We see an increase in overall accuracy and a significant improvement for class 1 in particular. However, the decision region plot would indicate we are overfitting the data. This is evident by the hard, "choppy" decision boundary, and small pockets of blue everywhere. We can soften the decision boundary and decrease overfitting by increasing the number of nearest neighbors.

3. Train a KNN model with `n_neighbors=25` by running the cell containing the following code:

```
knn = KNeighborsClassifier(n_neighbors=25)
knn.fit(X_train_std, y_train)
check_model_fit(knn, X_test_std, y_test)
```

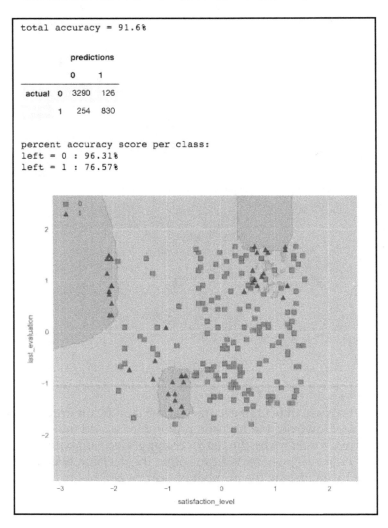

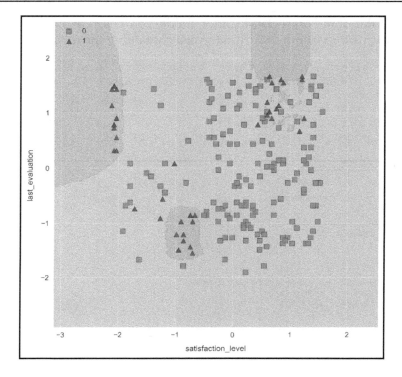

As we can see, the decision boundaries are significantly less choppy, and there are far less pockets of blue. The accuracy for class 1 is slightly less, but we would need to use a more comprehensive method such as k-fold cross-validation to decide if there's a significant difference between the two models.

Note that increasing n_neighbors has no effect on training time, as the model is simply memorizing the data. The prediction time, however, will be greatly affected.

 When doing machine learning with real-world data, it's important for the algorithms to run quick enough to serve their purposes. For example, a script to predict tomorrow's weather that takes longer than a day to run is completely useless! Memory is also a consideration that should be taken into account when dealing with substantial amounts of data.

# Training a Random Forest

Observe how similar it is to train and make predictions on each model, despite them each being so different internally.

1. Train a Random Forest classification model composed of 50 decision trees, each with a max depth of 5. Run the cell containing the following code:

```
from sklearn.ensemble import RandomForestClassifier
forest = RandomForestClassifier(n_estimators=50,
max_depth=5,
random_state=1)
forest.fit(X_train, y_train)
check_model_fit(forest, X_test, y_test)
```

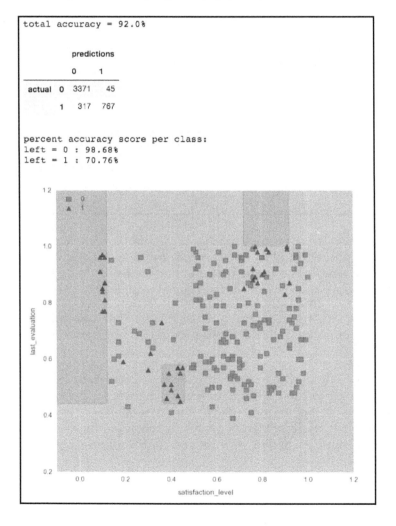

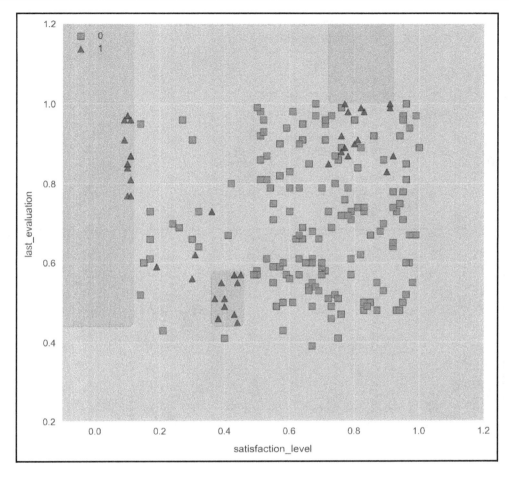

Note the distinctive axes-parallel decision boundaries produced by decision tree machine learning algorithms.

We can access any of the individual decision trees used to build the Random Forest. These trees are stored in the `estimators_attribute` of the model. Let's draw one of these decision trees to get a feel for what's going on. Doing this requires the **graph** viz dependency, which can sometimes be difficult to install.

2. Draw one of the decision trees in the Jupyter Notebook by running the cell containing the following code:

```
from sklearn.tree import export_graphviz
import graphviz
dot_data = export_graphviz(
    forest.estimators_[0],
    out_file=None,
    feature_names=features,
    class_names=['no', 'yes'],
    filled=True, rounded=True,
    special_characters=True)
graph = graphviz.Source(dot_data)
graph
```

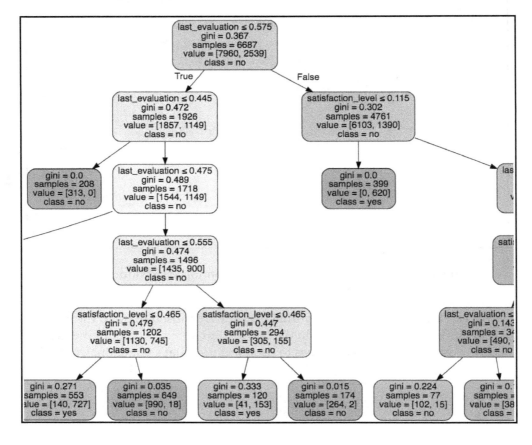

We can see that each path is limited to five nodes as a result of setting `max_depth=5`. The orange boxes represent predictions of `no` (has not left the company), and the blue boxes represent `yes` (has left the company). The shade of each box (light, dark, and so on) indicates the confidence level, which is related to the `gini` value.

To summarize, we have accomplished two of the learning objectives in this section:

- We gained a qualitative understanding of support vector machines (SVMs), k-Nearest Neighbor classifiers (kNNs), and Random Forest
- We are now able to train a variety of models using scikit-learn and Jupyter Notebooks so that we can confidently build and compare predictive models

In particular, we used the preprocessed data from our employee retention problem to train classification models to predict whether an employee has left the company or not. For the purposes of keeping things simple and focusing on the algorithms, we built models to predict this given only two features: the satisfaction level and last evaluation value. This two-dimensional feature space also allowed us to visualize the decision boundaries and identify what overfitting looks like.

In the following section, we will introduce two important topics in machine learning: k-fold cross-validation and validation curves

# Assessing Models with k-Fold Cross-Validation and Validation Curves

Thus far, we have trained models on a subset of the data and then assessed performance on the unseen portion, called the test set. This is good practice because the model performance on training data is not a good indicator of its effectiveness as a predictor. It's very easy to increase accuracy on a training dataset by overfitting a model, which can result in poorer performance on unseen data.

That said, simply training models on data split in this way is not good enough. There is a natural variance in data that causes accuracies to be different (if even slightly) depending on the training and test splits. Furthermore, using only one training/test split to compare models can introduce a bias towards certain models and lead to overfitting.

**k-fold cross validation** offers a solution to this problem and allows the variance to be accounted for by way of an error estimate on each accuracy calculation. This, in turn, naturally leads to the use of validation curves for tuning model parameters. These plots the accuracy as a function of a hyper parameter such as the number of decision trees used in a Random Forest or the max depth.

This is our first time using the term hyperparameter. It references a parameter that is defined when initializing a model, for example, the C parameter of the SVM. This is in contradistinction to a parameter of the trained model, such as the equation of the decision boundary hyperplane for a trained SVM.

The method is illustrated in the following diagram, where we see how the k-folds can be selected from the dataset:

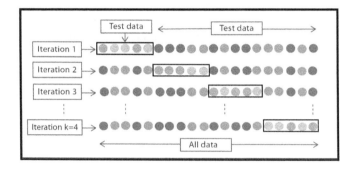

The k-fold cross-validation algorithm goes as follows:

1. Split data into k "folds" of near-equal size.
2. Test and train k models on different fold combinations. Each model will include $k - 1$ folds of training data and the left-out fold is used for testing. In this method, each fold ends up being used as the validation data exactly once.
3. Calculate the model accuracy by taking the mean of the k values. The standard deviation is also calculated to provide error bars on the value.

It's standard to set $k = 10$, but smaller values for k should be considered if using a big data set.

This validation method can be used to reliably compare model performance with different hyperparameters (for example, the C parameter for an SVM or the number of nearest neighbors in a KNN classifier). It's also suitable for comparing entirely different models.

Once the best model has been identified, it should be re-trained on the entirety of the dataset before being used to predict actual classifications.

When implementing this with scikit-learn, it's common to use a slightly improved variation of the normal k-fold algorithm instead. This is called stratified k-fold. The improvement is that stratified k-fold cross validation maintains roughly even class label populations in the folds. As you can imagine, this reduces the overall variance in the models and decreases the likelihood of highly unbalanced models causing bias.

Validation curves are plots of a training and validation metric as a function of some model parameter. They allow to us to make good model parameter selections. In this book, we will use the accuracy score as our metric for these plots.

 The documentation for plot validation curves is available here: `http://scikit-learn.org/stable/auto_examples/model_selecti on/plot_validation_curve.html`.

Consider this validation curve, where the accuracy score is plotted as a function of the gamma SVM parameter:

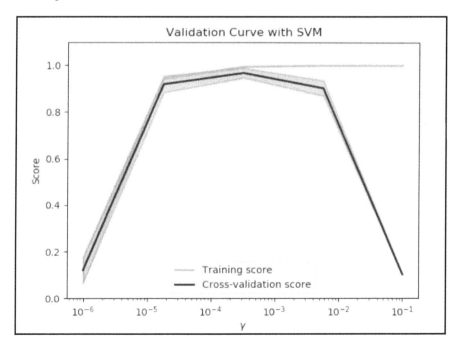

Starting on the left side of the plot, we can see that both sets of data are agreeing on the score, which is good. However, the score is also quite low compared to other gamma values, so therefore we say the model is underfitting the data. Increasing the gamma, we can see a point where the error bars of these two lines no longer overlap. From this point on, we see the classifier overfitting the data as the models behave increasingly well on the training set compared to the validation set. The optimal value for the gamma parameter can be found by looking for a high validation score with overlapping error bars on the two lines.

Keep in mind that a learning curve for some parameter is only valid while the other parameters remain constant. For example, if training the SVM in this plot, we could decide to pick gamma on the order of 10-4. However, we may want to optimize the C parameter as well. With a different value for C, the preceding plot would be different and our selection for gamma may no longer be optimal.

# Using k-fold cross-validation and validation curves in Python with scikit-learn

1. If you've not already done so, start the `NotebookApp` and open the `chapter-2-workbook.ipynb file.` Scroll down to Subtopic `K-fold cross-validation` and `validation curves`.

   The training data should already be in the notebook's memory, but let's reload it as a reminder of what exactly we're working with.

2. Load the data and select the `satisfaction_level` and `last_evaluation` features for the training/validation set. We will not use the train-test split this time because we are going to use k-fold validation instead. Run the cell containing the following code:

```
df = pd.read_csv('../data/hr-
analytics/hr_data_processed.csv')
features = ['satisfaction_level', 'last_evaluation']
X = df[features].values
y = df.left.values
```

3. Instantiate a Random Forest model by running the cell containing the following code:

```
clf = RandomForestClassifier(n_estimators=100, max_depth=5)
```

4. To train the model with stratified k-fold cross-validation, we'll use the `model_selection.cross_val_score` function.

   Train 10 variations of our model `clf` using stratified k-fold validation. Note that scikit-learn's `cross_val_score` does this type of validation by default. Run the cell containing the following code:

```
from sklearn.model_selection import cross_val_score
np.random.seed(1)
scores = cross_val_score(
    estimator=clf,
    X=X,
    y=y,
    cv=10)
print('accuracy = {:.3f} +/- {:.3f}'.format(scores.mean(),
scores.
    std()))
>> accuracy = 0.923 +/- 0.005
```

   Note how we use `np.random.seed` to set the seed for the random number generator, therefore ensuring reproducibility with respect to the randomly selected samples for each fold and decision tree in the Random Forest.

5. With this method, we calculate the accuracy as the average of each fold. We can also see the individual accuracies for each fold by printing scores. To see these, run `print(scores)`:

```
>> array([ 0.93404397, 0.91533333, 0.92266667, 0.91866667,
    0.92133333,
    0.92866667, 0.91933333, 0.92 , 0.92795197, 0.92128085])
```

   Using `cross_val_score` is very convenient, but it doesn't tell us about the accuracies within each class. We can do this manually with the `model_selection.StratifiedKFold` class. This class takes the number of folds as an initialization parameter, then the split method is used to build randomly sampled "masks" for the data. A mask is simply an array containing indexes of items in another array, where the items can then be returned by doing this: `data[mask]`.

6. Define a custom class for calculating k-fold cross validation class accuracies. Run the cell containing the following code:

```
from sklearn.model_selection import StratifiedKFold
...
    print('fold: {:d} accuracy: {:s}'.format(k+1, str(class_acc)))
return class_accuracy
```

7. We can then calculate the class accuracies with code that's very similar to step 4. Do this by running the cell containing the following code:

```
from sklearn.model_selection import cross_val_score
np.random.seed(1)
...
>> fold: 10 accuracy: [ 0.98861646 0.70588235]
>> accuracy = [ 0.98722476 0.71715647] +/- [ 0.00330026
0.02326823]
```

Now we can see the class accuracies for each fold! Pretty neat, right?

8. Let's move on to show how a validation curve can be calculated using `model_selection.validation_curve`. This function uses stratified k-fold cross-validation to train models for various values of a given parameter.

Do the calculations required to plot a validation curve by training Random Forests over a range of max_depth values. Run the cell containing the following code:

```
from sklearn.model_selection import validation_curve

clf = RandomForestClassifier(n_estimators=10)
max_depths = np.arange(3, 16, 3)
train_scores, test_scores = validation_curve(
    estimator=clf,
    X=X,
    y=y,
    param_name='max_depth',
    param_range=max_depths,
    cv=10);
```

This will return arrays with the cross-validation scores for each model, where the models have different max depths. In order to visualize the results, we'll leverage a function provided in the scikit-learn documentation.

9. Run the cell in which `plot_validation_curve` is defined. Then, run the cell containing the following code to draw the plot:

```
plot_validation_curve(train_scores, test_scores, max_depths,
xlabel='max_depth')
```

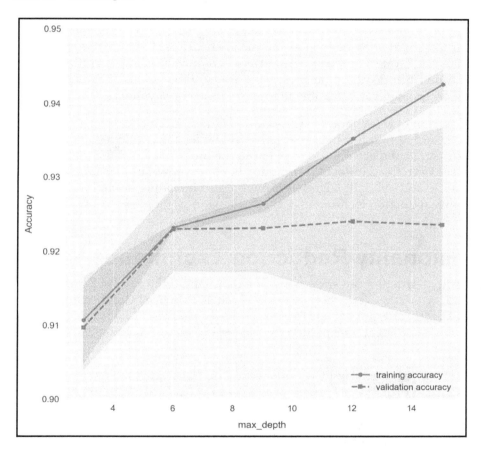

Recall how setting the max depth for decision trees limits the amount of overfitting? This is reflected in the validation curve, where we see overfitting taking place for large max depth values to the right. A good value for `max_depth` appears to be 6, where we see the training and validation accuracies in agreement. When `max_depth` is equal to 3, we see the model underfitting the data as training and validation accuracies are lower.

To summarize, we have learned and implemented two important techniques for building reliable predictive models. The first such technique was k-fold cross-validation, which is used to split the data into various train/test batches and generate a set accuracy. From this set, we then calculated the average accuracy and the standard deviation as a measure of the error. This is important so that we have a gauge of the variability of our model and we can produce trustworthy accuracy.

We also learned about another such technique to ensure we have trustworthy results: validation curves. These allow us to visualize when our model is overfitting based on comparing training and validation accuracies. By plotting the curve over a range of our selected hyperparameter, we are able to identify its optimal value.

In the final section of this chapter, we take everything we have learned so far and put it together in order to build our final predictive model for the employee retention problem. We seek to improve the accuracy, compared to the models trained thus far, by including all of the features from the dataset in our model. We'll see now-familiar topics such as k-fold cross-validation and validation curves, but we'll also introduce something new: dimensionality reduction techniques.

# Dimensionality Reduction Techniques

Dimensionality reduction can simply involve removing unimportant features from the training data, but more exotic methods exist, such as **Principal Component Analysis (PCA)** and **Linear Discriminant Analysis (LDA)**. These techniques allow for data compression, where the most important information from a large group of features can be encoded in just a few features.

In this subtopic, we'll focus on PCA. This technique transforms the data by projecting it into a new subspace of orthogonal "principal components," where the components with the highest eigenvalues encode the most information for training the model. Then, we can simply select a few of these principal components in place of the original high-dimensional dataset. For example, PCA could be used to encode the information from every pixel in an image. In this case, the original feature space would have dimensions equal to the number of pixels in the image. This high-dimensional space could then be reduced with PCA, where the majority of useful information for training predictive models might be reduced to just a few dimensions. Not only does this save time when training and using models, it allows them to perform better by removing noise in the dataset.

Like the models we've seen, it's not necessary to have a detailed understanding of PCA in order to leverage the benefits. However, we'll dig into the technical details of PCA just a bit further so that we can conceptualize it better. The key insight of PCA is to identify patterns between features based on correlations, so the PCA algorithm calculates the covariance matrix and then decomposes this into eigen vectors and eigenvalues. The vectors are then used to transform the data into a new subspace, from which a filed number of principal components can be selected.

In the following section, we'll see an example of how PCA can be used to improve our Random Forest model for the employee retention problem we have been working on. This will be done after training a classification model on the full feature space, to see how our accuracy is affected by dimensionality reduction.

# Training a predictive model for the employee retention problem

We have already spent considerable effort in planning a machine learning strategy, preprocessing the data, and building predictive models for the employee retention problem. Recall that our business objective was to help the client prevent employees from leaving. The strategy we decided upon was to build a classification model that would predict the probability of employees leaving. This way, the company can assess the likelihood of current employees leaving and take action to prevent it.

Given our strategy, we can summarize the type of predictive modeling we are doing as follows:

- Supervised learning on labeled training data
- Classification problems with two class labels (binary)

In particular, we are training models to determine whether an employee has left the company, given a set of continuous and categorical features. After preparing the data for machine learning in Activity, *Preparing to Train a Predictive Model for the Employee-Retention Problem*, we went on to implement SVM, k-Nearest Neighbors, and Random Forest algorithms using just two features. These models were able to make predictions with over 90% overall accuracy. When looking at the specific class accuracies, however, we found that employees who had left (`class-label 1`) could only be predicted with 70-80% accuracy. Let's see how much this can be improved by utilizing the full feature space.

1. In the `chapter-2-workbook.ipynb notebook`, scroll down to the code for this section. We should already have the preprocessed data loaded from the previous sections, but this can be done again, if desired, by executing `df = pd.read_csv('../data/hr-analytics/hr_data_processed.csv')`. Then, print the DataFrame columns with `print(df.columns)`.

2. Define a list of all the features by copy and pasting the output from `df.columns` into a new list (making sure to remove the target variable left). Then, define X and Y as we have done before. This goes as follows:

```
features = ['satisfaction_level', 'last_evaluation',
'number_project',
    'average_montly_hours', 'time_spend_company', 'work_accident',
        ...
        X = df[features].values
        y = df.left.values
```

Looking at the feature names, recall what the values look like for each one. Scroll up to the set of histograms we made in the first activity to help jog your memory. The first two features are continuous; these are what we used for training models in the previous two exercises. After that, we have a few discrete features, such as `number_ project` and `time_spend_company`, followed by some binary fields such as `work_ accident` and `promotion_last_5years`. We also have a bunch of binary features, such as `department_IT` and `department_accounting`, which were created by one-hot encoding.

Given a mix of features like this, Random Forests are a very attractive type of model. For one thing, they're compatible with feature sets composed of both continuous and categorical data, but this is not particularly special; for instance, an SVM can be trained on mixed feature types as well (given proper preprocessing).

 If you're interested in training an SVM or k-Nearest Neighbors classifier on mixed-type input features, you can use the data-scaling prescription from this StackExchange answer: `https://stats.stackexchange.com/questions/82923/mixing-continuous-and-binary-datawith-linear-svm/83086#83086`.

A simple approach would be to preprocess data as follows:

- Standardize continuous variables
- One-hot-encode categorical features
- Shift binary values to −1 and 1 instead of 0 and 1
- Then, the mixed-feature data could be used to train a variety of classification models

3. We need to figure out the best parameters for our Random Forest model. Let's start by tuning the max_depth hyperparameter using a validation curve. Calculate the training and validation accuracies by running the following code:

```
%%time
np.random.seed(1)
clf = RandomForestClassifier(n_estimators=20)
max_depths = [3, 4, 5, 6, 7,
9, 12, 15, 18, 21]
train_scores, test_scores = validation_curve(
estimator=clf,
    X=X,
    y=y,
param_name='max_depth',
param_range=max_depths,
cv=5);
```

We are testing 10 models with k-fold cross-validation. By setting k = 5, we produce five estimates of the accuracy for each model, from which we extract the mean and standard deviation to plot in the validation curve. In total, we train 50 models, and since n_estimators is set to 20, we are training a total of 1,000 decision trees! All in roughly 10 seconds!

4. Plot the validation curve using our custom plot_validation_curve function from the last exercise. Run the following code:

```
plot_validation_curve(train_scores, test_scores,
max_depths, xlabel='max_depth');
```

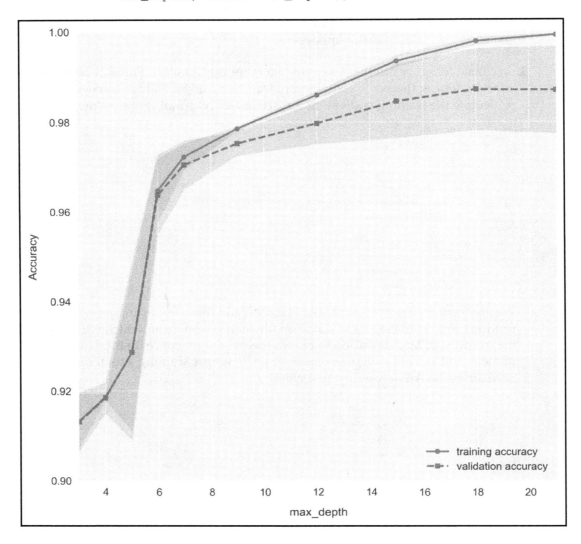

For small max depths, we see the model underfitting the data. Total accuracies dramatically increase by allowing the decision trees to be deeper and encode more complicated patterns in the data. As the max depth is increased further and the accuracy approaches 100%, we find the model overfits the data, causing the training and validation accuracies to grow apart. Based on this figure, let's select a `max_ depth` of 6 for our model.

We should really do the same for `n_estimators`, but in the spirit of saving time, we'll skip it. You are welcome to plot it on your own; you should find agreement between training and validation sets for a large range of values. Usually, it's better to use more decision tree estimators in the Random Forest, but this comes at the cost of increased training times. We'll use 200 estimators to train our model.

5. Use `cross_val_class_score`, the k-fold cross validation by class function we created earlier, to test the selected model, a Random Forest with `max_depth = 6` and `n_estimators = 200`:

```
np.random.seed(1)
clf = RandomForestClassifier(n_estimators=200, max_depth=6)
scores = cross_val_class_score(clf, X, y)
print('accuracy = {} +/- {}'\ .format(scores.mean(axis=0),
scores.std(axis=0)))
>> accuracy = [ 0.99553722 0.85577359] +/- [ 0.00172575
0.02614334]
```

The accuracies are way higher now that we're using the full feature set, compared to before when we only had the two continuous features!

6. Visualize the accuracies with a boxplot by running the following code:

```
fig = plt.figure(figsize=(5, 7))
sns.boxplot(data=pd.DataFrame(scores, columns=[0, 1]),
palette=sns.color_palette('Set1'))
plt.xlabel('Left')
plt.ylabel('Accuracy')
```

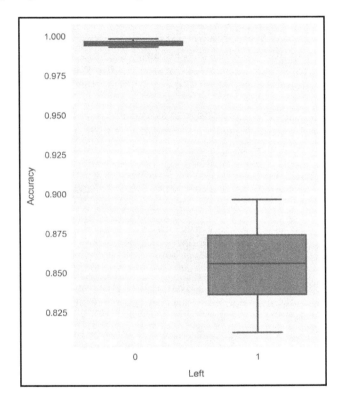

Random Forests can provide an estimate of the feature performances.

The feature importance in scikit-learn is calculated based on how the node impurity changes with respect to each feature. For a more detailed explanation, take a look at the following Stack Overflow thread about how feature importance is determined in Random Forest Classifier: `https://stackoverflow.com/questions/15810339/how-are-feature-importances-in-randomforestclassifier-determined` .

7. Plot the feature importance, as stored in the attribute `feature_importances_`, by running the following code:

```
pd.Series(clf.feature_importances_, name='Feature importance',
    index=df[features].columns)\
    .sort_values()\
    .plot.barh()
plt.xlabel('Feature importance')
```

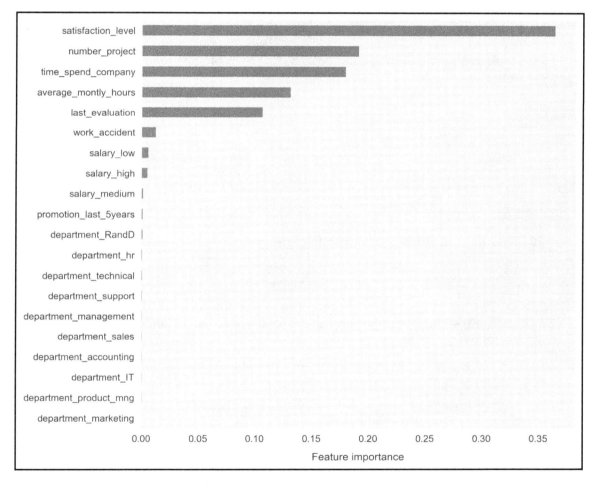

It doesn't look like we're getting much in the way of useful contribution from the one-hot encoded variables: department and salary. Also, the `promotion_last_5years` and `work_accident` features don't appear to be very useful.

Let's use Principal Component Analysis (PCA) to condense all of these weak features into just a few principal components.

8. Import the PCA class from scikit-learn and transform the features. Run the following code:

```
from sklearn.decomposition import PCA
pca_features = \
...
pca = PCA(n_components=3)
X_pca = pca.fit_transform(X_reduce)
```

9. Look at the string representation of X_pca by typing it alone and executing the cell:

```
>> array([[-0.67733089, 0.75837169, -0.10493685],
>> [ 0.73616575, 0.77155888, -0.11046422],
>> [ 0.73616575, 0.77155888, -0.11046422],
    >> ...,
>> [-0.67157059, -0.3337546 , 0.70975452],
>> [-0.67157059, -0.3337546 , 0.70975452],
>> [-0.67157059, -0.3337546 , 0.70975452]])
```

Since we asked for the top three components, we get three vectors returned.

10. Add the new features to our DataFrame with the following code:

```
df['first_principle_component'] = X_pca.T[0]
df['second_principle_component'] = X_pca.T[1]
df['third_principle_component'] = X_pca.T[2]
```

Select our reduced-dimension feature set to train a new Random Forest with. Run the following code:

```
features = ['satisfaction_level', 'number_project',
'time_spend_
    company',
'average_montly_hours', 'last_evaluation',
'first_principle_component',
'second_principle_component',
'third_principle_component']
X = df[features].values
y = df.left.values
```

11. Assess the new model's accuracy with k-fold cross-validation. This can be done by running the same code as before, where X now points to different features. The code is as follows:

```
np.random.seed(1)
clf = RandomForestClassifier(n_estimators=200, max_depth=6)
scores = cross_val_class_score(clf, X, y)
print('accuracy = {} +/- {}'\.format(scores.mean(axis=0),
scores.std(axis=0)))
>> accuracy = [ 0.99562463 0.90618594] +/- [ 0.00166047
0.01363927]
```

12. Visualize the result in the same way as before, using a box plot. The code is as follows:

```
fig = plt.figure(figsize=(5, 7))
sns.boxplot(data=pd.DataFrame(scores, columns=[0, 1]),
palette=sns.color_palette('Set1'))
plt.xlabel('Left')
plt.ylabel('Accuracy')
```

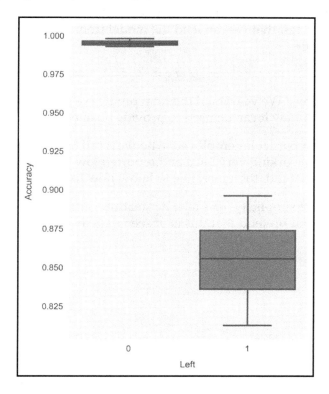

Comparing this to the previous result, we find an improvement in the class 1 accuracy! Now, the majority of the validation sets return an accuracy greater than 90%. The average accuracy of 90.6% can be compared to the accuracy of 85.6% prior to dimensionality reduction!

Let's select this as our final model. We'll need to re-train it on the full sample space before using it in production.

13. Train the final predictive model by running the following code:

```
np.random.seed(1)
clf = RandomForestClassifier(n_estimators=200, max_depth=6)
clf.fit(X, y)
```

14. Save the trained model to a binary file using `externals.joblib.dump`. Run the following code:

```
from sklearn.externals import joblib
joblib.dump(clf, 'random-forest-trained.pkl')
```

15. Check that it's saved into the working directory, for example, by running: `!ls *.pkl`. Then, test that we can load the model from the file by running the following code:

```
clf = joblib.load('random-forest-trained.pkl')
```

Congratulations! We've trained the final predictive model! Now, let's see an example of how it can be used to provide business insights for the client.

Say we have a particular employee, who we'll call Sandra. Management has noticed she is working very hard and reported low job satisfaction in a recent survey. They would, therefore, like to know how likely it is that she will quit.

For the sake of simplicity, let's take her feature values as a sample from the training set (but pretend that this is unseen data instead).

16. List the feature values for Sandra by running the following code:

```
sandra = df.iloc[573]
X = sandra[features]
    X
>> satisfaction_level 0.360000
>> number_project 2.000000
>> time_spend_company 3.000000
>> average_montly_hours 148.000000
>> last_evaluation 0.470000
>> first_principle_component 0.742801
>> second_principle_component -0.514568
>> third_principle_component -0.677421
```

The next step is to ask the model which group it thinks she should be in.

17. Predict the class label for Sandra by running the following code:

```
clf.predict([X])
>> array([1])
```

The model classifies her as having already left the company; not a good sign! We can take this a step further and calculate the probabilities of each class label.

18. Use `clf.predict_proba` to predict the probability of our model predicting that Sandra has quit. Run the following code:

```
clf.predict_proba([X])
>> array([[ 0.06576239, 0.93423761]])
```

We see the model predicting that she has quit with 93% accuracy. Since this is clearly a red flag for management, they decide on a plan to reduce her number of monthly hours to 100 and the time spent at the company to 1.

19. Calculate the new probabilities with Sandra's newly planned metrics. Run the following code:

```
X.average_montly_hours = 100
X.time_spend_company = 1
  clf.predict_proba([X])
    >> array([[ 0.61070329, 0.38929671]])
```

Excellent! We can now see that the model returns a mere 38% likelihood that she has quit! Instead, it now predicts she will not have left the company.

Our model has allowed management to make a data-driven decision. By reducing her amount of time with the company by this particular amount, the model tells us that she will most likely remain an employee at the company!

# Summary

In this chapter, we have seen how predictive models can be trained in Jupyter Notebooks.

To begin with, we talked about how to plan a machine learning strategy. We thought about how to design a plan that can lead to actionable business insights and stressed the importance of using the data to help set realistic business goals. We also explained machine learning terminologies such as supervised learning, unsupervised learning, classification, and regression.

Next, we discussed methods for preprocessing data using scikit-learn and pandas. This included lengthy discussions and examples of a surprisingly time-consuming part of machine learning: dealing with missing data.

In the latter half of the chapter, we trained predictive classification models for our binary problem, comparing how decision boundaries are drawn for various models such as the SVM, k-Nearest Neighbors, and Random Forest. We then showed how validation curves can be used to make good parameter choices and how dimensionality reduction can improve model performance. Finally, at the end of our activity, we explored how the final model can be used in practice to make data-driven decisions.

# Web Scraping and Interactive Visualizations

**3**

So far in this book, we have focused on using Jupyter to build reproducible data analysis pipelines and predictive models. We'll continue to explore these topics in this chapter, but the main focus here is data acquisition. In particular, we will show you how data can be acquired from the web using HTTP requests. This will involve scraping web pages by requesting and parsing HTML. We will then wrap up this chapter by using interactive visualization techniques to explore the data we've collected.

The amount of data available online is huge and relatively easy to acquire. It's also continuously growing and becoming increasingly important. Part of this continual growth is the result of an ongoing global shift from newspapers, magazines, and TV to online content. With customized news feeds available all the time on cell phones, and live-news sources such as Facebook, Reddit, Twitter, and YouTube, it's difficult to imagine the historical alternatives being relevant much longer. Amazingly, this accounts for only some of the increasingly massive amounts of data available online.

With this global shift toward consuming content using HTTP services (blogs, news sites, Netflix, and so on), there are plenty of opportunities to use data-driven analytics. For example, Netflix looks at the movies a user watches and predicts what they will like. This prediction is used to determine the suggested movies that appear. In this chapter, however, we won't be looking at "business-facing" data as such, but instead we will see how the client can leverage the internet as a database. Never before has this amount and variety of data been so easily accessible. We'll use web-scraping techniques to collect data, and then we'll explore it with interactive visualizations in Jupyter.

Interactive visualization is a visual form of data representation, which helps users understand the data using graphs or charts. Interactive visualization helps a developer or analyst present data in a simple form, which can be understood by non-technical personnel too.

By the end of this chapter, you will be able to:

- Analyze how HTTP requests work
- Scrape tabular data from a web page
- Build and transform Pandas Data Frames
- Create interactive visualizations

# Scraping Web Page Data

In the spirit of leveraging the internet as a database, we can think about acquiring data from web pages either by scraping content or by interfacing with web APIs. Generally, scraping content means getting the computer to read data that was intended to be displayed in a human-readable format. This is in contradistinction to web APIs, where data is delivered in machine-readable formats – the most common being JSON.

In this topic, we will focus on web scraping. The exact process for doing this will depend on the page and desired content. However, as we will see, it's quite easy to scrape anything we need from an HTML page so long as we have an understanding of the underlying concepts and tools. In this topic, we'll use Wikipedia as an example and scrape tabular content from an article. Then, we'll apply the same techniques to scrape data from a page on an entirely separate domain. But first, we'll take some time to introduce HTTP requests.

# Introduction to HTTP Requests

The Hypertext Transfer Protocol, or HTTP for short, is the foundation of data communication for the internet. It defies how a page should be requested and how the response should look. For example, a client can request an Amazon page of laptops for sale, a Google search of local restaurants, or their Facebook feed. Along with the URL, the request will contain the user agent and available browsing cookies among the contents of the **request header**. The user agent tells the server what browser and device the client is using, which is usually used to provide the most user-friendly version of the web page's response. Perhaps they have recently logged in to the web page; such information would be stored in a cookie that might be used to automatically log the user in.

These details of HTTP requests and responses are taken care of under the hood thanks to web browsers. Luckily for us, today the same is true when making requests with high level languages such as Python. For many purposes, the contents of request headers can be largely ignored.

Unless otherwise specified, these are automatically generated in Python when requesting a URL. Still, for the purposes of troubleshooting and understanding the responses yielded by our requests, it's useful to have a foundational understanding of HTTP.

There are many types of HTTP methods, such as GET, HEAD, POST, and PUT. The first two are used for requesting that data be sent from the server to the client, whereas the last two are used for sending data to the server.

These HTTP methods are summarized in the following table:

| HTTP method | Description |
| --- | --- |
| GET | Retrieves the information from the specified URL |
| HEAD | Retrieves the meta information from the HTTP header of the specified URL |
| POST | Sends the attached information for appending to the resource(s) at the specified URL |
| PUT | Sends the attached information for replacing the resource(s) at the specified URL |

A GET request is sent each time we type a web page address into our browser and press *Enter*. For web scraping, this is usually the only HTTP method we are interested in, and it's the only method we'll be using in this chapter.

Once the request has been sent, a variety of response types can be returned from the server. These are labeled with 100-level to 500-level codes, where the first digit in the code represents the response class. These can be described as follows:

- **1xx**: Informational response, for example, server is processing a request. It's uncommon to see this.
- **2xx**: Success, for example, page has loaded properly.
- **3xx**: Redirection, for example, the requested resource has been moved and we were redirected to a new URL.
- **4xx**: Client error, for example, the requested resource does not exist.
- **5xx**: Server error, for example, the website server is receiving too much traffic and could not fulfill the request.

For the purposes of web scraping, we usually only care about the response class, that is, the first digit of the response code. However, there exist subcategories of responses within each class that offer more granularity on what's going on. For example, a 401 code indicates an unauthorized response, whereas a 404 code indicates a *page not found* response.

This distinction is noteworthy because a 404 would indicate we've requested a page that does not exist, whereas 401 tells us we need to log in to view the particular resource.

Let's see how HTTP requests can be done in Python and explore some of these topics using the Jupyter Notebook.

# Making HTTP Requests in the Jupyter Notebook

Now that we've talked about how HTTP requests work and what type of responses we should expect, let's see how this can be done in Python. We'll use a library called **Requests**, which happens to be the most downloaded external library for Python. It's possible to use Python's built-in tools, such as `urllib`, for making HTTP requests, but Requests is far more intuitive, and in fact it's recommended over `urllib` in the official Python documentation.

Requests is a great choice for making simple and advanced web requests. It allows for all sorts of customization with respect to headers, cookies, and authorization. It tracks redirects and provides methods for returning specific page content such as JSON. Furthermore, there's an extensive suite of advanced features. However, it does not allow JavaScript to be rendered.

 Oftentimes, servers return HTML with JavaScript code snippets included, which are automatically run in the browser on load time. When requesting content with Python using Requests, this JavaScript code is visible, but it does not run. Therefore, any elements that would be altered or created by doing so are missing. Often, this does not affect the ability to get the desired information, but in some cases, we may need to render the JavaScript in order to scrape the page properly. For doing this, we could use a library like Selenium. This has a similar API to the Requests library, but provides support for rendering JavaScript using web drivers.

Let's dive into the following section using the Requests library with Python in a Jupyter Notebook.

## Handling HTTP requests with Python in a Jupyter Notebook

1. Start the `NotebookApp` from the project directory by executing `jupyter notebook`. Navigate to the *Chapter-3* directory and open up the `chapter-3-workbook.ipynb file`. Find the cell near the top where the packages are loaded and run it.

We are going to request a web page and then examine the response object. There are many different libraries for making requests and many choices for exactly how to do so with each. We'll only use the Requests library, as it provides excellent documentation, advanced features, and a simple API.

2. Scroll down to Subtopic `Introduction to HTTP requests` and run the first cell in that section to import the Requests library. Then, prepare a request by running the cell containing the following code:

```
url = 'https://jupyter.org/'
req = requests.Request('GET', url)
req.headers['User-Agent'] = 'Mozilla/5.0'
req = req.prepare()
```

We use the `Request class` to prepare a GET request to the jupyter.org homepage. By specifying the user agent as `Mozilla/5.0`, we are asking for a response that would be suitable for a standard desktop browser. Finally, we prepare the request.

3. Print the docstring for the "**prepared request**" req, by running the cell containing `req?`:

```
In [83]: req?

Type:        PreparedRequest
String form: <PreparedRequest [GET]>
File:        ~/anaconda/lib/python3.5/site-packages/requests/models.py
Docstring:
The fully mutable :class:`PreparedRequest <PreparedRequest>` object,
containing the exact bytes that will be sent to the server.

Generated from either a :class:`Request <Request>` object or manually.

Usage::

  >>> import requests
  >>> req = requests.Request('GET', 'http://httpbin.org/get')
  >>> r = req.prepare()
  <PreparedRequest [GET]>

  >>> s = requests.Session()
  >>> s.send(r)
  <Response [200]>
```

Looking at its usage, we see how the request can be sent using a session. This is similar to opening a web browser (starting a session) and then requesting a URL.

4. Make the request and store the response in a variable named page, by running the following code:

```
with requests.Session() as sess:
page = sess.send(req)
```

This code returns the HTTP response, as referenced by the page variable. By using the with statement, we initialize a session whose scope is limited to the indented code block. This means we do not have to worry about explicitly closing the session, as it is done automatically.

5. Run the next two cells in the notebook to investigate the response. The string representation of page should indicate a 200 status code response. This should agree with the status_code attribute.

6. Save the response text to the page_html variable and take a look at the head of the string with page_html[:1000]:

```
page_html = page.text

page_html[:1000]

'<!DOCTYPE html>\n<html>\n\n  <head>\n\n    <meta charset="utf-8">\n    <meta http-equiv="X-U
A-Compatible" content="IE=edge">\n    <meta name="viewport" content="width=device-width, init
ial-scale=1">\n    <meta name="description" content="">\n    <meta name="author" content="">\
n\n    <title>Project Jupyter | Home</title>\n    <meta property="og:title" content="Project
Jupyter" />\n    <meta property="og:description" content="The Jupyter Notebook is a web-based
interactive computing platform. The notebook combines live code, equations, narrative text, v
isualizations, interactive dashboards and other media.\n">\n    <meta property="og:url" conte
nt="http://www.jupyter.org" />\n    <meta property="og:image" content="http://jupyter.org/ass
ets/homepage.png" />\n    <!-- Bootstrap Core CSS -->\n    <script src="/cdn-cgi/apps/head/Mu
II14I_IVFkxldaVulmdWee9as.js"></script><link rel="stylesheet" href="/css/bootstrap.min.css">\
n    <link rel="stylesheet" href="/css/logo-nav.css">\n    <link rel="stylesheet" href="/c'
```

As expected, the response is HTML. We can format this output better with the help of BeautifulSoup, a library which will be used extensively for HTML parsing later in this section.

7. Print the head of the formatted HTML by running the following:

```
from bs4 import BeautifulSoup
print(BeautifulSoup(page_html, 'html.parser').prettify()[:1000])
```

We import BeautifulSoup and then print the pretty output, where newlines are indented depending on their hierarchy in the HTML structure.

8. We can take this a step further and actually display the HTML in Jupyter by using the IPython display module. Do this by running the following code:

```
from IPython.display import HTML
HTML(page_html)
```

circle of programming language icons
circle of programming language icons
circle of programming language icons
jupyter logo

white background

**Project Jupyter exists to develop open-source software, open-standards, and services for interactive computing across dozens of programming languages.**

**Ready to get started?**
Try it in your browser Install the Notebook

Here, we see the HTML rendered as well as possible, given that no JavaScript code has been run and no external resources have loaded. For example, the images that are hosted on the jupyter.org server are not rendered and we instead see the alt text: **circle of programming icons**, Jupyter logo, and so on.

9. Let's compare this to the live website, which can be opened in Jupyter using an IFrame. Do this by running the following code:

```
from IPython.display import IFrame
IFrame(src=url, height=800, width=800)
```

Here, we see the full site rendered, including JavaScript and external resources. In fact, we can even click on the hyperlinks and load those pages in the IFrame, just like a regular browsing session.

10. It's good practice to close the IFrame after using it. This prevents it from eating up memory and processing power. It can be closed by selecting the cell and clicking **Current Outputs | Clear** from the **Cell** menu in the Jupyter Notebook.

Recall how we used a prepared request and session to request this content as a string in Python. This is often done using a shorthand method instead. The drawback is that we do not have as much customization of the request header, but that's usually fine.

11. Make a request to `http://www.python.org/` by running the following code:

```
url = 'http://www.python.org/'
page = requests.get(url)
page
<Response [200]>
```

The string representation of the page (as displayed beneath the cell) should indicate a 200 status code, indicating a successful response.

12. Run the next two cells. Here, we print the `url` and `history` attributes of our page.

The URL returned is not what we input; notice the difference? We were redirected from the input URL, `http://www.python.org/`, to the secured version of that page, `https://www.python.org/`. The difference is indicated by an additional s at the start of the URL, in the protocol. Any redirects are stored in the history attribute; in this case, we find one page in here with status code 301 (permanent redirect), corresponding to the original URL requested.

Now that we're comfortable making requests, we'll turn our attention to parsing the HTML. This can be something of an art, as there are usually multiple ways to approach it, and the best method often depends on the details of the specific HTML in question.

# Parsing HTML in the Jupyter Notebook

When scraping data from a web page, after making the request, we must extract the data from the response content. If the content is HTML, then the easiest way to do this is with a high-level parsing library such as Beautiful Soup. This is not to say it's the only way; in principle, it would be possible to pick out the data using regular expressions or Python string methods such as `split`, but pursuing either of these options would be an inefficient use of time and could easily lead to errors. Therefore, it's generally frowned upon and instead, the use of a trustworthy parsing tool is recommended.

In order to understand how content can be extracted from HTML, it's important to know the fundamentals of HTML. For starters, HTML stands for **Hyper Text Markup Language**. Like Markdown or XML (**eXtensible Markup Language**), it's simply a language for marking up text.

In HTML, the display text is contained within the content section of HTML elements, where element attributes specify how that element should appear on the page.

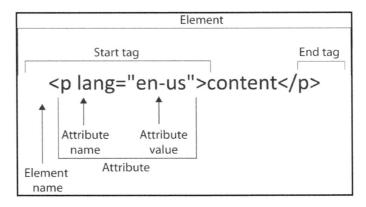

Looking at the anatomy of an HTML element, as seen in the preceding picture, we see the content enclosed between start and end tags. In this example, the tags are <p> for paragraph; other common tag types are <div> (text block), <table> (data table), <h1> (heading), <img> (image), and <a> (hyperlinks). Tags have attributes, which can hold important metadata. Most commonly, this metadata is used to specify how the element text should appear on the page. This is where CSS files come into play. The attributes can store other useful information, such as the hyperlink href in an <a> tag, which specifies a URL link, or the alternate alt label in an <img> tag, which specifies the text to display if the image resource cannot be loaded.

Now, let's turn our attention back to the Jupyter Notebook and parse some HTML! Although not necessary when following along with this section, it's very helpful in real-world situations to use the developer tools in Chrome or Firefox to help identify the HTML elements of interest. We'll include instructions for doing this with Chrome in the following section.

# Parsing HTML with Python in a Jupyter Notebook

1. In `chapter-3-workbook.ipynb` file, scroll to the top of Subtopic `Parsing HTML with Python`.

   In this section, we'll scrape the central bank interest rates for each country, as reported by Wikipedia. Before diving into the code, let's first open up the web page containing this data.

2. Open up the `https://en.wikipedia.org/wiki/List_of_countries_by_central_bank_interest_rates` URL in a web browser. Use Chrome, if possible, as later in this section we'll show you how to view and search the HTML with Chrome's developer tools.

   Looking at the page, we see very little content other than a big list of countries and their interest rates. This is the table we'll be scraping.

3. Return to the Jupyter Notebook and load the HTML as a Beautiful Soup object so that it can be parsed. Do this by running the following code:

```
from bs4 import BeautifulSoup
soup = BeautifulSoup(page.content, 'html.parser')
```

   We use Python's default `html.parser` as the parser, but third-party parsers such as `lxml` may be used instead, if desired.

   Usually, when working with a new object like this Beautiful Soup one, it's a good idea to pull up the docstring by doing `soup?`. However, in this case, the docstring is not particularly informative. Another tool for exploring Python objects is `pdir`, which lists all of an object's attributes and methods (this can be installed with `pip install pdir2`). It's basically a formatted version of Python's built-in `dir` function.

4. Display the attributes and methods for the BeautifulSoup object by running the following code. This will run, regardless of whether or not the `pdir` external library is installed:

```
try:
import pdir
dir = pdir
except:
print('You can install pdir with:\npip install pdir2')
dir(soup)
```

   Here, we see a list of methods and attributes that can be called on `soup`. The most commonly used function is probably `find_all`, which returns a list of elements that match the given criteria.

5. Get the h1 heading for the page with the following code:

```
h1 = soup.find_all('h1')
h1
>> [<h1 class="firstHeading" id="firstHeading" lang="en">
List of countries by central bank interest rates</h1>]
```

Usually, pages only have one H1 element, so it's obvious that we only find one here.

6. Run the next couple of cells. We redefine H1 to the first (and only) list element with h1 = h1[0], and then print out the HTML element attributes with h1.attrs:

```
>> {'class': ['firstHeading'], 'id': 'firstHeading', 'lang': 'en'}
```

We see the class and ID of this element, which can both be referenced by CSS code to define the style of this element.

7. Get the HTML element content (that is, the visible text) by printing h1.text.

8. Get all the images on the page by running the following code:

```
imgs = soup.find_all('img')
len(imgs)
>> 91
```

There are lots of images on the page. Most of these are for the country flags.

9. Print the source of each image by running the following code:

```
[element.attrs['src'] for element in imgs
    if 'src' in element.attrs.keys()]
```

```
['//upload.wikimedia.org/wikipedia/commons/thumb/3/36/Flag_of_Albania.svg/21px-Flag_of_Albania.svg.png',
 '//upload.wikimedia.org/wikipedia/commons/thumb/9/9d/Flag_of_Angola.svg/23px-Flag_of_Angola.svg.png',
 '//upload.wikimedia.org/wikipedia/commons/thumb/1/1a/Flag_of_Argentina.svg/23px-Flag_of_Argentina.svg.png',
 '//upload.wikimedia.org/wikipedia/commons/thumb/2/2f/Flag_of_Armenia.svg/23px-Flag_of_Armenia.svg.png',
 '//upload.wikimedia.org/wikipedia/en/thumb/b/b9/Flag_of_Australia.svg/23px-Flag_of_Australia.svg.png',
 '//upload.wikimedia.org/wikipedia/commons/thumb/d/dd/Flag_of_Azerbaijan.svg/23px-Flag_of_Azerbaijan.svg.png',
 '//upload.wikimedia.org/wikipedia/commons/thumb/9/93/Flag_of_the_Bahamas.svg/23px-Flag_of_the_Bahamas.svg.png',
 '//upload.wikimedia.org/wikipedia/commons/thumb/2/2c/Flag_of_Bahrain.svg/23px-Flag_of_Bahrain.svg.png',
 '//upload.wikimedia.org/wikipedia/commons/thumb/f/f9/Flag_of_Bangladesh.svg/23px-Flag_of_Bangladesh.svg.png',
 '//upload.wikimedia.org/wikipedia/commons/thumb/e/ef/Flag_of_Barbados.svg/23px-Flag_of_Barbados.svg.png',
 '//upload.wikimedia.org/wikipedia/commons/thumb/8/85/Flag_of_Belarus.svg/23px-Flag_of_Belarus.svg.png',
 '//upload.wikimedia.org/wikipedia/commons/thumb/f/fa/Flag_of_Botswana.svg/23px-Flag_of_Botswana.svg.png',
 '//upload.wikimedia.org/wikipedia/en/thumb/0/05/Flag_of_Brazil.svg/22px-Flag_of_Brazil.svg.png',
 '//upload.wikimedia.org/wikipedia/commons/thumb/9/9a/Flag_of_Bulgaria.svg/23px-Flag_of_Bulgaria.svg.png',
```

We use a list comprehension to iterate through the elements, selecting the `src` attribute of each (so long as that attribute is actually available).

Now, let's scrape the table. We'll use Chrome's developer tools to hunt down the element this is contained within.

10. If not already done, open the Wikipedia page we're looking at in Chrome. Then, in the browser, select **Developer Tools** from the `View` menu. A sidebar will open. The HTML is available to look at from the `Elements` tab in **Developer Tools**.

11. Select the little arrow in the top left of the tools sidebar. This allows us to hover over the page and see where the HTML element is located, in the Elements section of the sidebar:

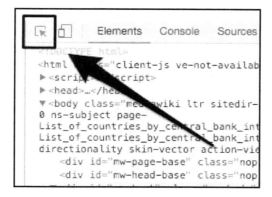

12. Hover over the body to see how the table is contained within the div that
    has `id="bodyContent"`:

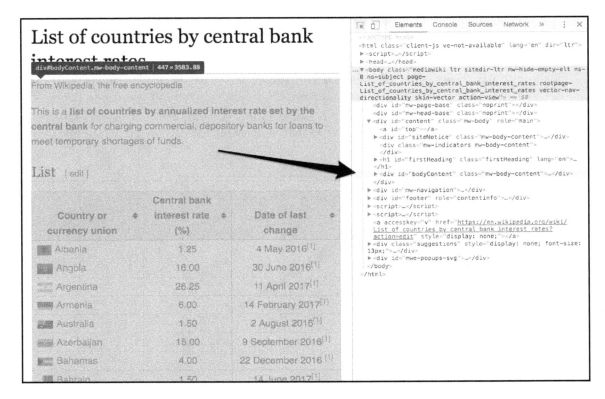

13. Select that div by running the following code:

```
body_content = soup.find('div', {'id': 'bodyContent'})
```

We can now seek out the table within this subset of the full HTML. Usually,
tables are organized into headers <th>, rows <tr>, and data entries <td>.

14. Get the table headers by running the following code:

```
table_headers = body_content.find_all('th')[:3]
table_headers
>>> [<th>Country or<br/>
currency union</th>, <th>Central bank<br/>
interest rate (%)</th>, <th>Date of last<br/>
change</th>]
```

Here, we see three headers. In the content of each is a break element `<br/>`, which will make the text a bit more difficult to cleanly parse.

15. Get the text by running the following code:

```
table_headers = [element.get_text().replace('\n', ' ')
for element in table_headers]
table_headers
>> ['Country or currency union',
'Central bank interest rate (%)',
'Date of last change']
```

Here, we get the content with the get_text method, and then run the replace string method to remove the newline resulting from the `<br/>` element. To get the data, we'll first perform some tests and then scrape all the data in a single cell.

16. Get the data for each cell in the second <tr> (row) element by running the following code:

```
row_number = 2
d1, d2, d3 = body_content.find_all('tr')[row_number]\.find_all('td')
```

We find all the row elements, pick out the third one, and then find the three data elements inside that.

Let's look at the resulting data and see how to parse the text from each row.

17. Run the next couple of cells to print d1 and its `text` attribute:

```
d1

<td align="left"><span class="flagicon"><img alt="" class="thumbborder" data-file-height="300
" data-file-width="450" height="15" src="//upload.wikimedia.org/wikipedia/commons/thumb/9/9d/
Flag_of_Angola.svg/23px-Flag_of_Angola.svg.png" srcset="//upload.wikimedia.org/wikipedia/comm
ons/thumb/9/9d/Flag_of_Angola.svg/35px-Flag_of_Angola.svg.png 1.5x, //upload.wikimedia.org/wi
kipedia/commons/thumb/9/9d/Flag_of_Angola.svg/45px-Flag_of_Angola.svg.png 2x" width="23"/> </
span><a href="/wiki/Angola" title="Angola">Angola</a></td>

d1.text

'\xa0Angola'
```

We're getting some undesirable characters at the front. This can be solved by searching for only the text of the <a> tag.

18. Run d1.find('a').text to return the properly cleaned data for that cell.
19. Run the next couple of cells to print d2 and its text. This data appears to be clean enough to convert directly into a flat.
20. Run the next couple of cells to print d3 and its text:

```
d3

<td><span class="sortkey" style="display:none;speak:none">000000002016-06-30-0000</span><span
style="white-space:nowrap">30 June 2016</span><sup class="reference" id="cite_ref-CentralBank
News_1-1"><a href="#cite_note-CentralBankNews-1">[1]</a></sup></td>

d3.text

'000000002016-06-30-000030 June 2016[1]'
```

Similar to d1, we see that it would be better to get only the span element's text.

21. Properly parse the date for this table entry by running the following code:

```
d3.find_all('span')[0].text
>> '30 June 2016'
```

22. Now, we're ready to perform the full scrape by iterating over the row elements <th>. Run the following code:

```
data = []
for i, row in enumerate(body_content.find_all('tr')):
    ...
    ...
>> Ignoring row 101 because len(data) != 3
>> Ignoring row 102 because len(data) != 3
```

We iterate over the rows, ignoring any that contain more than three data elements. These rows will not correspond to data in the table we are interested in. Rows that do have three data elements are assumed to be in the table, and we parse the text from these as identified during the testing. T

The text parsing is done inside a `try/except` statement, which will catch any errors and allow this row to be skipped without stopping the iteration. Any rows that raise errors due to this statement should be looked at. The data for these could be recorded manually or accounted for by altering the scraping loop and re-running it. In this case, we'll ignore any errors for the sake of time.

23. Print the head of the scraped data list by running print(data[:10]):

```
>> [['Albania', 1.25, '4 May 2016'],
['Angola', 16.0, '30 June 2016'],
['Argentina', 26.25, '11 April 2017'],
['Armenia', 6.0, '14 February 2017'],
['Australia', 1.5, '2 August 2016'],
['Azerbaijan', 15.0, '9 September 2016'],
['Bahamas', 4.0, '22 December 2016'],
['Bahrain', 1.5, '14 June 2017'],
['Bangladesh', 6.75, '14 January 2016'],
['Belarus', 12.0, '28 June 2017']]
```

24. We'll visualize this data later in the chapter. For now, save the data to a CSV file by running the following code:

```
f_path = '../data/countries/interest-rates.csv'
with open(f_path, 'w') as f:
  f.write('{};{};{}\n'.format(*table_headers))
  for d in data:
    f.write('{};{};{}\n'.format(*d))
```

Note that we are using semicolons to separate the fields.

# Activity: Web Scraping with Jupyter Notebooks

We are going to get the population of each country. Then, in the next topic, this will be visualized along with the interest rate data scraped in the previous section.

The page we look at in this activity is available here: `http://www.worldometers.info/world-population/population-by-country/`. Now that we've seen the basics of web scraping, let's apply the same techniques to a new web page and scrape some more data!

 This page may have changed since this document was created. If this URL no longer leads to a table of country populations, please use this Wikipedia page instead: `https://en.wikipedia.org/wiki/List_of_countries_by_population` (United_Nations).

1. For this page, the data can be scraped using the following code snippet:

```
data = []
for i, row in enumerate(soup.find_all('tr')):
    row_data = row.find_all('td')
        try:
            d1, d2, d3 = row_data[1], row_data[5], row_data[6]
            d1 = d1.find('a').text
            d2 = float(d2.text)
            d3 = d3.find_all('span')[1].text.replace('+', '')
        data.append([d1, d2, d3])
    except:
print('Ignoring row {}'.format(i))
```

2. In the `chapter-3-workbook.ipynb` Jupyter Notebook, scroll to `Activity Web scraping with Python`.

3. Set the `url` variable and load an IFrame of our page in the notebook by running the following code:

```
url ='http://www.worldometers.info/world-population/
            population-bycountry/'
IFrame(url, height=300, width=800)
```

4. Close the IFrame by selecting the cell and clicking **Current Outputs | Clear from the Cell** menu in the Jupyter Notebook.

5. Request the page and load it as a `BeautifulSoup` object by running the following code:

```
page = requests.get(url)
soup = BeautifulSoup(page.content, 'html.parser')
```

We feed the page content to the `BeautifulSoup` constructor. Recall that previously, we used `page.text` here instead. The difference is that `page.content` returns the raw binary response content, whereas `page.text` returns the `UTF-8` decoded content. It's usually best practice to pass the bytes object and let `BeautifulSoup` decode it, rather than doing it with Requests using `page.text`.

6. Print the `H1` for the page by running the following code:

```
soup.find_all('h1')
>> [<h1>Countries in the world by population (2017)</h1>]
```

We'll scrape the table by searching for `<th>`, `<tr>`, and `<td>` elements, as in the previous section.

7. Get and print the table headings by running the following code:

```
table_headers = soup.find_all('th')
table_headers
>> [<th>#</th>,
   <th>Country (or dependency)</th>,
   <th>Population<br/> (2017)</th>,
   <th>Yearly<br/> Change</th>,
   <th>Net<br/> Change</th>,
   <th>Density<br/> (P/Km²)</th>,
   <th>Land Area<br/> (Km²)</th>,
   <th>Migrants<br/> (net)</th>,
   <th>Fert.<br/> Rate</th>,
   <th>Med.<br/> Age</th>,
   <th>Urban<br/> Pop %</th>,
   <th>World<br/> Share</th>]
```

8. We are only interested in the first three columns. Select these and parse the text with the following code:

```
table_headers = table_headers[1:4]
table_headers = [t.text.replace('\n', '') for t in table_headers]
```

After selecting the subset of table headers we want, we parse the text content from each and remove any newline characters.

Now, we'll get the data. Following the same prescription as the previous section, we'll test how to parse the data for a sample row.

9. Get the data for a sample row by running the following code:

```
row_number = 2
row_data = soup.find_all('tr')[row_number]\.find_all('td')
```

10. How many columns of data do we have? Print the length of `row_data` by running `print(len(row_data))`.

11. Print the first elements by running `print(row_data[:4])`:

```
>> [<td>2</td>,
<td style="font-weight: bold; font-size:15px; text-align:left"><a
href="/world-population/india-population/">India</a></td>,
<td style="font-weight: bold;">1,339,180,127</td>,
<td>1.13 %</td>]
```

It's pretty obvious that we want to select list indices 1, 2, and 3. The first data value can be ignored, as it's simply the index.

12. Select the data elements we're interested in parsing by running the following code:

```
d1, d2, d3 = row_data[1:4]
```

13. Looking at the `row_data` output, we can find out how to correctly parse the data. We'll want to select the content of the `<a>` element in the first data element, and then simply get the text from the others. Test these assumptions by running the following code:

```
print(d1.find('a').text)
print(d2.text)
print(d3.text)
>> India
>> 1,339,180,127
>> 1.13 %
```

Excellent! This looks to be working well. Now, we're ready to scrape the entire table.

14. Scrape and parse the table data by running the following code:

```
ata = []
for i, row in enumerate(soup.find_all('tr')):
    try:
        d1, d2, d3 = row.fid_all('td')[1:4]
        d1 = d1.fid('a').text
        d2 = d2.text
        d3 = d3.text
        data.append([d1, d2, d3])
    except:
        print('Error parsing row {}'.format(i))

>> Error parsing row 0
```

This is quite similar to before, where we try to parse the text and skip the row if there's some error.

15. Print the head of the scraped data by running print(data[:10]):

```
>> [['China', '1,409,517,397', '0.43 %'],
['India', '1,339,180,127', '1.13 %'],
['U.S.', '324,459,463', '0.71 %'],
['Indonesia', '263,991,379', '1.10 %'],
['Brazil', '209,288,278', '0.79 %'],
['Pakistan', '197,015,955', '1.97 %'],
['Nigeria', '190,886,311', '2.63 %'],
['Bangladesh', '164,669,751', '1.05 %'],
['Russia', '143,989,754', '0.02 %'],
['Mexico', '129,163,276', '1.27 %']]
```

It looks like we have managed to scrape the data! Notice how similar the process was for this table compared to the Wikipedia one, even though this web page is completely different. Of course, it will not always be the case that data is contained within a table, but regardless, we can usually use find_all as the primary method for parsing.

16. Finally, save the data to a CSV file for later use. Do this by running the following code:

```
f_path = '../data/countries/populations.csv'
with open(f_path, 'w') as f:
  f.write('{};{};{}\n'.format(*table_headers))
  for d in data:
    f.write('{};{};{}\n'.format(*d))
```

To summarize, we've seen how Jupyter Notebooks can be used for web scraping. We started this chapter by learning about HTTP methods and status codes. Then, we used the Requests library to actually perform HTTP requests with Python and saw how the Beautiful Soup library can be used to parse the HTML responses.

Our Jupyter Notebook turned out to be a great tool for this type of work. We were able to explore the results of our web requests and experiment with various HTML parsing techniques. We were also able to render the HTML and even load a live version of the web page inside the notebook!

In the next topic of this chapter, we shift to a completely new topic: interactive visualizations. We'll see how to create and display interactive charts right inside the notebook, and use these charts as a way to explore the data we've just collected.

# Interactive Visualizations

Visualizations are quite useful as a means of extracting information from a dataset. For example, with a bar graph it's very easy to distinguish the value distribution, compared to looking at the values in a table. Of course, as we have seen earlier in this book, they can be used to study patterns in the dataset that would otherwise be quite difficult to identify. Furthermore, they can be used to help explain a dataset to an unfamiliar party. If included in a blog post, for example, they can boost reader interest levels and be used to break up blocks of text.

When thinking about interactive visualizations, the benefits are similar to static visualizations, but enhanced because they allow for active exploration on the viewer's part. Not only do they allow the viewer to answer questions they may have about the data, they also think of new questions while exploring. This can benefit a separate party such as a blog reader or co-worker, but also a creator, as it allows for easy ad hoc exploration of the data in detail, without having to change any code.

In this topic, we'll discuss and show how to use Bokeh to build interactive visualizations in Jupyter. Prior to this, however, we'll briefly revisit pandas Data Frames, which play an important role in doing data visualization with Python.

# Building a DataFrame to Store and Organize Data

As we've seen time and time again in this book, pandas is an integral part of doing data science with Python and Jupyter Notebooks. DataFrames offer a way to organize and store labeled data, but more importantly, pandas provides time saving methods for transforming data within a DataFrame. Examples we have seen in this book include dropping duplicates, mapping dictionaries to columns, applying functions over columns, and filing in missing values.

With respect to visualizations, DataFrames offer methods for creating all sorts of matplotlib graphs, including `df.plot.barh()`, `df.plot.hist()`, and more. The interactive visualization library Bokeh previously relied on pandas DataFrames for their *high-level* charts. These worked similar to Seaborn, as we saw earlier in the previous chapter, where a DataFrame is passed to the plotting function along with the specific columns to plot. The most recent version of Bokeh, however, has dropped support for this behavior. Instead, plots are now created in much the same way as matplotlib, where the data can be stored in simple lists or NumPy arrays. The point of this discussion is that DataFrames are not entirely necessary, but still very helpful for organizing and manipulating the data prior to visualization.

## Building and merging Pandas DataFrames

Let's dive right into an exercise, where we'll continue working on the country data we scraped earlier. Recall that we extracted the central bank interest rates and populations of each country, and saved the results in CSV files. We'll load the data from these files and merge them into a DataFrame, which will then be used as the data source for the interactive visualizations to follow.

1. In the `chapter-3-workbook.ipynb` Jupyter Notebook, scroll to the Subtopic `Building a DataFrame to store and organize data`.

   We are first going to load the data from the `CSV files`, so that it's back to the state it was in after scraping. This will allow us to practice building DataFrames from Python objects, as opposed to using the `pd.read_csv function`.

    When using `pd.read_csv`, the datatype for each column will be inferred from the string input. On the other hand, when using `pd.DataFrame` as we do here, the datatype is instead taken as the type of the input variables. In our case, as will be seen, we read the file and do not bother converting the variables to numeric or date-time until after instantiating the DataFrame.

2. Load the CSV files into lists by running the following code:

```
with open('../data/countries/interest-rates.csv', 'r') as f:
    int_rates_col_names = next(f).split(',')
    int_rates = [line.split(',') for line in f.read().splitlines()]
with open('../data/countries/populations.csv', 'r') as f:
    populations_col_names = next(f).split(',')
    populations = [line.split(',') for line in f.read().splitlines()]
```

3. Check what the resulting lists look like by running the next two cells. We should see an output similar to the following:

```
print(int_rates_col_names)
int_rates[:5]
>> ['Country or currency union', 'Central bank interest ...
...
['Indonesia', '263', '991', '379', '1.10 %'],
['Brazil', '209', '288', '278', '0.79 %']]
```

Now, the data is in a standard Python list structure, just as it was after scraping from the web pages in the previous sections. We're now going to create two DataFrames and merge them, so that all of the data is organized within one object.

4. Use the standard DataFrame constructor to create the two DataFrames by running the following code:

```
df_int_rates = pd.DataFrame(int_rates, columns=int_rates_col_names)
df_populations = pd.DataFrame(populations,
                    columns=populations_col_names)
```

This isn't the first time we've used this function in this book. Here, we pass the lists of data (as seen previously) and the corresponding column names. The input data can also be of dictionary type, which can be useful when each column is contained in a separate list.

Next, we're going to clean up each DataFrame. Starting with the interest rates one, let's print the head and tail, and list the data types.

5. When displaying the entire DataFrame, the default maximum number of rows is 60 (for version 0.18.1). Let's reduce this to 10 by running the following code:

```
pd.options.display.max_rows = 10
```

6. Display the head and tail of the interest rates DataFrame by running the following code:

```
df_int_rates
```

|  | Country or currency union | Central bank interest rate (%) | Date of last change |
| --- | --- | --- | --- |
| 0 | Albania | 1.25 | 4 May 2016 |
| 1 | Angola | 16.0 | 30 June 2016 |
| 2 | Argentina | 26.25 | 11 April 2017 |
| 3 | Armenia | 6.0 | 14 February 2017 |
| 4 | Australia | 1.5 | 2 August 2016 |
| ... | ... | ... | ... |
| 84 | United States | 1.25 | 14 June 2017 |
| 85 | Uzbekistan | 9.0 | 1 January 2015 |
| 86 | Vietnam | 6.25 | 7 July 2017 |
| 87 | West African States | 3.5 | 16 September 2013 |
| 88 | Zambia | 12.5 | 17 May 2017 |

89 rows × 3 columns

7. Print the data types by running:

```
df_int_rates.dtypes
>> Country or currency union object
>> Central bank interest rate (%) object
>> Date of last change object
>> dtype: object
```

Pandas has assigned each column as a string datatype, which makes sense because the input variables were all strings. We'll want to change these to string, float, and date-time, respectively.

8. Convert to the proper datatypes by running the following code:

```
df_int_rates['Central bank interest rate (%)'] = \
df_int_rates['Central bank interest rate (%)']\
.astype(float,copy=False)
df_int_rates['Date of last change'] = \
pd.to_datetime(df_int_rates['Date of last change'])
```

We use `astype` to cast the Interest Rate values as floats, setting `copy=False` to save memory. Since the date values are given in such an easy-to-read format, these can be converted simply by using `pd.to_datetime`.

9. Check the new datatypes of each column by running the following code:

```
df_int_rates.dtypes
>> Country or currency union            object
>> Central bank interest rate (%)       float64
>> Date of last change          datetime64[ns]
>> dtype: object
```

As can be seen, everything is now in the proper format.

10. Let's apply the same procedure to the other DataFrame. Run the next few cells to repeat the preceding steps for `df_populations`:

**df_populations**

|       | Country (or dependency) | Population (2017) | Yearly Change |
|-------|-------------------------|-------------------|---------------|
| 0     | China                   | 1,409,517,397     | 0.43 %        |
| 1     | India                   | 1,339,180,127     | 1.13 %        |
| 2     | U.S.                    | 324,459,463       | 0.71 %        |
| 3     | Indonesia               | 263,991,379       | 1.10 %        |
| 4     | Brazil                  | 209,288,278       | 0.79 %        |
| ...   | ...                     | ...               | ...           |
| 228   | Saint Helena            | 4,049             | 0.35 %        |
| 229   | Falkland Islands        | 2,910             | 0.00 %        |
| 230   | Niue                    | 1,618             | -0.37 %       |
| 231   | Tokelau                 | 1,300             | 1.40 %        |
| 232   | Holy See                | 792               | -1.12 %       |

Then, run this code:

```
df_populations['Population (2017)'] = df_populations['Population
(2017)']\.str.replace(',', '')\
.astype(float, copy=False)
df_populations['Yearly Change'] = df_populations['Yearly Change']\
.str.rstrip('%')\
.astype(float, copy=False)
```

To cast the numeric columns as a float, we had to first apply some modifications to the strings in this case. We stripped away any commas from the populations and removed the percent sign from the Yearly Change column, using string methods.

Now, we're going to merge the DataFrames on the country name for each row. Keep in mind that these are still the raw country names as scraped from the web, so there might be some work involved with matching the strings.

11. Merge the DataFrames by running the following code:

```
df_merge = pd.merge(df_populations,
    df_int_rates,
    left_on='Country (or dependency)',
    right_on='Country or currency union',
    how='outer'
df_merge
```

We pass the population data in the left DataFrame and the interest rates in the right one, performing an outer match on the country columns. This will result in NaN values where the two do not overlap.

12. For the sake of time, let's just look at the most populated countries to see whether we missed matching any. Ideally, we would want to check everything. Look at the most populous countries by running the following code:

```
df_merge.sort_values('Population (2017)', ascending=False)\ .head(10)
```

| | Country (or dependency) | Population (2017) | Yearly Change | Country or currency union | Central bank interest rate (%) | Date of last change |
|---|---|---|---|---|---|---|
| 0 | China | 1.409517e+09 | 0.43 | China | 1.75 | 2015-10-23 |
| 1 | India | 1.339180e+09 | 1.13 | India | 6.00 | 2017-08-02 |
| 2 | U.S. | 3.244595e+08 | 0.71 | NaN | NaN | NaT |
| 3 | Indonesia | 2.639914e+08 | 1.10 | Indonesia | 4.75 | 2016-10-20 |
| 4 | Brazil | 2.092883e+08 | 0.79 | Brazil | 7.25 | 2017-07-26 |
| 5 | Pakistan | 1.970160e+08 | 1.97 | Pakistan | 5.75 | 2016-05-21 |
| 6 | Nigeria | 1.908863e+08 | 2.63 | Nigeria | 14.00 | 2016-07-26 |
| 7 | Bangladesh | 1.646698e+08 | 1.05 | Bangladesh | 6.75 | 2016-01-14 |
| 8 | Russia | 1.439898e+08 | 0.02 | Russia | 9.00 | 2017-06-16 |
| 9 | Mexico | 1.291633e+08 | 1.27 | Mexico | 7.00 | 2017-06-22 |

It looks like U.S. didn't match up. This is because it's listed as United States in the interest rates data. Let's remedy this.

13. Fix the label for U.S. in the populations table by running the following code:

```
col = 'Country (or dependency)'
df_populations.loc[df_populations[col] == 'U.S.'] = 'United States'
```

We rename the country for the populations DataFrame with the use of the `loc` method to locate that row. Now, let's merge the DataFrames properly.

14. Re-merge the DataFrames on the country names, but this time use an inner merge to remove the NaN values:

```
df_merge = pd.merge(df_populations,
            df_int_rates,
            left_on='Country (or dependency)',
            right_on='Country or currency union',
            how='inner')
```

15. We are left with two identical columns in the merged DataFrame. Drop one of them by running the following code:

```
del df_merge['Country or currency union']
```

16. Rename the columns by running the following code:

```
name_map = {'Country (or dependency)': 'Country',
    'Population (2017)': 'Population',
    'Central bank interest rate (%)': 'Interest rate'}

df_merge = df_merge.rename(columns=name_map)
```

We are left with the following merged and cleaned DataFrame:

|    | Country       | Population    | Yearly Change | Interest rate | Date of last change |
|----|---------------|---------------|---------------|---------------|---------------------|
| 0  | China         | 1.409517e+09  | 0.43          | 1.75          | 2015-10-23          |
| 1  | India         | 1.339180e+09  | 1.13          | 6.00          | 2017-08-02          |
| 2  | United States | 3.244595e+08  | 0.71          | 1.25          | 2017-06-14          |
| 3  | Indonesia     | 2.639914e+08  | 1.10          | 4.75          | 2016-10-20          |
| 4  | Brazil        | 2.092883e+08  | 0.79          | 7.25          | 2017-07-26          |
| ...| ...           | ...           | ...           | ...           | ...                 |
| 76 | Mauritius     | 1.265138e+06  | 0.24          | 4.00          | 2016-07-20          |
| 77 | Fiji          | 9.055020e+05  | 0.75          | 0.50          | 2011-11-02          |
| 78 | Bahamas       | 3.953610e+05  | 1.06          | 4.00          | 2016-12-22          |
| 79 | Iceland       | 3.350250e+05  | 0.77          | 4.50          | 2017-06-14          |
| 80 | Samoa         | 1.964400e+05  | 0.67          | 0.14          | 2016-07-01          |

81 rows × 5 columns

17. Now that we have all the data in a nicely organized table, we can move on to the fun part: visualizing it. Let's save this table to a CSV file for later use, and then move on to discuss how visualizations can be created with Bokeh. Write the merged data to a CSV file for later use with the following code:

```
df_merge.to_csv('../data/countries/merged.csv', index=False)
```

# Introduction to Bokeh

Bokeh is an interactive visualization library for Python. Its goal is to provide similar functionality to D3, the popular interactive visualization library for JavaScript. Bokeh functions very differently than D3, which is not surprising given the differences between Python and JavaScript. Overall, it's much simpler and it doesn't allow nearly as much customization as D3 does. This works to its advantage though, as it's much easier to use, and it still boasts an excellent suite of features that we'll explore in this section.

Let's dive right into a quick exercise with the Jupyter Notebook and introduce Bokeh by example.

There is good documentation online for Bokeh, but much of it is outdated. Searching something like `Bokeh bar plot` in Google still tends to turn up documentation for legacy modules that no longer exist, for example, the high-level plotting tools that used to be available through `bokeh.charts` (prior to version 0.12.0). These are the ones that take pandas DataFrames as input in much the same way that Seaborn plotting functions do. Removing the high-level plotting tools module has simplified Bokeh, and will allow for more focused development going forward. Now, the plotting tools are largely grouped into the bokeh. `plotting module`, as will be seen in the next exercise and following activity.

# Introduction to interactive visualizations with Bokeh

We'll load the required Bokeh modules and show some simple interactive plots that can be made with Bokeh. Please note that the examples in this book have been designed using version 0.12.10 of Bokeh.

1. In the `chapter-3-workbook.ipynb` Jupyter notebook, scroll to Subtopic `Introduction to Bokeh`.

2. Like scikit-learn, Bokeh modules are usually loaded in pieces (unlike pandas, for example, where the whole library is loaded at once). Import some basic plotting modules by running the following code:

```
from bokeh.plotting
import figure, show, output_notebook output_notebook()
```

We need to run `output_notebook()` in order to render the interactive visuals within the Jupyter notebook.

3. Generate random data to plot by running the following code:

```
np.random.seed(30)
data = pd.Series(np.random.randn(200),
index=list(range(200)))\
.cumsum()
x = data.index
y = data.values
```

The random data is generated using the cumulative sum of a random set of numbers that are distributed about zero. The effect is a trend that looks similar to a stock price time series, for example.

4. Plot the data with a line plot in Bokeh by running the following code:

```
p = figure(title='Example plot', x_axis_label='x', y_axis_label='y')
p.line(x, y, legend='Random trend') show(p)
```

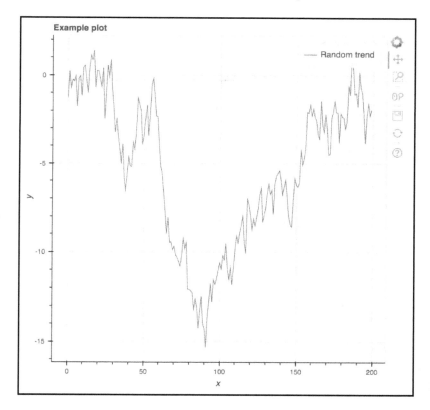

We instantiate the figure, as referenced by the variable p, and then plot a line. Running this in Jupyter yields an interactive figure with various options along the right-hand side.

The top three options (as of version 0.12.10) are **Pan**, **Box Zoom**, and **Wheel Zoom**. Play around with these and experiment with how they work. Use the reset option to re-load the default plot limits.

5. Other plots can be created with the alternative methods of `figure`. Draw a scatter plot by running the following code, where we replace `line` in the preceding code with `circle`:

```
size = np.random.rand(200) * 5
p = figure(title='Example plot', x_axis_label='x', y_axis_label='y')
p.circle(x, y, radius=size, alpha=0.5, legend='Random dots')
show(p)
```

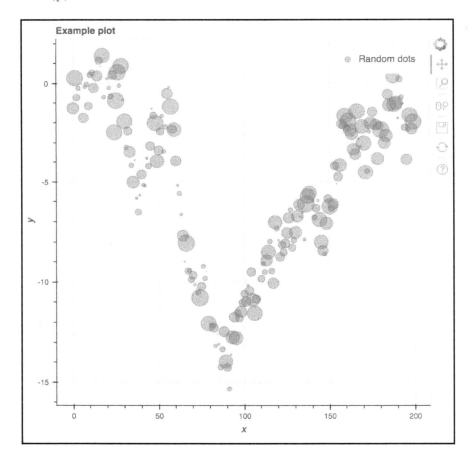

Here, we've specified the size of each circle using a random set of numbers.

A very enticing feature of interactive visualizations is the tooltip. This is a hover tool that allows the user to get information about a point by hovering over it.

6. In order to add this tool, we're going to use a slightly different method for creating the plot. This will require us to import a couple of new libraries. Run the following code:

```
p.circle(x, y, radius=size, alpha=0.5, legend='Random dots') show(p)
```

This time, we'll create a data source to pass to the plotting method. This can contain metadata, which can be included in the visualization via the hover tool.

7. Create random labels and plot the interactive visualization with a hover tool by running the following code:

```
source = ColumnDataSource(data=dict(
x=x,
y=y,
...
...
source=source,
  legend='Random dots')
show(p)
```

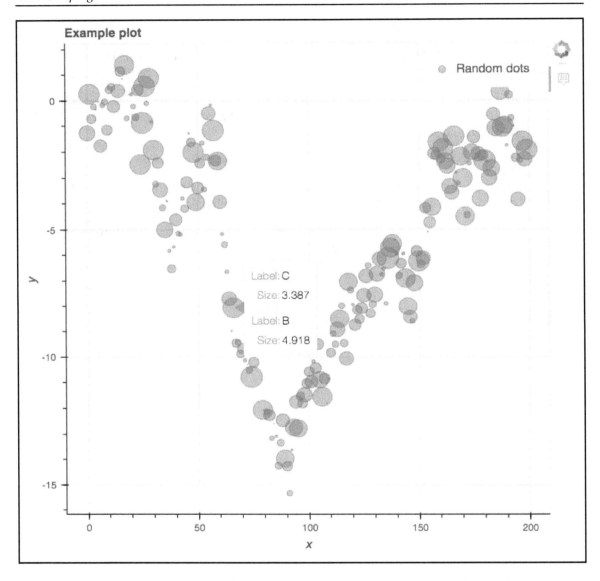

We define a data source for the plot by passing a dictionary of key/value pairs to the `ColumnDataSource` constructor. This source includes the *x* location, *y* location, and size of each point, along with the random letter *A*, *B*, or *C* for each point. These random letters are assigned as labels for the hover tool, which will also display the size of each point.

The **Hover Tool** is then added to the figure, and the data is retrieved from each element through the specific plotting method, which is circle in this case.

The result is that we are now able to hover over the points and see the data we've selected for the **Hover Tool**!

We notice, by looking at the toolbar to the right of the plot, that by explicitly including the **Hover Tool**, the others have disappeared. These can be included by manually adding them to the list of tool objects that gets passed to bokeh. plotting.figure.

8.  Add pan, zoom, and reset tools to the plot by running the following code:

```
from bokeh.models
import PanTool, BoxZoomTool, WheelZoomTool, ResetTool
...

...
    legend='Random dots')
    show(p)
```

This code is identical to what was previously shown except for the tools variable, which now references several new tools we've imported from the Bokeh library.

We'll stop the introductory exercise here, but we'll continue creating and exploring plots in the following activity.

# Activity: Exploring Data with Interactive Visualizations

We'll pick up using Bokeh right where we left off with the previous exercise, except instead of using the randomly generated data seen there, we'll instead use the data we scraped from the web in the first part of this chapter.

To use Bokeh to create interactive visualizations of our scraped data.

1. In the `chapter-3-workbook.ipynb` file, scroll to the **Activity: Interactive visualizations with Bokeh** section.

2. Load the previously scraped, merged, and cleaned web page data by running the following code:

```
df = pd.read_csv('../data/countries/merged.csv')
df['Date of last change'] = pd.to_datetime(df['Date of last change'])
```

3. Recall what the data looks like by displaying the DataFrame:

|  | Country | Population | Yearly Change | Interest rate | Date of last change |
|---|---|---|---|---|---|
| 0 | China | 1.409517e+09 | 0.43 | 1.75 | 2015-10-23 |
| 1 | India | 1.339180e+09 | 1.13 | 6.00 | 2017-08-02 |
| 2 | United States | 3.244595e+08 | 0.71 | 1.25 | 2017-06-14 |
| 3 | Indonesia | 2.639914e+08 | 1.10 | 4.75 | 2016-10-20 |
| 4 | Brazil | 2.092883e+08 | 0.79 | 7.25 | 2017-07-26 |
| ... | ... | ... | ... | ... | ... |
| 76 | Mauritius | 1.265138e+06 | 0.24 | 4.00 | 2016-07-20 |
| 77 | Fiji | 9.055020e+05 | 0.75 | 0.50 | 2011-11-02 |
| 78 | Bahamas | 3.953610e+05 | 1.06 | 4.00 | 2016-12-22 |
| 79 | Iceland | 3.350250e+05 | 0.77 | 4.50 | 2017-06-14 |
| 80 | Samoa | 1.964400e+05 | 0.67 | 0.14 | 2016-07-01 |

81 rows × 5 columns

Whereas in the previous exercise we were interested in learning how Bokeh worked, now we are interested in what this data looks like. In order to explore this dataset, we are going to use interactive visualizations.

4. Draw a scatter plot of the population as a function of the interest rate by running the following code:

```
source = ColumnDataSource(data=dict(
    x=df['Interest rate'],
    y=df['Population'],
    desc=df['Country'],
))
hover = HoverTool(tooltips=[
    ('Country', '@desc'),
    ('Interest Rate (%)', '@x'),
    ('Population', '@y')
```

```
])
tools = [hover, PanTool(), BoxZoomTool(),
WheelZoomTool(), ResetTool()]
    p = figure(tools=tools,
    x_axis_label='Interest Rate (%)',
    y_axis_label='Population')
p.circle('x', 'y', size=10, alpha=0.5, source=source)
show(p)
```

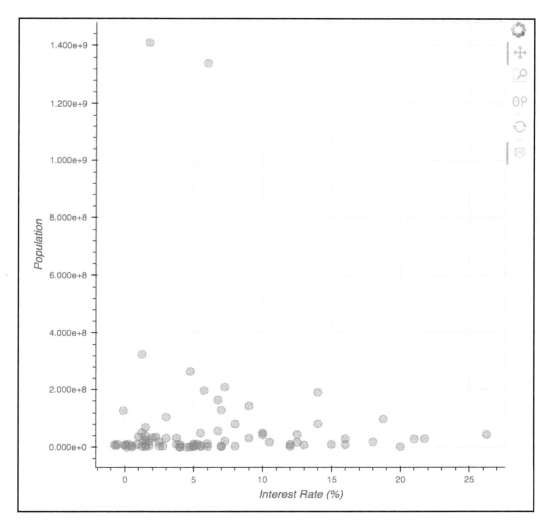

This is quite similar to the final examples we looked at when introducing Bokeh in the previous exercise. We set up a customized data source with the x and y coordinates for each point, along with the country name. This country name is passed to the **Hover Tool**, so that it's visible when hovering the mouse over the dot. We pass this tool to the figure, along with a set of other useful tools.

5. In the data, we see some clear outliers with high populations. Hover over these to see what they are:

We see they belong to India and China. These countries have fairly average interest rates. Let's focus on the rest of the points by using the **Box Zoom** tool to modify the view window size.

6. Select the Box Zoom tool and alter the viewing window to better see the majority of the data:

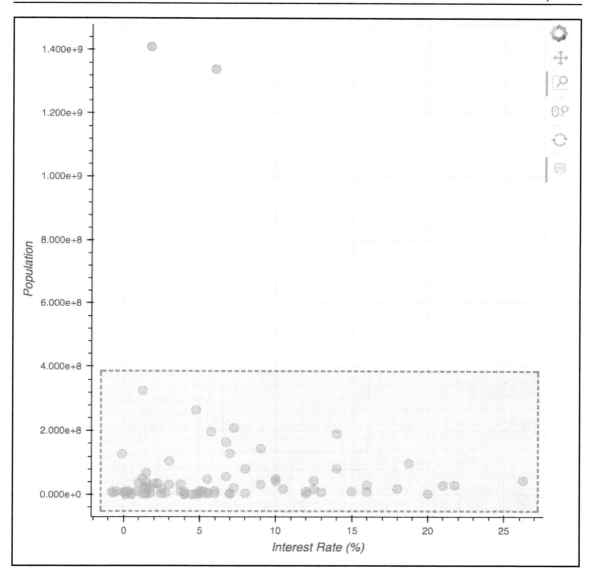

Explore the points and see how the interest rates compare for various countries. What are the countries with the highest interest rates?

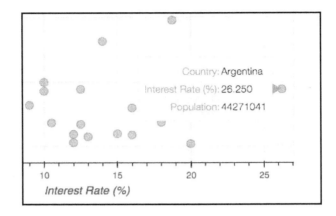

7. Some of the lower population countries appear to have negative interest rates. Select the **Wheel Zoom** tool and use it to zoom in on this region. Use the **Pan** tool to re-center the plot, if needed, so that the negative interest rate samples are in view. Hover over some of these and see what countries they correspond to:

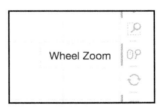

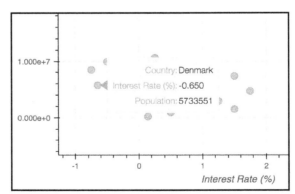

Let's re-plot this, adding a color based on the date of last interest rate change. This will be useful to search for relations between the date of last change and the interest rate or population size.

8. Add a Year of last change column to the DataFrame by running the following code:

```
def get_year(x):
  year = x.strftime('%Y')
  if year in ['2018', '2017', '2016']:
      return year
else:
      return 'Other'
df['Year of last change'] = df['Date of last change'].apply(get_year)
```

We first define a function to group the samples based on year of last change, and then apply that function to the **Date of last change** column. Next, we need to map these values to colors for the visualization.

9. Create a map to group the last change date into color categories by running the following code:

```
year_to_color = {
'2018': 'black',
'2017': 'blue',
'2016': 'orange',
'Other':'red'
}
```

Once mapped to the Year of last change column, this will assign values to colors based on the available categories: 2018, 2017, 2016, and Other. The colors here are standard strings, but they could alternatively by represented by hexadecimal codes.

10. Create the colored visualization by running the following code:

```
source = ColumnDataSource(data=dict(
x=df['Interest rate'],
...
...
    fill_color='colors', line_color='black',
    legend='label')
show(p)
```

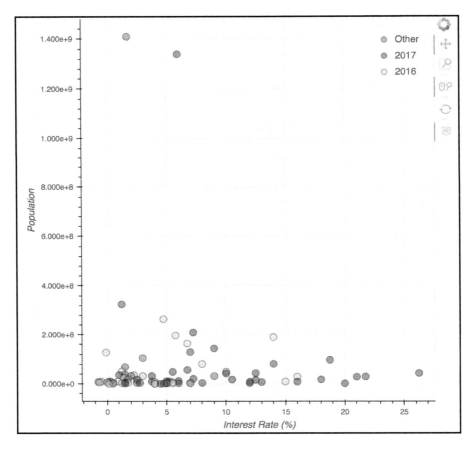

There are some technical details that are important here. First of all, we add the colors and labels for each point to the `ColumnDataSource`. These are then referenced when plotting the circles by setting the `fill_color` and legend arguments.

11. Looking for patterns, zoom in on the lower population countries:

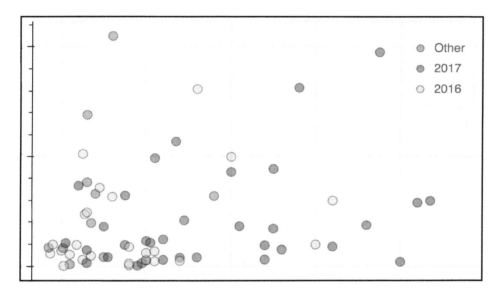

We can see how the dark dots are more prevalent to the right-hand side of the plot. This indicates that countries that have higher interest rates are more likely to have been recently updated.

The one data column we have not yet looked at is the year-over-year change in population. Let's visualize this compared to the interest rate and see if there is any trend. We'll also enhance the plot by setting the circle size based on the country population.

12. Plot the interest rate as a function of the year-over-year population change by running the following code:

```
source = ColumnDataSource(data=dict(
    x=df['Yearly Change'],
...
...
p.circle('x', 'y', size=10, alpha=0.5, source=source,
radius='radii')
show(p)
```

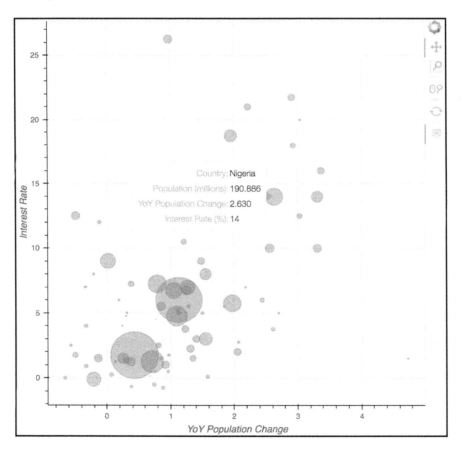

Here, we use the square root of the population for the radii, making sure to also scale down the result to a good size for the visualization.

We see a strong correlation between the year-over-year population change and the interest rate. This correlation is especially strong when we take the population sizes into account, by looking primarily at the bigger circles. Let's add a line of best fit to the plot to illustrate this correlation.

We'll use scikit-learn to create the line of best fit, using the country populations (as visualized in the preceding plot) as weights.

13. Determine the line of best fit for the previously plotted relationship by running the following code:

```
from sklearn.linear_model import LinearRegression
X = df['Yearly Change'].values.reshape(-1, 1)
y = df['Interest rate'].values
weights = np.sqrt(df['Population'])/1e5
lm = LinearRegression()
lm.fit(X, y, sample_weight=weights)
lm_x = np.linspace(X.flatten().min(), X.flatten().max(), 50)
lm_y = lm.predict(lm_x.reshape(-1, 1))
```

The scikit-learn code should be familiar from earlier in this book. As promised, we are using the transformed populations, as seen in the previous plot, as the weights. The line of best fit is then calculated by predicting the linear model values for a range of *x* values.

To plot the line, we can reuse the preceding code, adding an extra call to the line module in Bokeh. We'll also have to set a new data source for this line.

14. Re-plot the preceding figure, adding a line of best fi, by running the following code:

```
source = ColumnDataSource(data=dict(
    x=df['Yearly Change'],
    y=df['Interest rate'],
 ...
 ...
p.line('x', 'y', line_width=2, line_color='red',
    source=lm_source)
    show(p)
```

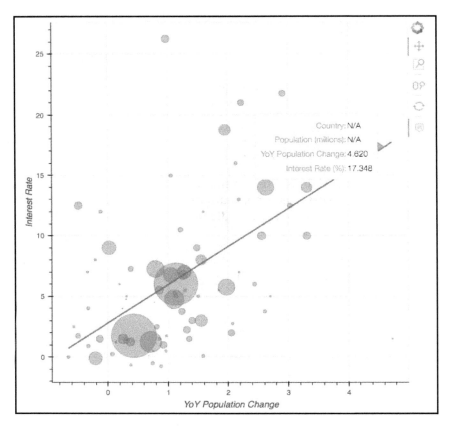

For the line source, `lm_source`, we include N/A as the country name and population, as these are not applicable values for the line of best fit. As can be seen by hovering over the line, they indeed appear in the tooltip.

The interactive nature of this visualization gives us a unique opportunity to explore outliers in this dataset, for example, the tiny dot in the lower-right corner.

15. Explore the plot by using the zoom tools and hovering over interesting samples. Note the following:

- Ukraine has an unusually high interest rate, given the low year-over-year population change:

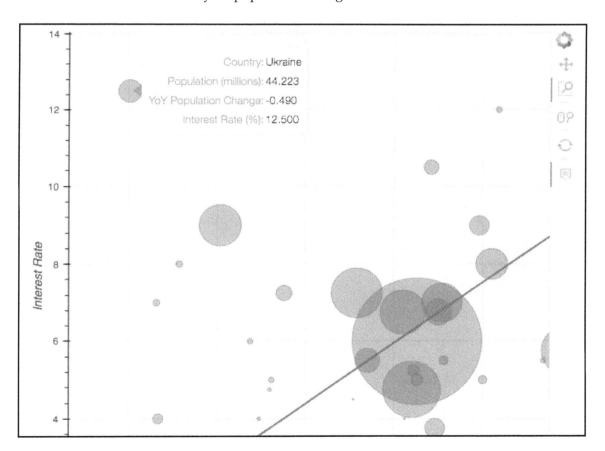

- The small country of Bahrain has an unusually low interest rate, given the high year-over-year population change:

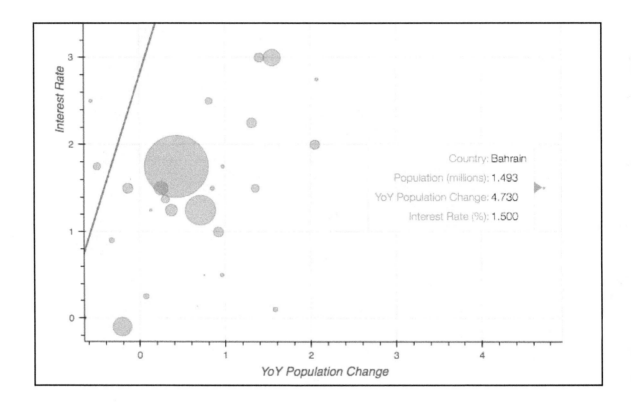

# Summary

In this chapter, we scraped web page tables and then used interactive visualizations to study the data.

We started by looking at how HTTP requests work, focusing on GET requests and their response status codes. Then, we went into the Jupyter Notebook and made HTTP requests with Python using the Requests library. We saw how Jupyter can be used to render HTML in the notebook, along with actual web pages that can be interacted with. After making requests, we saw how Beautiful Soup can be used to parse text from the HTML, and used this library to scrape tabular data.

After scraping two tables of data, we stored them in pandas DataFrames. The first table contained the central bank interest rates for each country and the second table contained the populations. We combined these into a single table that was then used to create interactive visualizations.

Finally, we used Bokeh to render interactive visualizations in Jupyter. We saw how to use the Bokeh API to create various customized plots and made scatter plots with specific interactive abilities such as zoom, pan, and hover. In terms of customization, we explicitly showed how to set the point radius and color for each data sample. Furthermore, when using Bokeh to explore the scraped population data, the tooltip was utilized to show country names and associated data when hovering over the points.

Congratulations for completing this introductory course on data science using Jupyter Notebooks! Regardless of your experience with Jupyter and Python coming into the book, you've learned some useful and applicable skills for practical data science!

# 4
# Introduction to Neural Networks and Deep Learning

The MNIST dataset does not contain numbers on the edges of images. Hence, neither network assigns relevant values to the pixels located in that region. Both networks are much better at classifying numbers correctly if we draw them closer to the center of the designated area. This shows that neural networks can only be as powerful as the data that is used to train them. If the data used for training is very different than what we are trying to predict, the network will most likely produce disappointing results. In this chapter, we will cover the basics of neural networks and how to set up a deep learning programming environment. We will also explore the common components of a neural network and its essential operations. We will conclude this chapter by exploring a trained neural network created using TensorFlow.

This chapter is about understanding what neural networks can do. We will not cover mathematical concepts underlying deep learning algorithms, but will instead describe the essential pieces that make a deep learning system. We will also look at examples where neural networks have been used to solve real-world problems.

This chapter will give you a practical intuition on how to engineer systems that use neural networks to solve problems—including how to determine if a given problem can be solved at all with such algorithms. At its core, this chapter challenges you to think about your problem as a mathematical representation of ideas. By the end of this chapter, you will be able to think about a problem as a collection of these representations and then start to recognize how these representations may be learned by deep learning algorithms.

By the end of this chapter, you will be able to:

- Cover the basics of neural networks
- Set up a deep learning programming environment
- Explore the common components of a neural network and its essential operations
- Conclude this chapter by exploring a trained neural network created using TensorFlow

# What are Neural Networks?

Neural networks—also known as **Artificial Neural Networks**—were first proposed in the 40s by MIT professors Warren McCullough and Walter Pitts.

 For more information refer, Explained: Neural networks. MIT News Office, April 14, 2017. Available at: `http://news.mit.edu/2017/explained-neural-networksdeep-learning-0414`.

Inspired by advancements in neuroscience, they proposed to create a computer system that reproduced how the brain works (human or otherwise). At its core was the idea of a computer system that worked as an interconnected network. That is, a system that has many simple components. These components both interpret data and influence each other on how to interpret data. This same core idea remains today.

Deep learning is largely considered the contemporary study of neural networks. Think of it as a current name given to neural networks. The main difference is that the neural networks used in deep learning are typically far greater in size—that is, they have many more nodes and layers—than earlier neural networks. Deep learning algorithms and applications typically require resources to achieve success, hence the use of the word *deep* to emphasize its size and the large number of interconnected components.

# Successful Applications

Neural networks have been under research since their inception in the 40s in one form or another. It is only recently, however, that deep learning systems have been successfully used in large-scale industrial applications.

Contemporary proponents of neural networks have demonstrated great success in speech recognition, language translation, image classification, and other fields. Its current prominence is backed by a significant increase in available computing power and the emergence of **Graphics Processing Units (GPUs)** and **Tensor Processing Units (TPUs)**— which are able to perform many more simultaneous mathematical operations than regular CPUs, as well as a much greater availability of data.

Power consumption of different AlphaGo algorithms. AlphaGo is an initiative by DeepMind to develop a series of algorithms to beat the game Go. It is considered a prime example of the power of deep learning. TPUs are a chipset developed by Google for the use in deep learning programs.

The graphic depicts the number of GPUs and TPUs used to train different versions of the AlphaGo algorithm. Source: `https://deepmind.com/blog/alphago-zero-learning-scratch/`

In this book, we will not be using GPUs to fulfill our activities. GPUs are not required to work with neural networks. In a number of simple examples—like the ones provided in this book—all computations can be performed using a simple laptop's CPU. However, when dealing with very large datasets, GPUs can be of great help given that the long time to train a neural network would be unpractical.

Here are a few examples of fields in which neural networks have had a great impact:

- **Translating text**: In 2017, Google announced that it was releasing a new algorithm for its translation service called **Transformer**. The algorithm consisted of a recurrent neural network (LSTM) that is trained used bilingual text. Google showed that its algorithm had gained notable accuracy when comparing to industry standards (BLEU) and was also computationally efficient. At the time of writing, Transformer is reportedly used by Google Translate as its main translation algorithm.

Google Research Blog. Transformer: A Novel Neural Network Architecture for Language Understanding. August 31, 2017. Available at: `https://research.googleblog.com/2017/08/transformernovel-neural-network.html`.

- **Self-driving vehicles**: Uber, NVIDIA, and Waymo are believed to be using deep learning models to control different vehicle functions that control driving. Each company is researching a number of possibilities, including training the network using humans, simulating vehicles driving in virtual environments, and even creating a small city-like environment in which vehicles can be trained based on expected and unexpected events.

> Alexis C. Madrigal: Inside Waymo's Secret World for Training SelfDriving Cars. The Atlantic. August 23, 2017. Available at: `https://www.theatlantic.com/technology/archive/2017/08/ inside-waymos-secret-testing-and-simulationfacilities/537648/.`
> NVIDIA: *End-to-End Deep Learning for Self-Driving Cars.* August 17, 2016. Available at: `https://devblogs.nvidia.com/ parallelforall/deep-learning-self-driving-cars/.`
> Dave Gershgorn: Uber's new AI team is looking for the shortest route to self-driving cars. Quartz. December 5, 2016. Available at: `https://qz.com/853236/ubers-new-ai-team-is-looking-for-theshortest-route-to-self-driving-cars/.`

- **Image recognition**: Facebook and Google use deep learning models to identify entities in images and automatically tag these entities as persons from a set of contacts. In both cases, the networks are trained with previously tagged images as well as with images from the target friend or contact. Both companies report that the models are able to suggest a friend or contact with a high level of accuracy in most cases.

While there are many more examples in other industries, the application of deep learning models is still in its infancy. Many more successful applications are yet to come, including the ones that you create.

# Why Do Neural Networks Work So Well?

Why are neural networks so powerful? Neural networks are powerful because they can be used to predict any given function with reasonable approximation. If one is able to represent a problem as a mathematical function and also has data that represents that function correctly, then a deep learning model can, in principle—and given enough resources—be able to approximate that function. This is typically called the *universality principle of neural networks*.

For more information refer, Michael Nielsen: Neural Networks and Deep Learning: A visual proof that neural nets can compute any function. Available at: `http://neuralnetworksanddeeplearning.com/chap4.html`.

We will not be exploring mathematical proofs of the universality principle in this book. However, two characteristics of neural networks should give you the right intuition on how to understand that principle: representation learning and function approximation.

 For more information refer, Kai Arulkumaran, Marc Peter Deisenroth, Miles Brundage, and Anil Anthony Bharath. A Brief Survey of Deep Reinforcement Learning. arXiv. September 28, 2017. Available at: `https://www.arxiv-vanity.com/papers/1708.05866/` .

# Representation Learning

The data used to train a neural network contains representations (also known as *features*) that explain the problem you are trying to solve. For instance, if one is interested in recognizing faces from images, the color values of each pixel from a set of images that contain faces will be used as a starting point. The model will then continuously learn higher-level representations by combining pixels together as it goes through its training process.

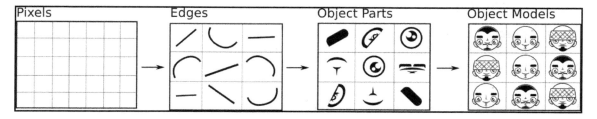

Figure 1: Series of higher-level representations that begin on input data. Derivate image based on original image from: Yann LeCun, Yoshua Bengio & Geoffrey Hinton. "Deep Learning". Nature 521, 436–444 (28 May 2015) doi:10.1038/ nature14539

In formal words, neural networks are computation graphs in which each step computes higher abstraction representations from input data.

Each one of these steps represents a progression into a different abstraction layer. Data progresses through these layers, building continuously higher-level representations. The process finishes with the highest representation possible: the one the model is trying to predict.

# Function Approximation

When neural networks learn new representations of data, they do so by combining weights and biases with neurons from different layers. They adjust the weights of these connections every time a training cycle takes place using a mathematical technique called backpropagation. The weights and biases improve at each round, up to the point that an optimum is achieved. This means that a neural network can measure how wrong it is on every training cycle, adjust the weights and biases of each neuron, and try again. If it determines that a certain modification produces better results than the previous round, it will invest in that modification until an optimal solution is achieved.

In a nutshell, that procedure is the reason why neural networks can approximate functions. However, there are many reasons why a neural network may not be able to predict a function with perfection, chief among them being that:

- Many functions contain stochastic properties (that is, random properties)
- There may be overfitting to peculiarities from the training data
- There may be a lack of training data

In many practical applications, simple neural networks are able to approximate a function with reasonable precision. These sorts of applications will be our focus.

# Limitations of Deep Learning

Deep learning techniques are best suited to problems that can be defiled with formal mathematical rules (that is, as data representations). If a problem is hard to define this way, then it is likely that deep learning will not provide a useful solution. Moreover, if the data available for a given problem is either biased or only contains partial representations of the underlying functions that generate that problem, then deep learning techniques will only be able to reproduce the problem and not learn to solve it.

Remember that deep learning algorithms are learning different representations of data to approximate a given function. If data does not represent a function appropriately, it is likely that a function will be incorrectly represented by a neural network. Consider the following analogy: you are trying to predict the national prices of gasoline (that is, fuel) and create a deep learning model. You use your credit card statement with your daily expenses on gasoline as an input data for that model. The model may eventually learn the patterns of your gasoline consumption, but it will likely misrepresent price fluctuations of gasoline caused by other factors only represented weekly in your data such as government policies, market competition, international politics, and so on. The model will ultimately yield incorrect results when used in production.

To avoid this problem, make sure that the data used to train a model represents the problem the model is trying to address as accurately as possible.

For an in-depth discussion of this topic, refer to François Chollet's upcoming book Deep Learning with Python. François is the creator of Keras, a Python library used in this book. The chapter, The limitations of deep learning, is particularly important for understanding this topic. The working version of that book is available at: `https://blog.keras.io/the-limitations-of-deeplearning.html`.

# Inherent Bias and Ethical Considerations

Researchers have suggested that the use of the deep learning model without considering the inherent bias in the training data can lead not only to poor performing solutions, but also to ethical complications.

For instance, in late 2016, researchers from the Shanghai Jiao Tong University in China created a neural network which correctly classified criminals using only pictures from their faces. The researchers used 1,856 images of Chinese men in which half had been convicted.

Their model identified inmates with 89.5 percent accuracy. (`https://blog.keras.io/the-limitations-of-deep-learning.html`). MIT Technology Review. Neural Network Learns to Identify Criminals by Their Faces. November 22, 2016. Available at: `https://www.technologyreview.com/s/602955/neuralnetwork-learns-to-identify-criminals-by-their-faces/`.

The paper resulted in great furor within the scientific community and popular media. One key issue with the proposed solution is that it fails to properly recognize the bias inherent in the input data. Namely, the data used in this study came from two different sources: one for criminals and one for non-criminals. Some researchers suggest that their algorithm identifies patterns associated with the different data sources used in the study instead of identifying relevant patterns from people's faces. While there are technical considerations one can make about the reliability of the model, the key criticism is on ethical grounds: one ought to clearly recognize the inherent bias in input data used by deep learning algorithms and consider how its application will have an impact on people's lives.

Timothy Revell. Concerns as face recognition tech used to 'identify' criminals. New Scientist. December 1, 2016. Available at: `https://www.newscientist.com/article/2114900-concernsas-face-recognition-tech-used-to-identify-criminals/`. For understanding more about the topic of ethics in learning algorithms (including deep learning), refer to the work done by the AI Now Institute (`https://ainowinstitute.org/`), an organization created for the understanding of the social implications of intelligent systems.

# Common Components and Operations of Neural Networks

Neural networks have two key components: layers and nodes. Nodes are responsible for specific operations, and layers are groups of nodes used to differentiate different stages of the system.

Typically, neural networks have the following three categories of layers:

- **Input**: Where the input data is received and first interpreted
- **Hidden**: Where computations take place, modifying data as it goes through
- **Output**: Where an output is assembled and evaluated

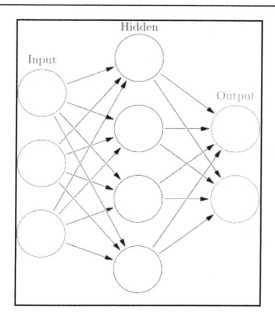

Figure 2: Illustration of the most common layers in a neural network. By Glosser.ca - Own work, Derivative of File: Artificial neural network.svg, CC BY-SA 3.0, https://commons.wikimedia.org/w/index.php?curid=24913461

Hidden layers are the most important layers in neural networks. They are referred to as *hidden* because the representations generated in them are not available in the data, but are learned from it. It is within these layers where the main computations take place in neural networks.

Nodes are where data is represented in the network. There are two values associated with nodes: biases and weights. Both of these values affect how data is represented by the nodes and passed on to other nodes. When a network learns, it effectively adjusts these values to satisfy an optimization function.

Most of the work in neural networks happens in the hidden layers. Unfortunately, there isn't a clear rule for determining how many layers or nodes a network should have. When implementing a neural network, one will probably spend time experimenting with different combinations of layers and nodes. It is advised to always start with a single layer and also with a number of nodes that reflect the number of features the input data has (that is, how many *columns* are available in a dataset). One will then continue to add layers and nodes until satisfactory performance is achieved—or whenever the network starts overfitting to the training data.

Contemporary neural network practice is generally restricted to the experimentation with the number of nodes and layers (for example, how deep the network is), and the kinds of operations performed at each layer. There are many successful instances in which neural networks outperformed other algorithms simply by adjusting these parameters.

As an intuition, think about data entering a neural network system via the input layer, then moving through the network from node to node. The path that data takes will depend on how interconnected the nodes are, the weights and the biases of each node, the kind of operations that are performed in each layer, and the state of data at the end of such operations. Neural networks often require many "runs" (or epochs) in order to keep tuning the weights and biases of nodes, meaning that data flows over the different layers of the graph multiple times.

This section offered you an overview of neural networks and deep learning. Additionally, we discussed a starter's intuition to understand the following key concepts:

- Neural networks can, in principle, approximate most functions, given that it has enough resources and data.
- Layers and nodes are the most important structural components of neural networks. One typically spends a lot of time altering those components to find a working architecture.
- Weights and biases are the key properties that a network "learns" during its training process.

Those concepts will prove useful in our next section as we explore a real-world trained neural network and make modifications to train our own.

# Configuring a Deep Learning Environment

Before we finish this chapter, we want you to interact with a real neural network. We will start by covering the main software components used throughout this book and make sure that they are properly installed. We will then explore a pre-trained neural network and explore a few of the components and operations discussed earlier in the What are Neural Networks? section.

# Software Components for Deep Learning

We'll use the following software components for deep learning:

## Python 3

We will be using Python 3. Python is a general-purpose programming language which is very popular with the scientific community—hence its adoption in deep learning. Python 2 is not supported in this book but can be used to train neural networks instead of Python 3. Even if you chose to implement your solutions in Python 2, consider moving to Python 3 as its modern feature set is far more robust than that of its predecessor.

## TensorFlow

TensorFlow is a library used for performing mathematical operations in the form of graphs. TensorFlow was originally developed by Google and today it is an open-source project with many contributors. It has been designed with neural networks in mind and is among the most popular choices when creating deep learning algorithms.

TensorFlow is also well-known for its production components. It comes with TensorFlow Serving (`https://github.com/tensorflow/serving`), a high-performance system for serving deep learning models. Also, trained TensorFlow models can be consumed in other high-performance programming languages such as Java, Go, and C. This means that one can deploy these models in anything from a micro-computer (that is, a RaspberryPi) to an Android device.

## Keras

In order to interact efficiently with TensorFlow, we will be using Keras (`https://keras.io/`), a Python package with a high-level API for developing neural networks. While TensorFlow focuses on components that interact with each other in a computational graph, Keras focuses specifically on neural networks. Keras uses TensorFlow as its backend engine and makes developing such applications much easier.

As of November 2017 (TensorFlow version 1.4), Keras is distributed as part of TensorFlow. It is available under the `tf.keras` namespace. If you have TensorFlow 1.4 or higher installed, you already have Keras available in your system.

# TensorBoard

TensorBoard is a data visualization suite for exploring TensorFlow models and is natively integrated with TensorFlow. TensorBoard works by consuming checkpoint and summary files created by TensorFlow as it trains a neural network. Those can be explored either in near real-time (with a 30-second delay) or after the network has finished training.

TensorBoard makes the process of experimenting and exploring a neural network much easier—plus it's quite exciting to follow the training of your network!

# Jupyter Notebooks, Pandas, and NumPy

When working to create deep learning models with Python, it is common to start working interactively, slowly developing a model that eventually turns into more structured software. Three Python packages are used frequently during that process: Jupyter Notebooks, Pandas, and NumPy:

- Jupyter Notebooks create interactive Python sessions that use a web browser as its interface
- Pandas is a package for data manipulation and analysis
- NumPy is frequently used for shaping data and performing numerical computations

These packages are used occasionally. They typically do not form part of a production system, but are often used when exploring data and starting to build a model. We focus on the other tools in much more detail.

 The book *Learning Pandas* by Michael Heydt (June 2017, Packt Publishing) and *Learning Jupyter* by Dan Toomey (November 2016, Packt Publishing) offer a comprehensive guide on how to use these technologies. These books are good references for continuing to learn more.

| Component | Description | Minimum Version |
|-----------|-------------|-----------------|
| Python | General-purpose programming language. A popular language used in the development of deep learning applications. | 3.6 |
| TensorFlow | Open-source graph computation Python package typically used for developing deep learning systems. | 1.4 |
| Keras | Python package that provides a high-level interface to TensorFlow. | 2.0.8-tf (distributed with TensorFlow) |
| TensorBoard | Browser-based software for visualizing neural network statistics. | 0.4.0 |
| Jupyter Notebook | Browser-based software for working interactively with Python sessions. | 5.2.1 |

| Pandas | Python package for analyzing and manipulating data. | 0.21.0 |
| NumPy | Python package for high-performance numerical computations. | 1.13.3 |

Table 1: Software components necessary for creating a deep learning environment

# Activity: Verifying Software Components

Before we explore a trained neural network, let's verify that all the software components that we need are available. We have included a script that verifies these components work. Let's take a moment to run the script and deal with any eventual problems we may find.

We will now be testing if the software components required for this book are available in your working environment. First, we suggest the creation of a Python virtual environment using Python's native module `venv`. Virtual environments are used for managing project dependencies. We advise each project you create to have its own virtual environments. Let's create one now.

 If you are more comfortable with `conda` environments, feel free to use those instead.

1. A Python virtual environment can be created by using the following command:

```
$ python3 -m venv venv
$ source venv/bin/activate
```

2. The latter command will append the string (venv) to the beginning of your command line. Use the following command to deactivate your virtual environment:

```
$ deactivate
```

Make sure to always activate your Python virtual environment when working on a project.

3. After activating your virtual environment, make sure that the right components are installed by executing pip over the file `requirements.txt`. This will attempt to install the models used in this book in that virtual environment. It will do nothing if they are already available:

```
(venv) ~/Programs/book  pip install -r requirements.txt
Requirement already satisfied: bleach==1.5.0 in ./venv/lib/python3.6/site-packages (from -r requirements.txt (line 1))
Requirement already satisfied: cycler==0.10.0 in ./venv/lib/python3.6/site-packages (from -r requirements.txt (line 2))
Requirement already satisfied: html5lib==0.9999999 in ./venv/lib/python3.6/site-packages (from -r requirements.txt (line 3))
Requirement already satisfied: Keras==2.0.8 in ./venv/lib/python3.6/site-packages (from -r requirements.txt (line 4))
Requirement already satisfied: Markdown==2.6.9 in ./venv/lib/python3.6/site-packages (from -r requirements.txt (line 5))
Requirement already satisfied: matplotlib==2.1.0 in ./venv/lib/python3.6/site-packages (from -r requirements.txt (line 6))
Requirement already satisfied: numpy==1.13.3 in ./venv/lib/python3.6/site-packages (from -r requirements.txt (line 7))
Requirement already satisfied: pandas==0.21.0 in ./venv/lib/python3.6/site-packages (from -r requirements.txt (line 8))
Requirement already satisfied: protobuf==3.4.0 in ./venv/lib/python3.6/site-packages (from -r requirements.txt (line 9))
Requirement already satisfied: pyparsing==2.2.0 in ./venv/lib/python3.6/site-packages (from -r requirements.txt (line 10))
Requirement already satisfied: python-dateutil==2.6.1 in ./venv/lib/python3.6/site-packages (from -r requirements.txt (line 11))
Requirement already satisfied: pytz==2017.3 in ./venv/lib/python3.6/site-packages (from -r requirements.txt (line 12))
Requirement already satisfied: PyYAML==3.12 in ./venv/lib/python3.6/site-packages (from -r requirements.txt (line 13))
Requirement already satisfied: scipy==0.19.1 in ./venv/lib/python3.6/site-packages (from -r requirements.txt (line 14))
Requirement already satisfied: seaborn==0.8.1 in ./venv/lib/python3.6/site-packages (from -r requirements.txt (line 15))
Requirement already satisfied: six==1.11.0 in ./venv/lib/python3.6/site-packages (from -r requirements.txt (line 16))
Requirement already satisfied: tensorflow==1.3.0 in ./venv/lib/python3.6/site-packages (from -r requirements.txt (line 17))
Requirement already satisfied: tensorflow-tensorboard==0.1.8 in ./venv/lib/python3.6/site-packages (from -r requirements.txt (line 18))
Requirement already satisfied: tqdm==4.19.4 in ./venv/lib/python3.6/site-packages (from -r requirements.txt (line 19))
Requirement already satisfied: Werkzeug==0.12.2 in ./venv/lib/python3.6/site-packages (from -r requirements.txt (line 20))
Requirement already satisfied: setuptools in ./venv/lib/python3.6/site-packages (from protobuf==3.4.0->-r requirements.txt (line 9))
Requirement already satisfied: wheel>=0.26 in ./venv/lib/python3.6/site-packages (from tensorflow==1.3.0->-r requirements.txt (line 17))
(venv) ~/Programs/book  
```

Figure 3: Image of a terminal running pip to install dependencies from requirements.txt

Install dependencies by running the following command:

```
$ pip install -r requirements.txt
```

This will install all the required dependencies for your system. If they are already installed, this command should simply inform you.

These dependencies are essential for working with all code activities.

As a final step on this activity, let's execute the script `test_stack.py`. That script formally verifies that all the required packages for this book are installed and available in your system.

4. Students, run the script `Chapter_4/activity_1/test_stack.py` to check if the dependencies Python 3, TensorFlow, and Keras are available. Use the following command:

```
$ python3 chapter_4/activity_1/test_stack.py
```

The script returns helpful messages stating what is installed and what needs to be installed.

5. Run the following script command in your terminal:

```
$ tensorboard --help
```

You should see a help message that explains what each command does. If you do not see that message – or see an error message instead – please ask for assistance from your instructor:

Figure 4: Image of a terminal running `python3 test_stack.py`. The script returns messages informing that all dependencies are installed correctly.

If a similar message to the following appears, there is no need to worry: Runtime Warning: compile time version 3.5 of module `'tensorflow.python.framework.fast_tensor_util'` does not match runtime version 3.6 return f(*args, **kwds) That message appears if you are running Python 3.6 and the distributed TensorFlow wheel was compiled under a different version (in this case, 3.5). You can safely ignore that message.

Once we have verified that Python 3, TensorFlow, Keras, TensorBoard, and the packages outlined in `requirements.txt` have been installed, we can continue to a demo on how to train a neural network and then go on to explore a trained network using these same tools.

# Exploring a Trained Neural Network

In this section, we explore a trained neural network. We do that to understand how a neural network solves a real-world problem (predict handwritten digits) and also to get familiar with the TensorFlow API. When exploring that neural network, we will recognize many components introduced in previous sections such as nodes and layers, but we will also see many that we don't recognize (such as activation functions)—we will explore those in further sections. We will then walk through an exercise on how that neural network was trained and then train that same network on our own.

The network that we will be exploring has been trained to recognize numerical digits (integers) using images of handwritten digits. It uses the MNIST dataset (http:// yann. lecun.com/exdb/mnist/), a classic dataset frequently used for exploring pattern recognition tasks.

## MNIST Dataset

The **Modified National Institute of Standards and Technology (MNIST)** dataset contains a training set of 60,000 images and a test set of 10,000 images. Each image contains a single handwritten number. This dataset—which is a derivate from one created by the US Government—was originally used to test different approaches to the problem of recognizing handwritten text by computer systems. Being able to do that was important for the purpose of increasing the performance of postal services, taxation systems, and government services. The MNIST dataset is considered too naïve for contemporary methods. Different and more recent datasets are used in contemporary research (for example, CIFAR). However, the MNIST dataset is still very useful for understanding how neural networks work because known models can achieve a high level of accuracy with great efficiency.

The CIFAR dataset is a machine learning dataset that contains images organized in different classes. Different than the MNIST dataset, the CIFAR dataset contains classes in many different areas such as animals, activities, and objects. The CIFAR dataset is available at: `https://www.cs.toronto.edu/~kriz/cifar.html`.

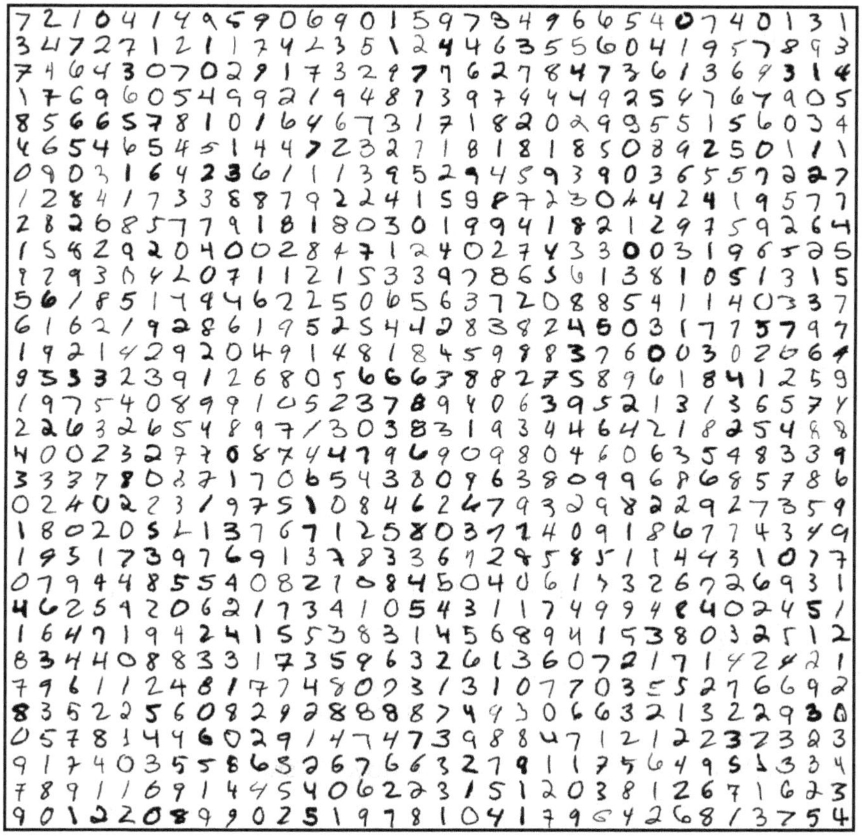

Figure 5: Excerpt from the training set of the MNIST dataset. Each image is a separate 20x20 pixels image with a single handwritten digit. The original dataset is available at: http://yann.lecun.com/exdb/mnist/.

# Training a Neural Network with TensorFlow

Now, let's train a neural network to recognize new digits using the MNIST dataset.

We will be implementing a special-purpose neural network called "Convolutional Neural Network" to solve this problem (we will discuss those in more detail in further sections). Our network contains three hidden layers: two fully connected layers and a convolutional layer. The convolutional layer is defined by the following TensorFlow snippet of Python code:

```
W = tf.Variable(
    tf.truncated_normal([5, 5, size_in, size_out],
    stddev=0.1),
    name="Weights")
B = tf.Variable(tf.constant(0.1, shape=[size_out]),
    name="Biases")

convolution = tf.nn.conv2d(input, W, strides=[1, 1, 1, 1],
padding="SAME")
activation = tf.nn.relu(convolution + B)

tf.nn.max_pool(
activation,
ksize=[1, 2, 2, 1],
strides=[1, 2, 2, 1],
padding="SAME")
```

We execute that snippet of code only once during the training of our network.

The variables W and B stand for weights and biases. These are the values used by the nodes within the hidden layers to alter the network's interpretation of the data as it passes through the network. Do not worry about the other variables for now.

The **fully connected layers** are defined by the following snippet of Python code:

```
W = tf.Variable(
    tf.truncated_normal([size_in, size_out], stddev=0.1),
    name="Weights")
B = tf.Variable(tf.constant(0.1, shape=[size_out]),
    name="Biases")
    activation = tf.matmul(input, W) + B
```

Here, we also have the two TensorFlow variables W and B. Notice how simple the initialization of these variables is: W is initialized as a random value from a pruned Gaussian distribution (pruned with `size_in and size_out`) with a standard deviation of 0.1, and B (the bias term) is initialized as `0.1,` a constant. Both these values will continuously change during each run. That snippet is executed twice, yielding two fully connected networks— one passing data to the other.

Those 11 lines of Python code represent our complete neural network. We will go into a lot more detail in *Chapter 5, Model Architecture* about each one of those components using Keras. For now, focus on understanding that the network is altering the values of W and B in each layer on every run and how these snippets form different layers. These 11 lines of Python are the culmination of dozens of years of neural network research.

Let's now train that network to evaluate how it performs in the MNIST dataset.

# Training a Neural Network

Follow the following steps to set up this exercise:

1. Open two terminal instances.
2. In both of them, navigate to the directory `chapter_4/exercise_a`.
3. In both of them, make sure that your Python 3 virtual environment is active and that the requirements outlined in `requirements.txt` are installed.
4. In one of them, start a TensorBoard server with the following command:
   `$ tensorboard --logdir=mnist_example/`
5. In the other, run the `train_mnist.py` script from within that directory.
6. Open your browser in the TensorBoard URL provided when you start the server.

In the terminal that you ran the script `train_mnist.py`, you will see a progress bar with the epochs of the model. When you open the browser page, you will see a couple of graphs. Click on the one that reads `Accuracy`, enlarge it and let the page refresh (or click on the `refresh` button). You will see the model gaining accuracy as epochs go by.

Use that moment to explain the power of neural networks in reaching a high level of accuracy very early in the training process.

We can see that in about 200 epochs (or steps), the network surpassed 90 percent accuracy. That is, the network is getting 90 percent of the digits in the test set correctly. The network continues to gain accuracy as it trains up to the 2,000th step, reaching a 97 percent accuracy at the end of that period.

Now, let's also test how well those networks perform with unseen data. We will use an open-source web application created by Shafeen Tejani to explore if a trained network correctly predicts handwritten digits that we create.

## Testing Network Performance with Unseen Data

Visit the website `http://mnist-demo.herokuapp.com/` in your browser and draw a number between 0 and 9 in the designated white box:

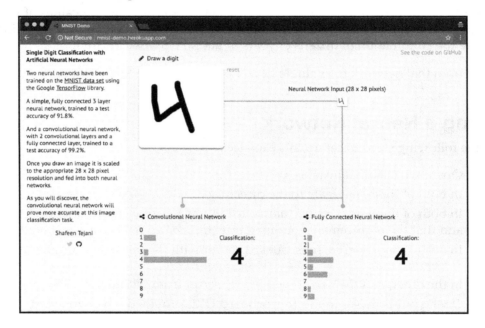

Figure 6: Web application in which we can manually draw digits and test the accuracy of two trained networks

  Source: `https://github.com/ShafeenTejani/mnist-demo` .

In the application, you can see the results of two neural networks. The one that we have trained is on the left (called CNN). Does it classify all your handwritten digits correctly? Try drawing numbers at the edge of the designated area.

For instance, try drawing the number **1** close to the right edge of that area:

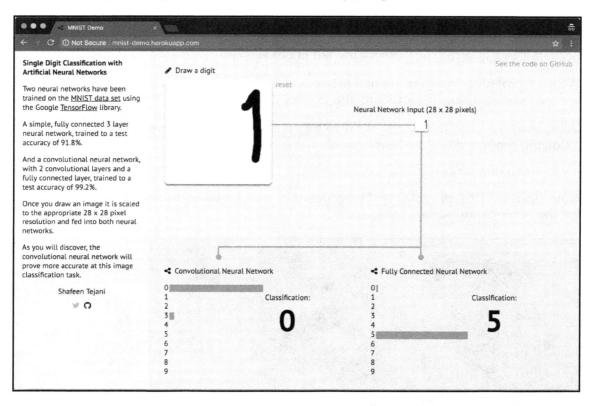

Figure 7: Both networks have a difficult time estimating values drawn on the edges of the area

In this example, we see the number **1** drawn to the right side of the drawing area. The probability of this number being a **1** is **0** in both networks.

The MNIST dataset does not contain numbers on the edges of images. Hence, neither network assigns relevant values to the pixels located in that region. Both networks are much better at classifying numbers correctly if we draw them closer to the center of the designated area. This shows that neural networks can only be as powerful as the data that is used to train them. If the data used for training is very different than what we are trying to predict, the network will most likely produce disappointing results.

# Activity: Exploring a Trained Neural Network

In this section, we will explore the neural network that we have trained during our exercise. We will also train a few other networks by altering hyper parameters from our original one. Let's start by exploring the network trained in our exercise.

We have provided that same trained network as binary files in the directory. Let's open that trained network using TensorBoard and explore its components.

Using your terminal, navigate to the directory `chapter_4/activity_2` and execute the following command to start TensorBoard:

```
$ tensorboard --logdir=mnist_example/
```

Now, open the URL provided by TensorBoard in your browser. You should be able to see the TensorBoard scalars page:

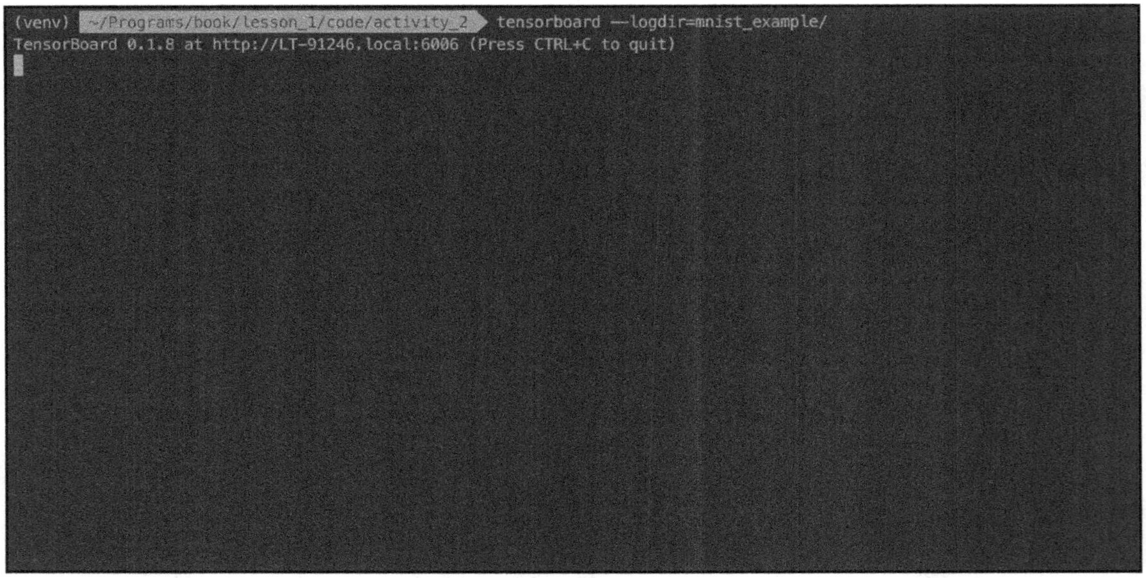

```
(venv)  ~/Programs/book/lesson_1/code/activity_2   tensorboard --logdir=mnist_example/
TensorBoard 0.1.8 at http://LT-91246.local:6006 (Press CTRL+C to quit)
```

Figure 8: Image of a terminal after starting a TensorBoard instance

After you open the URL provided by the `tensorboard` command, you should be able to see the following TensorBoard page:

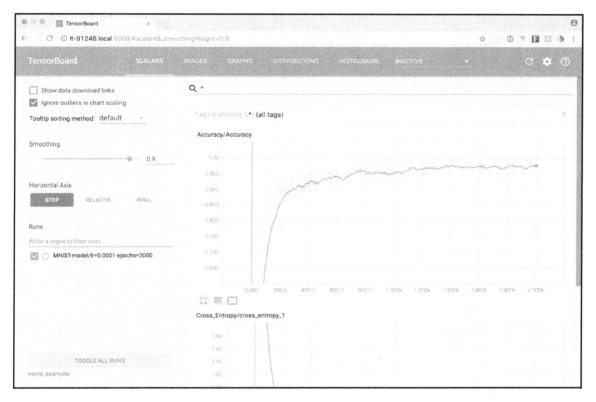

Figure 9: Image of the TensorBoard landing page

Let's now explore our trained neural network and see how it performed.

On the TensorBoard page, click on the **Scalars** page and enlarge the **Accuracy** graph. Now, move the **Smoothing** slider to **0.9**.

The accuracy graph measures how accurate the network was able to guess the labels of a test set. At first, the network guesses those labels completely wrong. This happens because we have initialized the weights and biases of our network with random values, so its first attempts are a guess. The network will then change the weights and biases of its layers on a second run; the network will continue to invest in the nodes that give positive results by altering their weights and biases, and penalize those that don't by gradually reducing their impact on the network (eventually reaching 0). As you can see, this is a really efficient technique that quickly yields great results.

Let's focus our attention on the **Accuracy** graph. See how the algorithm manages to reach great accuracy (> 95 percent) after around 1,000 epochs? What happens between 1,000 and 2,000 epochs?

Would it get more accurate if we continued to train with more epochs? Between 1,000 and 2,000 is when the accuracy of the network continues to improve, but at a decreasing rate. The network may improve slightly if trained with more epochs, but it will not reach 100 percent accuracy with the current architecture.

The script is a modified version of an official Google script that was created to show how TensorFlow works. We have divided the script into functions that are easier to understand and added many comments to guide your learning. Try running that script by modifying the variables at the top of the script:

```
LEARNING_RATE = 0.0001
EPOCHS = 2000
```

Now, try running that script by modifying the values of those variables. For instance, try modifying the learning rate to **0.1** and the epochs to **100**. Do you think the network can achieve comparable results?

There are many other parameters that you can modify in your neural network. For now, experiment with the epochs and the learning rate of your network. You will notice that those two on their own can greatly change the output of your network—but only by so much. Experiment to see if you can train this network faster with the current architecture just by altering those two parameters.

Verify how your network is training using TensorBoard. Alter those parameters a few more times by multiplying the starting values by 10 until you notice that the network is improving. This process of tuning the network and finding improved accuracy is similar to what is used in industrial applications today to improve existing neural network models.

# Summary

In this chapter, we explored a TensorFlow-trained neural network using TensorBoard and trained our own modified version of that network with different epochs and learning rates. This gave you hands-on experiences on how to train a highly performant neural network and also allowed you to explore some of its limitations.

Do you think we can achieve similar accuracy with real Bitcoin data? We will attempt to predict future Bitcoin prices using a common neural network algorithm during *Chapter 5, Model Architecture*. In *Chapter 6, Model Evaluation and Optimization*, we will evaluate and improve that model and, finally, in *Chapter 7, Productization*, we will create a program that serves the prediction of that system via an HTTP API.

# 5
# Model Architecture

Building on fundamental concepts from *Chapter 4*, Introduction to Neural Networks and Deep Learning, we now move into a practical problem: can we predict Bitcoin prices using a deep learning model? In this chapter, we will learn how to build a deep learning model that attempts to do that. We will conclude this chapter by putting all of these components together and building a bare-bones yet complete first version of a deep learning application.

By the end of this chapter, you will be able to:

- Prepare data for a deep learning model
- Choose the right model architecture
- Use Keras, a TensorFlow abstraction library
- Make predictions with a trained model

## Choosing the Right Model Architecture

Deep learning is a filled undergoing intense research activity. Among other things, researchers are devoted to inventing new neural network architectures that can either tackle new problems or increase the performance of previously implemented architectures. In this section, we study both old and new architectures.

Older architectures have been used to solve a large array of problems and are generally considered the right choice when starting a new project. Newer architectures have shown great successes in specific problems, but are harder to generalize. The latter is interesting as references for what to explore next but is hardly a good choice when starting a project.

# Common Architectures

Considering the many architecture possibilities, there are two popular architectures that have often been used as starting points for a number of applications: **convolutional neural networks (CNNs)** and **recurrent neural networks (RNNs)**. These are foundational networks and should be considered starting points for most projects. We also include descriptions of another three networks, due to their relevance in the field: **Long-short term memory (LSTM)** networks, an RNN variant; **generative adversarial networks (GANs)**; and deep reinforcement learning. These latter architectures have shown great success in solving contemporary problems, but are somewhat more difficult to use.

## Convolutional Neural Networks

Convolutional neural networks have gained notoriety for working with problems that have a grid-like structure. They were originally created to classify images, but have been used in a number of other areas, ranging from speech recognition to self-driving vehicles.

CNN's essential insight is to use closely related data as an element of the training process, instead of only individual data inputs. This idea is particularly effective in the context of images, where a pixel located to the right of another pixel is related to that pixel as well, given that they form part of a larger composition. In this case, that composition is what the network is training to predict. Hence, combining a few pixels together is better than using an individual pixel on its own.

The name **convolution** is given to the mathematical representation of this process:

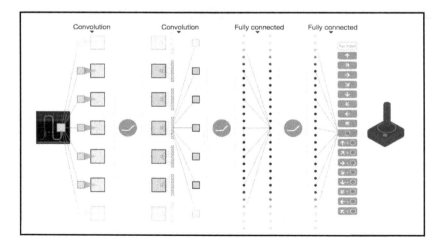

Figure 1: Illustration of the convolution process Image source: Volodymyr Mnih, et al.

For more information, refer Human-level control through deep reinforcement learning. February 2015, Nature. Available at: `https:// storage. googleapis.com/deepmind-media/dqn/DQNNaturePaper.pdf`.

# Recurrent Neural Networks

Convolutional neural networks work with a set of inputs that keep altering the weights and biases of the networks' respective layers and nodes. A known limitation of this approach is that its architecture ignores the sequence of these inputs when determining how to change the networks' weights and biases.

Recurrent neural networks were created precisely to address that problem. RNNs are designed to work with sequential data. This means that at every epoch, layers can be influenced by the output of previous layers. The memory of previous observations in a given sequence plays a role in the evaluation of posterior observations.

RNNs have had successful applications in speech recognition due to the sequential nature of that problem. Also, they are used for translation problems. Google Translate's current algorithm—called **Transformer**—uses an RNN to translate text from one language to another.

 For more information, refer Transformer: A Novel Neural Network Architecture for Language Understanding, by Jakob Uszkoreit, Google Research Blog, August 2017. Available at: `https://ai.googleblog.com/ 2017/08/transformer-novel-neural-network.html`.

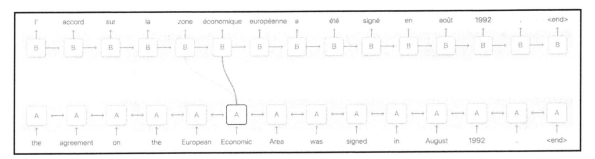

Figure 2: Illustration from distill.pub (https://distill.pub/2016/augmented-rnns/)

Figure 2 shows that words in English are related to words in French, based on where they appear in a sentence. RNNs are very popular in language translation problems.

Long-short term memory networks are RNN variants created to address the vanishing gradient problem. The vanishing gradient problem is caused by memory components that are too distant from the current step and would receive lower weights due to their distance. LSTMs are a variant of RNNs that contain a memory component—called **forget gate**. That component can be used to evaluate how both recent and old elements affect the weights and biases, depending on where the observation is placed in a sequence.

For more details refer, The LSTM architecture was first introduced by Sepp Hochreiter and Jürgen Schmidhuber in 1997. Current implementations have had several modifications. For a detailed mathematical explanation of how each component of an LSTM works, we suggest the article *Understanding LSTM Networks* by Christopher Olah, August 2015, available at http://colah.github.io/posts/2015- 08-Understanding-LSTMs/.

# Generative Adversarial Networks

**Generative adversarial networks** (**GANs**) were invented in 2014 by Ian Goodfellow and his colleagues at the University of Montreal. GANs suggest that, instead of having one neural network that optimizes weights and biases with the objective to minimize its errors, there should be two neural networks that compete against each other for that purpose.

For more details refer, Generative Adversarial Networks by Ian Goodfellow, et al, arXiv. June 10, 2014. Available at: https://arxiv.org/abs/1406.2661.

GANs have a network that generates new data (that is, "fake" data) and a network that evaluates the likelihood of the data generated by the first network to be real or "fake". They compete because both learn: one learns how to better generate "fake" data, and the other learns how to distinguish if the data it is presented with is real or not. They iterate on every epoch until they both converge. That is the point when the network that evaluates generated data cannot distinguish between "fake" and real data any longer.

GANs have been successfully used in fields where data has a clear topological structure. Its original implementation used a GAN to create synthetic images of objects, people's faces, and animals that were similar to real images of those things. This domain of image creation is where GANs are used the most frequently, but applications in other domains occasionally appear in research papers.

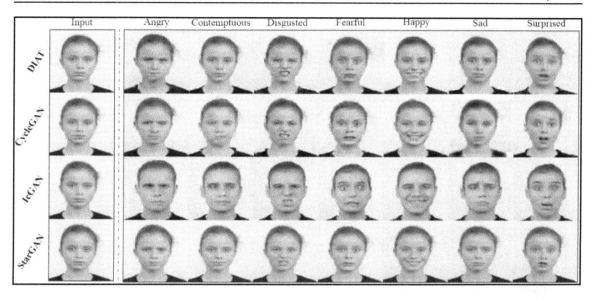

Figure 3: Image that shows the result of different GAN algorithms in changing people's faces based on a given emotion. Source: StarGAN Project. Available at https://github.com/yunjey/StarGAN.

# Deep Reinforcement Learning

The original DRL architecture was championed by DeepMind, a Google-owned artificial intelligence research organization based in the UK.

The key idea of DRL networks is that they are unsupervised in nature and that they learn from trial-and-error, only optimizing for a reward function. That is, different than other networks (which use supervised approaches to optimize for how wrong the predictions are, compared to what is known to be right), DRL networks do not know of a correct way of approaching a problem. They are simply given the rules of a system and are then rewarded every time they perform a function correctly. This process, which takes a very large number of iterations, eventually trains networks to excel in a number of tasks.

For more information, refer Human-level control through deep reinforcement learning, by Volodymyr Mnih et al., February 2015, Nature. Available at: https://storage.googleapis.com/deepmind-media/dqn/DQNNaturePaper.pdf.

Deep Reinforcement Learning models gained popularity after DeepMind created AlphaGo, a system that plays the game Go better than professional players. DeepMind also created DRL networks that learn how to play video games at a superhuman level, entirely on their own:

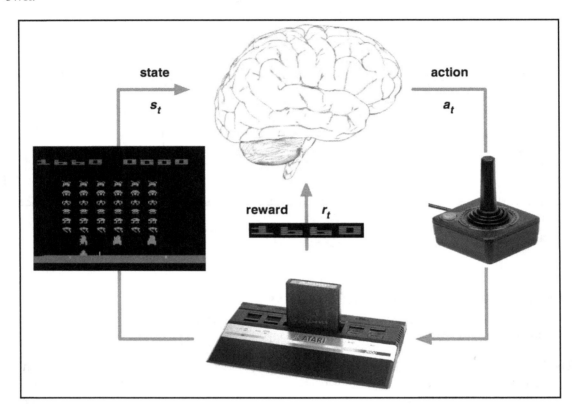

Figure 4: Image that represents how the DQN algorithm works

 For more information refer, DQN was created by DeepMind to beat Atari games. The algorithm uses a deep reinforcement learning solution to continuously increase its reward. Image source: `https://keon.io/ deep-q-learning/`.

| Architecture | Data Structure | Successful Applications |
|---|---|---|
| Convolutional neural networks (CNNs) | Grid-like topological structure (that is, images) | Image recognition and classification |
| Recurrent neural network (RNN) and long-short term memory (LSTM) networks | Sequential data (that is, time-series data) | Speech recognition, text generation, and translation |
| Generative adversarial networks (GANs) | Grid-like topological structure (that is, images) | Image generation |
| Deep reinforcement learning (DRL) | System with clear rules and a clearly defined reward function | Playing video games and self-driving vehicles |

Table 1: Different neural network architectures have shown success in different fields. The network's architecture is typically related to the structure of the problem at hand.

# Data Normalization

Before building a deep learning model, one more step is necessary: data normalization.

Data normalization is a common practice in machine learning systems. Particularly regarding neural networks, researchers have proposed that normalization is an essential technique for training RNNs (and LSTMs), mainly because it decreases the network's training time and increases the network's overall performance.

 For more information refer, *Batch Normalization: Accelerating Deep Network Training by Reducing Internal Covariate Shift* by Sergey Ioffe et. al., arXiv, March 2015. Available at: `https://arxiv.org/abs/1502.03167`.

Deciding on a normalization technique varies, depending on the data and the problem at hand. The following techniques are commonly used.

# Z-score

When data is normally distributed (that is, Gaussian), one can compute the distance between each observation as a standard deviation from its mean.

This normalization is useful when identifying how distant data points are from more likely occurrences in the distribution. The Z-score is defiled by:

$$z_i = \frac{x_i - \mu}{\sigma}$$

Here, $x_i$ is the $i^{th}$ observation, $\mu$ the mean, and $\sigma$ the standard deviation of the series.

For more information, refer Standard score article (Z-score). Wikipedia.Available at: `https://en.wikipedia.org/wiki/Standard_score`.

## Point-Relative Normalization

This normalization computes the difference of a given observation in relation to the first observation of the series. This kind of normalization is useful to identify trends in relation to a starting point. The point-relative normalization is defined by:

$$n_i = \left(\frac{o_i}{o_0}\right) - 1$$

Here, $o_i$ is the $i^{th}$ observation and $o_0$ is the first observation of the series.

As suggested by Siraj Raval in his video, *How to Predict Stock Prices Easily Intro to Deep Learning #7*, available on YouTube at `https://www.youtube.com/watch?v=ftMq5ps503w`.

## Maximum and Minimum Normalization

This normalization computes the distance between a given observation and the maximum and minimum values of the series. This normalization is useful when working with a series in which the maximum and minimum values are not outliers and are important for future predictions.

This normalization technique can be applied with:

$$n_i = \frac{o_i - \min(O)}{\max(O) - \min(O)}$$

Here, $o_i$ is the $i^{th}$ observation, $O$ represents a vector with all O values, and the functions min (O) and max (O) represent the minimum and maximum values of the series, respectively.

During the next Activity, Exploring the Bitcoin Dataset and Preparing Data for Model, we will prepare available Bitcoin data to be used in our LSTM model. That includes selecting variables of interest, selecting a relevant period, and applying the preceding point-relative normalization technique.

# Structuring Your Problem

Compared to researchers, practitioners spend much less time determining which architecture to choose when starting a new deep learning project. Acquiring data that represents a given problem correctly is the most important factor to consider when developing these systems, followed by the understanding of the datasets inherent biases and limitations.

When starting to develop a deep learning system, consider the following questions for reflection:

- **Do I have the right data?** This is the hardest challenge when training a deep learning model. First, define your problem with mathematical rules. Use precise definitions and organize the problem in either category (classification problems) or a continuous scale (regression problems). Now, how can you collect data about those metrics?

- **Do I have enough data?** Typically, deep learning algorithms have shown to perform much better in large datasets than in smaller ones. Knowing how much data is necessary to train a high-performance algorithm depends on the kind of problem you are trying to address, but aim to collect as much data as you can.

- **Can I use a pre-trained model?** If you are working on a problem that is a subset of a more general application—but within the same domain—consider using a pre-trained model. Pretrained models can give you a head start on tackling the specific patterns of your problem, instead of the more general characteristics of the domain at large. A good place to start is the official TensorFlow repository (`https://github.com/tensorflow/models`).

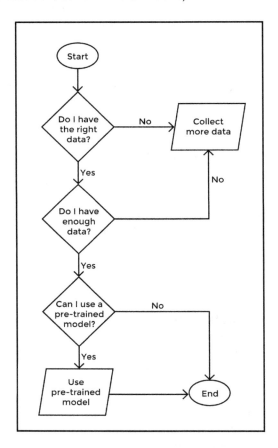

Figure 5: Decision-tree of key reflection questions to be made at the beginning of a deep learning project

In certain circumstances, data may simply not be available. Depending on the case, it may be possible to use a series of techniques to effectively create more data from your input data. This process is known as **data augmentation** and has a successful application when working with image recognition problems.

Classifying plankton with deep neural networks is a good reference article, available at `http://benanne.github.io/2015/03/17/plankton.html`. The authors show a series of techniques for augmenting a small set of image data in order to increase the number of training samples the model has.

# Activity: Exploring the Bitcoin Dataset and Preparing Data for Model

We will be using a public dataset originally retrieved from CoinMarketCap, a popular website that tracks different cryptocurrency statistics. The dataset has been provided alongside this chapter and will be used.

We will be exploring the dataset using Jupyter Notebooks. Jupyter Notebooks provide Python sessions via a web browser that allows you to work with data interactively. They are a popular tool for exploring datasets. They will be used in activities throughout this book.

Using your terminal, navigate to the directory `Chapter_5/activity_3` and execute the following command to start a Jupyter Notebook instance:

```
$ jupyter notebook
```

Now, open the URL provided by the application in your browser. You should be able to see a Jupyter Notebook page with a number of directories from your file system. You should see the following output:

```
(venv) x ~/Programs/book/lesson_2/activity_3  jupyter notebook
[I 00:25:49.252 NotebookApp] Serving notebooks from local directory: /Users/lcapelo/Programs/book/lesson_2/activity_3
[I 00:25:49.252 NotebookApp] 0 active kernels
[I 00:25:49.252 NotebookApp] The Jupyter Notebook is running at:
[I 00:25:49.252 NotebookApp] http://localhost:8888/?token=2a5f88a7e4eedadd758a342ba1310013610353560df95a32
[I 00:25:49.252 NotebookApp] Use Control-C to stop this server and shut down all kernels (twice to skip confirmation).
[C 00:25:49.253 NotebookApp]

    Copy/paste this URL into your browser when you connect for the first time,
    to login with a token:
        http://localhost:8888/?token=2a5f88a7e4eedadd758a342ba1310013610353560df95a32
[I 00:25:49.451 NotebookApp] Accepting one-time-token-authenticated connection from ::1
```

Figure 6: Terminal image after starting a Jupyter Notebook instance. Navigate to the URL shown in a browser, and you should be able to see the Jupyter Notebook landing page.

Now, navigate to the directories and click on the file Activity `Exploring_Bitcoin_` `Dataset.ipynb`. This is a Jupyter Notebook file that will be opened in a new browser tab. The application will automatically start a new Python interactive session for you.

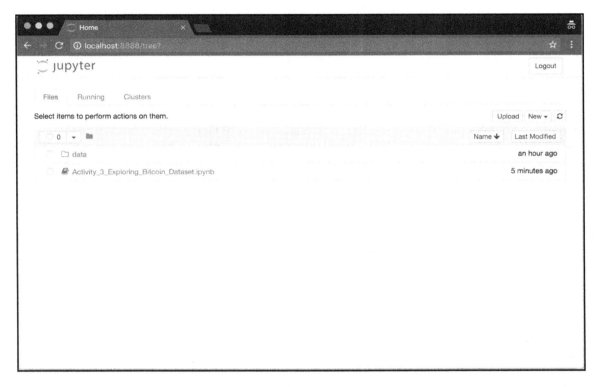

Figure 7: Landing page of your Jupyter Notebook instance

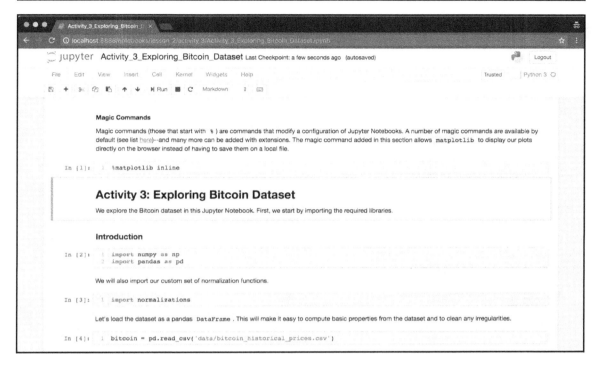

Figure 8: Image of the Notebook Activity_Exploring_Bitcoin_Dataset.ipynb. You can now interact with that Notebook and make modifications.

After opening our Jupyter Notebook, let's now explore the Bitcoin data made available with this chapter.

The dataset `data/bitcoin_historical_prices.csv` contains measurements of Bitcoin prices since early 2013. The most recent observation is on November 2017—the dataset comes from `CoinMarketCap`, an online service that is updated daily. It contains eight variables, two of which (date and week) describe a time period of the data—these can be used as indices—and six others (`open`, `high`, `low`, `close`, `volume`, and `market_capitalization`) that can be used to understand how the price and value of Bitcoin has changed over time:

| Variable | Description |
|----------|-------------|
| date | Date of the observation. |
| iso_week | Week number for a given year. |
| open | Open value for a single Bitcoin coin. |
| high | Highest value achieved during a given day period. |
| low | Lowest value achieved during a given day period. |
| close | Value at the close of the transaction day. |

| | |
|---|---|
| `volume` | The total volume of Bitcoin that was exchanged during that day. |
| `market_capitalization` | Market capitalization, which is explained by Market Cap = Price *Circulating Supply. |

Table 2: Available variables (that is, columns) in the Bitcoin historical prices dataset

Using the open Jupyter Notebook instance, let's now explore the time-series of two of those variables: `close` and `volume`. We will start with those time-series to explore price-fluctuation patterns.

Navigate to the open instance of the Jupyter Notebook Activity `Exploring_Bitcoin_Dataset.ipynb`. Now, execute all cells under the header Introduction. This will import the required libraries and import the dataset into memory.

After the dataset has been imported into memory, move to the Exploration section. You will find a snippet of code that generates a time-series plot for the close variable. Can you generate the same plot for the `volume` variable?

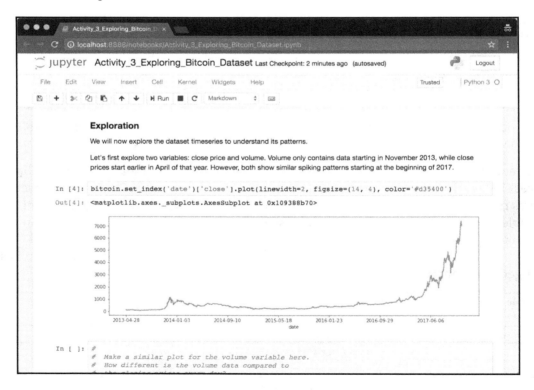

Figure 9: Time-series plot of the closing price for Bitcoin from the close variable. Reproduce this plot, but using the volume variable in a new cell below this one.

You will have most certainly noticed that both variables surge in 2017. This reflects the current phenomenon that both the prices and value of Bitcoin have been continuously growing since the beginning of that year.

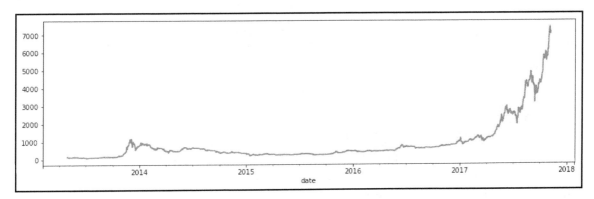

Figure 10: Closing price of Bitcoin coins in USD. Notice an early spike by late 2013 and early 2014. Also, notice how the recent prices have skyrocketed since the beginning of 2017.

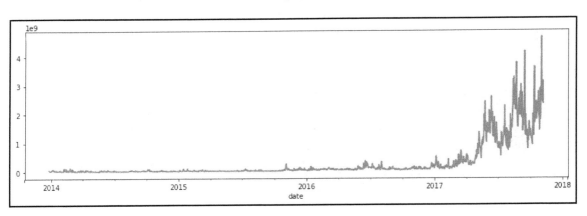

Figure 11: The volume of transactions of Bitcoin coins (in USD) shows that starting in 2017, a trend starts in which a significantly larger amount of Bitcoin is being transacted in the market. The total daily volume varies much more than daily closing prices.

Also, we notice that for many years, Bitcoin prices did not fluctuate as much as in recent years. While those periods can be used by a neural network to understand certain patterns, we will be excluding older observations, given that we are interested in predicting future prices for not-too-distant periods. Let's filter the data for 2016 and 2017 only.

Navigate to the Preparing Dataset for Model section. We will use the pandas API for filtering the data for the years 2016 and 2017. Pandas provide an intuitive API for performing this operation:

```
bitcoin_recent = bitcoin[bitcoin['date'] >= '2016-01-01']
```

The variable `bitcoin_recent` now has a copy of our original bitcoin dataset, but filtered to the observations that are newer or equal to January 1, 2016.

As our final step, we now normalize our data using the point-relative normalization technique described in the *Data Normalization* section. We will only normalize two variables (close and volume) because those are the variables that we are working to predict.

In the same directory containing this chapter, we have placed a script called `normalizations.py`. That script contains the three normalization techniques described in this chapter. We import that script into our Jupyter Notebook and apply the functions to our series.

Navigate to the Preparing Dataset for Model section. Now, use the `iso_week` variable to group all the day observations from a given week using the pandas method `groupby()`. We can now apply the normalization function `normalizations.point_relative_normalization()` directly to the series within that week. We store the output of that normalization as a new variable in the same pandas dataframe using:

```
bitcoin_recent['close_point_relative_normalization'] =
bitcoin_recent.groupby('iso_week')['close'].apply(
lambda x: normalizations.point_relative_normalization(x))
```

The variable `close_point_relative_normalization` now contains the normalized data for the variable `close`. Do the same with the variable `volume`:

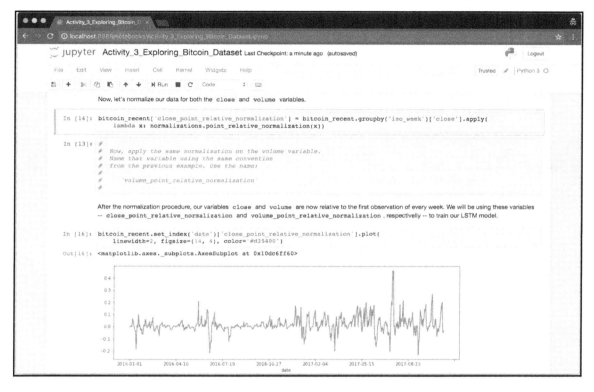

Figure 12: Image of Jupyter Notebook focusing on the section where the normalization function is applied.

The normalized close variable contains an interesting variance pattern every week. We will be using that variable to train our LSTM model.

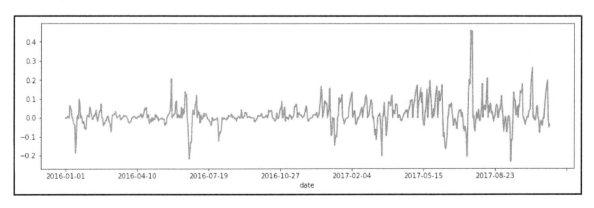

Figure 13: Plot that displays the series from the normalized variable close_point_relative_normalization.

In order to evaluate how well our model performs, we need to test its accuracy versus some other data. We do that by creating two datasets: a training set and a test set. In this activity, we will use 80 percent of the dataset to train our LSTM model and 20 percent to evaluate its performance.

Given that the data is continuous and in the form of a time series, we use the last 20 percent of available weeks as a test set and the first 80 percent as a training set:

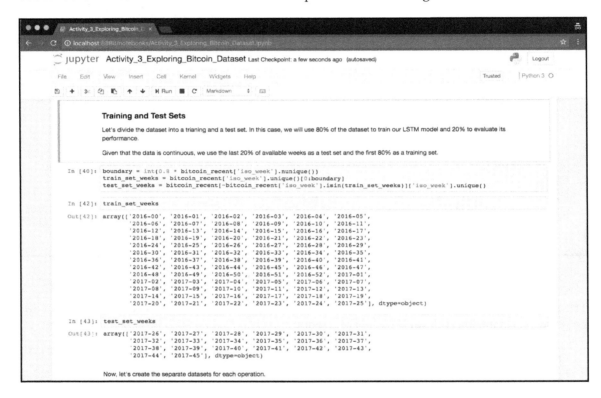

Figure 14: Using weeks to create a training and a test set

Finally, navigate to the Storing Output section and save the filtered variable to disk, as follows:

```
test_dataset.to_csv('data/test_dataset.csv', index=False)
train_dataset.to_csv('data/train_dataset.csv', index=False)
bitcoin_recent.to_csv('data/bitcoin_recent.csv', index=False)
```

In this section, we explored the Bitcoin dataset and prepared it for a deep learning model.

We learned that during the year 2017, the prices of Bitcoin skyrocketed. This phenomenon takes a long time to take place—and may be influenced by a number of external factors that this data alone doesn't explain (for instance, the emergence of other cryptocurrencies). We also used the point-relative normalization technique to process the Bitcoin dataset in weekly chunks. We do this to train an LSTM network to learn the weekly patterns of Bitcoin price changes so that it can predict a full week into the future. However, Bitcoin statistics show significant fluctuations on a weekly basis. Can we predict the price of Bitcoin in the future?

What will those prices be seven days from now? We will be building a deep learning model to explore that question in our next section using Keras.

# Using Keras as a TensorFlow Interface

This section focuses on Keras. We are using Keras because it simplifies the TensorFlow interface into general abstractions. In the backend, the computations are still performed in TensorFlow—and the graph is still built using TensorFlow components—but the interface is much simpler. We spend less time worrying about individual components, such as variables and operations, and spend more time building the network as a computational unit. Keras makes it easy to experiment with different architectures and hyperparameters, moving more quickly towards a performant solution.

As of TensorFlow 1.4.0 (November 2017), Keras is now officially distributed with TensorFlow as `tf.keras`. This suggests that Keras is now tightly integrated with TensorFlow and that it will likely continue to be developed as an open source tool for a long period of time.

# Model Components

As we have seen in *Chapter 4*, *Introduction to Neural Networks and Deep Learning*, LSTM networks also have input, hidden, and output layers. Each hidden layer has an activation function that evaluates that layer's associated weights and biases. As expected, the network moves data sequentially from one layer to another and evaluates the results by the output at every iteration (that is, an epoch).

Keras provides intuitive classes that represent each one of those components:

| Component | Keras Class |
|---|---|
| High-level abstraction of a complete sequential neural network. | `keras.models.Sequential()` |
| Dense, fully-connected layer. | `keras.layers.core.Dense()` |
| Activation function. | `keras.layers.core.Activation()` |
| LSTM recurrent neural network. This class contains components that are exclusive to this architecture, most of which are abstracted by Keras. | `keras.layers.recurrent.LSTM()` |

Table 3: Description of key components from the Keras API. We will be using these components to build a deep learning model.

Keras' `keras.models.Sequential()` component represents a whole sequential neural network. That Python class can be instantiated on its own, then have other components added to it subsequently.

We are interested in building an LSTM network because those networks perform well with sequential data—and time-series is a kind of sequential data. Using Keras, the complete LSTM network would be implemented as follows:

```
from keras.models import Sequential
from keras.layers.recurrent import LSTM
from keras.layers.core import Dense, Activation

model = Sequential()

model.add(LSTM(
units=number_of_periods,
input_shape=(period_length, number_of_periods)
return_sequences=False), stateful=True)
model.add(Dense(units=period_length))
model.add(Activation("linear"))
model.compile(loss="mse", optimizer="rmsprop")
```

*Snippet 1*: LSTM implementation using Keras

This implementation will be further optimized in *Chapter 6, Model Evaluation and Optimization*.

Keras abstraction allows for one to focus on the key elements that make a deep learning system more performant: what the right sequence of components is, how many layers and nodes to include, and which activation function to use. All of these choices are determined by either the order in which components are added to the instantiated `keras.models.Sequential()` class or by parameters passed to each component instantiation (that is, `Activation("linear")` ). The final `model.compile()` step builds the neural network using TensorFlow components.

After the network is built, we train our network using the `model.fit()` method. This will yield a trained model that can be used to make predictions:

```
model.fit(
X_train, Y_train,
batch_size=32, epochs=epochs)
```

*Snippet* 2.1: Usage of `model.fit()`

The variables `X_train` and `Y_train` are, respectively, a set used for training and a smaller set used for evaluating the loss function (that is, testing how well the network predicts data).

Finally, we can make predictions using the `model.predict()` method:

```
model.predict(x=X_train)
```

*Snippet* 2.2: Usage of `model.predict()`

The previous steps cover the Keras paradigm for working with neural networks. Despite the fact that different architectures can be dealt with in very different ways, Keras simplifies the interface for working with different architectures by using three components - network architecture, fit, and predict:

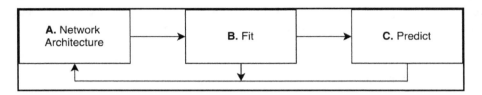

Figure 15: The Keras neural network paradigm: A. design a neural network architecture, B. Train a neural network (or Fit), and C. Make predictions

Keras allows for much greater control within each of those steps. However, its focus is to make it as easy as possible for users to create neural networks in as little time as possible. That means that we can start with a simple model, then add complexity to each one of the steps above to make that initial model perform better.

We will take advantage of that paradigm during our upcoming activity and chapters. In the next activity, we will create the simplest LSTM network possible. Then, in *Chapter 6, Model Evaluation and Optimization*, we will continuously evaluate and alter that network to make it more robust and performant.

# Activity: Creating a TensorFlow Model Using Keras

In this activity, we will create an LSTM model using Keras.

Keras serves as an interface for lower-level programs; in this case, TensorFlow. When we use Keras to design our neural network, that neural network is *compiled* as a TensorFlow computation graph.

Navigate to the open instance of the Jupyter Notebook `Activity_4_Creating_a_ TensorFlow_Model_Using_Keras.ipynb`. Now, execute all cells under the header **Building a Model**. In that section, we build our first LSTM model parametrizing two values: the input size of the training observation (1 equivalent for a single day) and the output size for the predicted period—in our case, seven days:

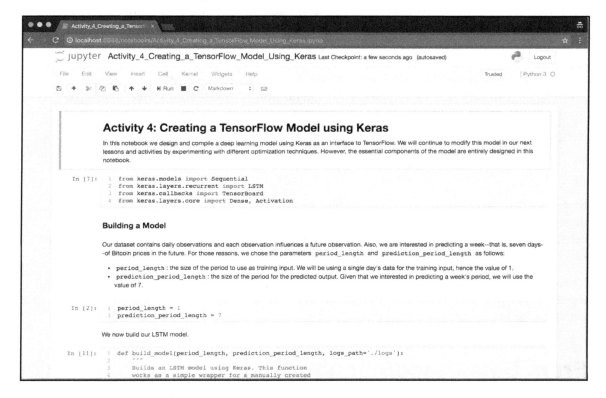

Use the Jupyter Notebook `Activity_4_Creating_a_TensorFlow_Model_Using_Keras.ipynb` to build the same model from the *Model Components* section, parametrizing the period length of input and of output to allow for experimentation.

After the model is compiled, we proceed to store it as an `h5 file` on disk. It is a good practice to store versions of your model on disk occasionally so that you keep a version of the model architecture alongside its predictive capabilities.

Still, on the same Jupyter Notebook, navigate to the header **Saving Model**. In that section, we will store the model as a file on disk with the following command:

```
model.save('bitcoin_lstm_v0.h5')
```

The model 'bitcoin_lstm_v0.h5' hasn't been trained yet. When saving a model without prior training, one effectively only saves the architecture of the model. That same model can later be loaded by using Keras' load_model() function, as follows:

```
1 model = keras.models.load_model('bitcoin_lstm_v0.h5')
```

You may encounter the following warning when loading the Keras library: Using TensorFlow backend. Keras can be configured to use the other backend instead of TensorFlow (that is, Theano). In order to avoid this message, you can create a file called keras.json and configure its backend there. The correct configuration of that file depends on your system. Hence, it is recommended that you visit Keras' official documentation on the topic at https://keras.io/backend/.

In this section, we have learned how to build a deep learning model using Keras, an interface for TensorFlow. We studied core components from Keras and used those components to build the first version of our Bitcoin price-predicting system based on an LSTM model.

In our next section, we will discuss how to put all the components from this chapter together into a (nearly complete) deep learning system. That system will yield our very first predictions, serving as a starting point for future improvements.

# From Data Preparation to Modeling

This section focuses on the implementation aspects of a Deep Learning system. We will use the Bitcoin data from, *Choosing the Right Model Architecture* and the Keras knowledge from, *Using Keras as a TensorFlow Interface* to put both of these components together. This section concludes the chapter by building a system that reads data from a disk and feeds it into a model as a single piece of software.

# Training a Neural Network

Neural networks can take long periods of time to train. Many factors affect how long that process may take. Among them, three factors are commonly considered the most important:

- The network's architecture
- How many layers and neurons the network has
- How much data there is to be used in the training process

Other factors may also greatly impact how long a network takes to train, but most of the optimization that a neural network can have when addressing a business problem comes from exploring those three.

We will be using the normalized data from our previous section. Recall that we have stored the training data in a file called `train_dataset.csv`. We will load that dataset into memory using pandas for easy exploration:

```
import pandas as pd
train = pd.read_csv('data/train_dataset.csv')
```

|   | date | iso_week | close | volume | close_point_relative_normalization | volume_point_relative_normalization |
|---|------|----------|-------|--------|-----------------------------------|-------------------------------------|
| 0 | 2016-01-01 | 2016-00 | 434.33 | 36278900.0 | 0.000000 | 0.000000 |
| 1 | 2016-01-02 | 2016-00 | 433.44 | 30096600.0 | -0.002049 | -0.170410 |
| 2 | 2016-01-03 | 2016-01 | 430.01 | 39633800.0 | 0.000000 | 0.000000 |
| 3 | 2016-01-04 | 2016-01 | 433.09 | 38477500.0 | 0.007163 | -0.029175 |
| 4 | 2016-01-05 | 2016-01 | 431.96 | 34522600.0 | 0.004535 | -0.128961 |

Figure 17: Table showing the first five rows of the training dataset loaded from the `train_d-ataset.csv` file

We will be using the series from the variable `close_point_relative_normalization`, which is a normalized series of the Bitcoin closing prices—from the variable close—since the beginning of 2016.

The variable `close_point_relative_normalization` has been normalized on a weekly basis. Each observation from the week's period is made relative to the difference from the closing prices on the first day of the period. This normalization step is important and will help our network train faster.

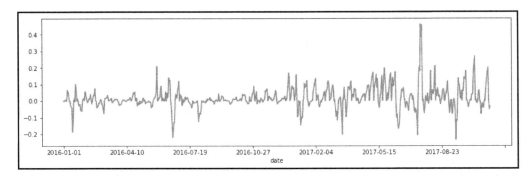

Figure 18: Plot that displays the series from the normalized variable close_point_relative_normalization. This variable will be used to train our LSTM model.

# Reshaping Time-Series Data

Neural networks typically work with vectors and tensors, both mathematical objects that organize data in a number of dimensions. Each neural network implemented in Keras will have either a vector or a tensor that is organized according to a specification as input. At first, understanding how to reshape the data into the format expected by a given layer can be confusing. To avoid confusion, it is advised to start with a network with as little components as possible, then add components gradually. Keras' official documentation (under the section **Layers**) is essential for learning about the requirements for each kind of layer.

The Keras official documentation is available at `https://keras.io/layers/core/`. That link takes you directly to the Layers section.

`NumPy` is a popular Python library used for performing numerical computations. It is used by the deep learning community to manipulate vectors and tensors and prepare them for deep learning systems. In particular, the `numpy.reshape()` method is very important when adapting data for deep learning models. That model allows for the manipulation of NumPy arrays, which are Python objects analogous to vectors and tensors.

We now organize the prices from the variable `close_point_relative_normalization` using the weeks of both 2016 and 2017. We create distinct groups containing seven observations each (one for each day of the week) for a total of 77 complete weeks.

We do that because we are interested in predicting the prices of a week's worth of trading.

 We use the ISO standard to determine the beginning and the end of a week. Other kinds of organizations are entirely possible. This one is simple and intuitive to follow, but there is room for improvement.

LSTM networks work with three-dimensional tensors. Each one of those dimensions represents an important property for the network. These dimensions are:

- **Period length**: The period length, that is, how many observations there are on a period
- **Number of periods**: How many periods are available in the dataset
- **Number of features**: Number of features available in the dataset

Our data from the variable `close_point_relative_normalization` is currently a one-dimensional vector—we need to reshape it to match those three dimensions.

We will be using a week's period. Hence, our period length is seven days (period length = 7). We have 77 complete weeks available in our data. We will be using the very last of those weeks to test our model against during its training period. That leaves us with 76 distinct weeks (number of periods = 76). Finally, we will be using a single feature in this network (number of features = 1)—we will include more features in future versions.

How can we reshape the data to match those dimensions? We will be using a combination of base Python properties and the `reshape()` from the `numpy library`. First, we create the 76 distinct week groups with seven days each using pure Python:

```
group_size = 7
samples = list()
for i in range(0, len(data), group_size):
sample = list(data[i:i + group_size])
if len(sample) == group_size:
samples.append(np.array(sample).reshape(group_size, 1).tolist())

data = np.array(samples)
```

Snippet 3: Python code snippet that creates distinct week groups

The resulting variable data is a variable that contains all the right dimensions. The Keras LSTM layer expects these dimensions to be organized in a specific order: number of features, number of observations, and period length.

Let's reshape our dataset to match that format:

```
X_train = data[:-1,:].reshape(1, 76, 7)
Y_validation = data[-1].reshape(1, 7)
```

Snippet 4: Python code snippet that creates distinct week groups

 Each Keras layer will expect its input to be organized in specific ways. However, Keras will reshape data accordingly in most cases. Always refer to the Keras documentation on layers (`https://keras.io/layers/ core/`) before adding a new layer or if you encounter issues with the shape layers expect.

*Snippet 4* also selects the very last week of our set as a validation set (via `data[-1]`). We will be attempting to predict the very last week in our dataset by using the preceding 76 weeks. The next step is to use those variables to fit our model:

```
model.fit(x=X_train, y=Y_validation, epochs=100)
```

*Snippet 5*: Snippet shows how to train our model

LSTMs are computationally expensive models. They may take up to file minutes to train with our dataset on a modern computer. Most of that time is spent at the beginning of the computation when the algorithm creates the full computation graph. The process gains speed after it starts training:

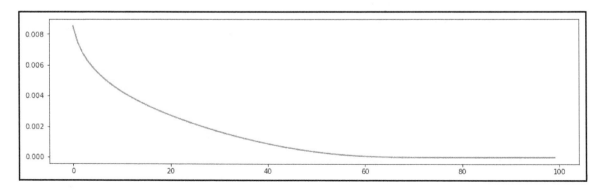

Figure 19: Graph that shows the results of the loss function evaluated at each epoch

This compares what the model predicted at each epoch, then compares with the real data using a technique called mean-squared error. This plot shows those results.

At a glance, our network seems to perform very well: it starts with a very small error rate that continuously decreases. Now, what do our predictions tell us?

# Making Predictions

After our network has been trained, we can now proceed to make predictions. We will be making predictions for a future week beyond our time period.

Once we have trained our model with model.fit(), making predictions is trivial:

```
model.predict(x=X_train)
```

*Snippet 6*: Making a prediction using the same data that we previously used for training

We use the same data for making predictions as the data used for training (the X_train variable). If we have more data available, we can use that instead—given that we reshape it to the format the LSTM requires.

# Overfitting

When a neural network overfits to a validation set, it means that it learns patterns present in the training set, but is unable to generalize it to unseen data (for instance, the test set). During our next chapter, we will learn how to avoid over-fitting and create a system for both evaluating our network and increasing its performance:

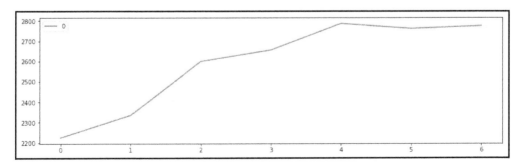

Figure 20: After de-normalization, our LSTM model predicted that in late July 2017, the prices of Bitcoin would increase from $2,200 to roughly $2,800, a 30 percent increase in a single week

# Activity: Assembling a Deep Learning System

In this activity, we bring together all the essential pieces for building a basic deep learning system: data, model, and prediction.

We will continue to use Jupyter Notebooks and will use the data prepared in previous exercises (`data/train_dataset.csv`) as well as the model that we stored locally (`bitcoin_ lstm_v0.h5`).

1. After starting a Jupyter Notebook instance, navigate to the Notebook called `Activity_5_Assembling_a_Deep_Learning_System.ipynb` and open it. Execute the cells from the header to load the required components and then navigate to the header **Shaping Data**:

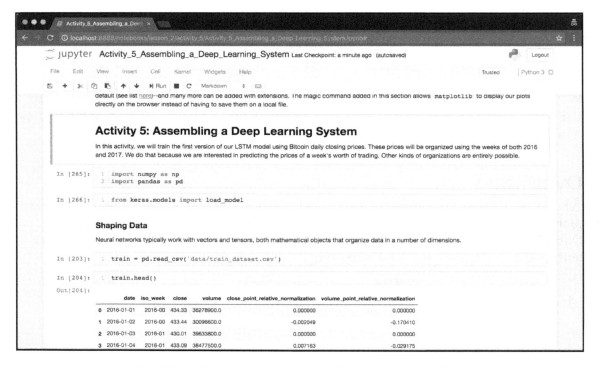

Figure 21: Plot that displays the series from the normalized variable close_point_relative_normalization

The `close_point_relative_normalization` variable will be used to train our LSTM model.

We will start by loading the dataset we prepared during our previous activities. We use pandas to load that dataset into memory.

2. Load the training dataset into memory using pandas, as follows:

```
train = pd.read_csv('data/train_dataset.csv')
```

3. Now, quickly inspect the dataset by executing the following command:

```
train.head()
```

As explained in this chapter, LSTM networks require tensors with three dimensions. These dimensions are: period length, number of periods, and number of features.

Now, proceed to create weekly groups, then rearrange the resulting array to match those dimensions.

4. Feel free to use the provided function `create_groups()` to perform this operation:

```
create_groups(data=train, group_size=7)
```

The default values for that function are 7 days. What would happen if you changed that number to a different value, for instance, 10?

Now, make sure to segregate the data into two sets: training and validation. We do this by assigning the last week from the Bitcoin prices dataset to the evaluation set. We then train the network to evaluate that last week.

Separate the last week of the training data and reshape it using `numpy.reshape()`. Reshaping is important, as the LSTM model only accepts data organized in this way:

```
X_train = data[:-1,:].reshape(1, 76, 7)
Y_validation = data[-1].reshape(1, 7)
```

Our data is now ready to be used in training. Now we load our previously saved model and train it with a given number of epochs.

5. Navigate to the header **Load Our Model** and load our previously trained model:

```
model = load_model('bitcoin_lstm_v0.h5')
```

6. And now, train that model with our training data `X_train` and `Y_validation`:

```
history = model.fit(
x=X_train, y=Y_validation,
batch_size=32, epochs=100)
```

Notice that we store the logs of the model in a variable called history. The model logs are useful for exploring specific variations in its training accuracy and to understand how well the loss function is performing:

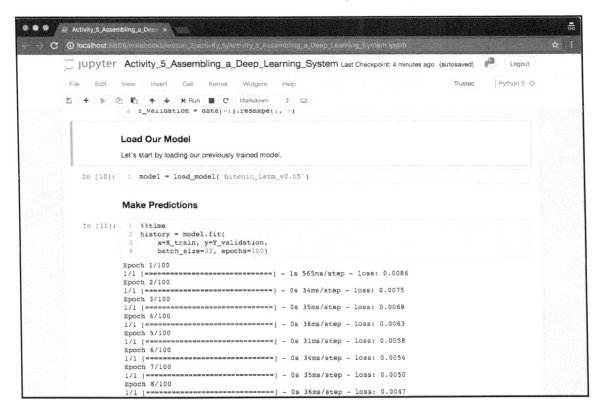

Figure 22: Section of Jupyter Notebook where we load our earlier model and train it with new data

Finally, let's make a prediction with our trained model.

7. Using the same `data X_train`, call the following method:

```
model.predict(x=X_train)
```

8. The model immediately returns a list of normalized values with the prediction for the next seven days. Use the `denormalize()` function to turn the data into US Dollar values. Use the latest values available as a reference for scaling the predicted results:

```
denormalized_prediction = denormalize(predictions, last_weeks_value)
```

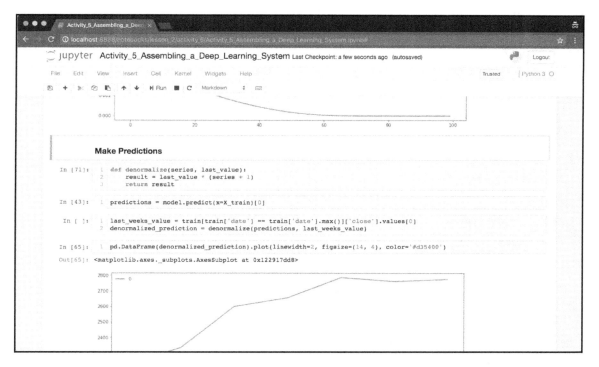

Figure 23: Section of Jupyter Notebook where we predict the prices of Bitcoin for the next seven days.

Our predictions suggest a great price surge of about 30 percent.

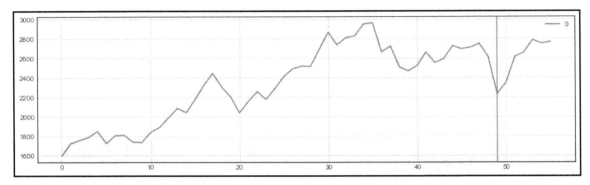

Figure 24: Projection of Bitcoin prices for seven days in the future using the LSTM model we just built

 We combine both time-series in this graph: the real data (before the line) and the predicted data (after the line). The model shows variance similar to the patterns seen before and it suggests a price increase during the following seven days period.

9. After you are done experimenting, save your model with the following command:

```
model.save('bitcoin_lstm_v0_trained.h5')
```

We will save this trained network for future reference and compare its performance with other models.

The network may have learned patterns from our data, but how can it do that with such a simple architecture and so little data? LSTMs are powerful tools for learning patterns from data. However, we will learn in our next sessions that they can also suffer from *overfitting*, a phenomenon common in neural networks in which they learn patterns from the training data that are useless when predicting real-world patterns. We will learn how to deal with that and how to improve our network to make useful predictions.

# Summary

In this chapter, we have assembled a complete deep learning system: from data to prediction. The model created in this activity needs a number of improvements before it can be considered useful. However, it serves as a great starting point from which we will continuously improve.

Our next chapter will explore techniques for measuring the performance of our model and will continue to make modifications until we reach a model that is both useful and robust.

# 6
# Model Evaluation and Optimization

This chapter focuses on how to evaluate a neural network model. Different than working with other kinds of models, when working with neural networks, we modify the network's hyper parameters to improve its performance. However, before altering any parameters, we need to measure how the model performs.

By the end of this chapter, you will be able to:

- Evaluate a model
    - Explore the types of problems addressed by neural networks
    - Explore loss functions, accuracy, and error rates
    - Use TensorBoard
    - Evaluate metrics and techniques
- Hyperparameter optimization
    - Add layers and nodes
    - Explore and add epochs
    - Implement activation functions
    - Use regularization strategies

## Model Evaluation

In machine learning, it is common to define two distinct terms: parameter and hyper **parameter**. Parameters are properties that affect how a model makes predictions from data. Hyper parameters refer to how a model learns from data. Parameters can be learned from the data and modified dynamically. Hyper parameters are higher-level properties and are not typically learned from data. For a more detailed overview, refer to the book Python Machine Learning, by Sebastian Raschka and Vahid Mirjalili (Packt, 2017).

# Problem Categories

Generally, there are two categories of problems solved by neural networks: classification and regression. Classification problems regard the prediction of the right categories from data; for instance, if the temperature is hot or cold. Regression problems are about the prediction of values in a continuous scalar; for instance, what the actual temperature value is?

Problems in these two categories are characterized by the following properties:

- **Classification**: Problems that are characterized by categories. The categories can be different, or not; they can also be about a binary problem. However, they must be clearly assigned to each data element. An example of a classification problem would be to assign the label *car* or *not car* to an image using a Convolutional Neural Network. The MNIST example explored in *Chapter 4, Introduction to Neural Networks and Deep Learning*, is another example of a classification problem.
- **Regression**: Problems that are characterized by a continuous variable (that is, a scalar). These problems are measured in terms of ranges, and their evaluations regard how close to the real values the network is. An example is a time-series classification problem in which a Recurrent Neural Network is used to predict the future temperature values. The Bitcoin price-prediction problem is another example of a regression problem.

While the overall structure of how to evaluate these models is the same for both of these problem categories, we employ different techniques for evaluating how models perform. In the following section, we explore these techniques for either classification or regression problems.

 All of the code snippets in this chapter are implemented in *Activities 6 and 7*. Feel free to follow along, but don't feel that it is mandatory, given that they will be repeated in more detail during the activities.

# Loss Functions, Accuracy, and Error Rates

Neural networks utilize functions that measure how the networks perform when compared to a validation set—that is, a part of the data separated to be used as part of the training process. These functions are called **loss functions**.

Loss functions evaluate how *wrong* a neural network's predictions are; then they will propagate those errors back and make adjustments to the network, modifying how individual neurons are activated. Loss functions are key components of neural networks, and choosing the right loss function can have a significant impact on how the network performs.

How are errors propagated to each neuron in a network?

Errors are propagated via a process called back propagation. Back propagation is a technique for propagating the errors returned by the loss function back to each neuron in a neural network. Propagated errors affect how neurons activate, and ultimately, how they influence the output of that network.

Many neural network packages, including Keras, use this technique by default.

 For more information about the mathematics of backpropagation, please refer to *Deep Learning* by Ian Goodfellow et. al., MIT Press, 2016.

We use different loss functions for regression and classification problems. For classification problems, we use accuracy functions (that is, the proportion of times the predictions were correct). While for regression problems, we use error rates (that is, how close the predicted values were to the observed ones).

The following table provides a summary of common loss functions to utilize, alongside their common applications:

| Problem Type | Loss Function | Problem | Example |
|---|---|---|---|
| Regression | Mean Squared Error (MSE) | Predicting a continuous function. That is, predicting value within a range of values. | Predicting the temperature in the future using temperature measurements from the past. |
| Regression | Root Mean Squared Error(RMSE) | Same as preceding, but deals with negative values. RMSE typically provides more interpretable results. | Same as preceding. |
| Regression | Mean Absolute Percentage Error (MAPE) | Prediction continuous functions. Has better in performance when working with de-normalized ranges. | Predicting the sales for a product using the product properties (for example, price, type, target audience, market conditions). |
| Classification | Binary Cross entropy | Classification between two categories or between two values (that is, `true` or `false`). | Predicting if the visitor of a website is male or female based on their browser activity. |

| Classification | Categorical Cross-entropy | Classification between many categories from a known set of categories. | Predicting the nationality of a speaker based on their accent when speaking a sentence in English. |
|---|---|---|---|

For regression problems, the MSE function is the most common choice. While for classification problems, Binary Cross-entropy (for binary category problems) and Categorical Cross-entropy (for multi-category problems) are common choices. It is advised to start with these loss functions, then experiment with other functions as you evolve your neural network, aiming to gain performance.

For regression problems, the MSE function is the most common choice. While for classification problems, Binary Cross-entropy (for binary category problems) and Categorical Cross-entropy (for multi-category problems) are common choices. It is advised to start with these loss functions, then experiment with other functions as you evolve your neural network, aiming to gain performance.

The network we develop in *Chapter 5, Model Architecture*, uses the MSE as its loss function. In the following section, we explore how that function performs as the network trains.

# Different Loss Functions, Same Architecture

Before moving ahead to the next section, let's explore, in practical terms, how these problems are different in the context of neural networks.

The TensorFlow Playground application is made available by the TensorFlow team to help us understand how neural networks work. Here, we see a neural network represented with its layers: input (on the left), hidden layers (in the middle), and output (on the right).

We can also choose different sample datasets to experiment with on the far-left side. And, finally, on the far-right side, we see the output of the network.

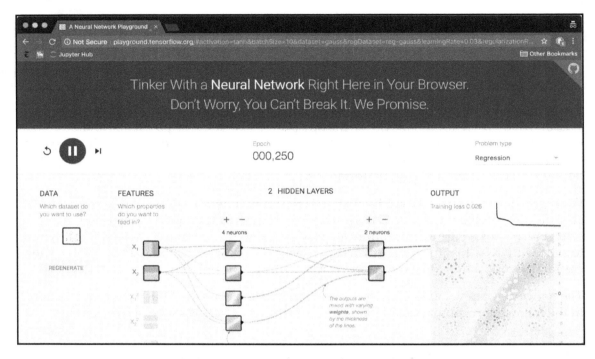

Figure 1: TensorFlow Playground web application. Take the parameters for a neural network in this visualization to gain some

intuition on how each parameter affects the model results.

This application helps us explore the different problem categories we discussed in our previous section. When we choose **Classification** as the **Problem type** (upper right-hand corner), the dots in the dataset are colored with only two color values: either blue or orange.

When we choose **Regression**, the colors of the dots are colored in a range of color values between orange and blue. When working on classification problems, the network evaluates its loss function based on how many blues and oranges the network has gotten wrong; and when working on classification problems, it checks how far away to the right color values for each dot the network was, as shown in the following image:

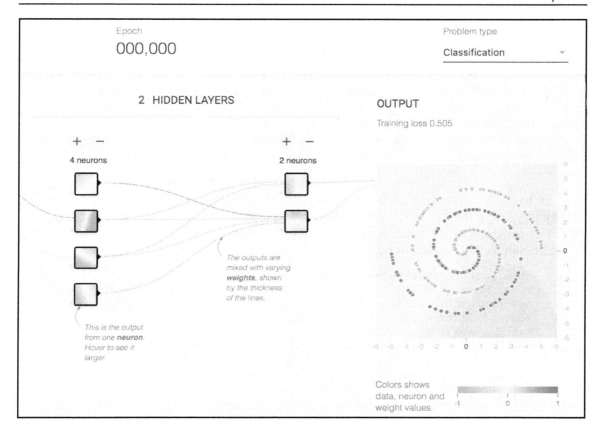

Figure 2: Detail of the TensorFlow Playground application. Different color values are assigned to the dots,

depending on the problem type.

After clicking on the play button, we notice that the numbers in the Training loss area keep going down as the network continuously trains. The numbers are very similar in each problem category because the loss functions play the same role in both neural networks. However, the actual loss function used for each category is different, and is chosen depending on the problem type.

# Using TensorBoard

Evaluating neural networks is where TensorBoard excels. As explained in *Chapter 4, Introduction to Neural Networks and Deep Learning*, TensorBoard is a suite of visualization tools shipped with TensorFlow. Among other things, one can explore the results of loss function evaluations after each epoch. A great feature of TensorBoard is that one can organize the results of each run separately and compare the resulting loss function metrics for each run. One can then make a decision on which hyper parameters to tune and have a general sense of how the network is performing. The best part is that it is all done in real time.

In order to use TensorBoard with our model, we will use a Keras callback function. We do that by importing the `TensorBoard` callback and passing it to our model when calling its `fit()` function. The following code shows an example of how it would be implemented in the Bitcoin model created in our preceding chapters:

```
from keras.callbacks import TensorBoard
model_name = 'bitcoin_lstm_v0_run_0'
tensorboard = TensorBoard(log_dir='./logs/{}'.format(model_name))
model.fit(x=X_train, y=Y_validate,
batch_size=1, epochs=100,
verbose=0, callbacks=[tensorboard])
```

*Snippet 1*: Snippet that implements a TensorBoard callback in our LSTM model

Keras callback functions are called at the end of each epoch run. In this case, Keras calls the TensorBoard callback to store the results from each run on the disk. There are many other useful callback functions available, and one can create custom ones using the Keras API.

 Please refer to the Keras callback documentation (`https://keras.io/callbacks/`) for more information.

After implementing the TensorBoard callback, the `loss` function metrics are now available in the TensorBoard interface. You can now run a TensorBoard process (`with tensorboard --logdir=./logs`) and leave it running while you train your network with `fit()`. The main graphic to evaluate is typically called *loss*. One can add more metrics by passing known metrics to the metrics parameter in the `fit()` function; these will then be available for visualization in TensorBoard, but will not be used to adjust the network weights.

The interactive graphics will continue to update in real time, which allows you to understand what is happening on every epoch.

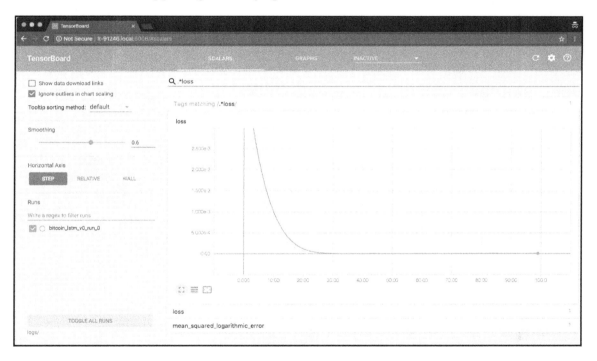

Figure 3: Screenshot of a TensorBoard instance showing the loss function results alongside other metrics added to the metrics parameter

# Implementing Model Evaluation Metrics

In both regression and classification problems, we split the input dataset into three other datasets: train, validation, and test. Both the train and the validation sets are used to train the network. The train set is used by the network as an input, and the validation set is used by the loss function to compare the output of the neural network to the real data, computing how wrong the predictions are. Finally, the test set is used after the network has been trained to measure how the network can perform on data it has never seen before.

 There isn't a clear rule for determining how the train, validation, and test datasets must be divided. It is a common approach to divide the original dataset as 80 percent train and 20 percent test, then to further divide the train dataset into 80 percent train and 20 percent validation. For more information about this problem, please refer to the book *Python Machine Learning*, by Sebastian Raschka and Vahid Mirjalili (Packt, 2017).

In classification problems, you pass both the data and the labels to the neural network as related but distinct data. The network then learns how data is related to each label. In regression problems, instead of passing data and labels, one passes the variable of interest as one parameter and the variables used for learning patterns as another. Keras provides an interface for both of those use cases with the `fit()` method. See *Snippet 2* for an example:

```
model.fit(x=X_train, y=Y_train,
batch_size=1, epochs=100,
verbose=0, callbacks=[tensorboard],
validation_split=0.1,
validation_data=(X_validation, Y_validation))
```

*Snippet 2*: Snippet that illustrates how to use the `validation_split` and `validation_data` parameters

 The `fit()` method can use either the `validation_split` or the `validation_data` parameter, but not both at the same time.

Loss functions evaluate the progress of models and adjust their weights on every run. However, loss functions only describe the relationship between training data and validation data. In order to evaluate if a model is performing correctly, we typically use a third set of data—which is not used to train the network—and compare the predictions made by our model to the values available in that set of data.

That is the role of the test set. Keras provides the method `model.evaluate()`, which makes the process of evaluating a trained neural network against a test set easy. See the following code for an example:

```
model.evaluate(x=X_test, y=Y_test)
```

*Snippet 3:* Snippet that illustrates how to use the `evaluate()` method

The `evaluate()` method returns both the results of the loss function and the results of the functions passed to the `metrics` parameter. We will be using that function frequently in the Bitcoin problem to test how the model performs on the test set.

You will notice that the Bitcoin model looks a bit different than the example above. That is because we are using an LSTM architecture. LSTMs are designed to predict sequences. Because of that, we do not use a set of variables to predict a different single variable—even if it is a regression problem. Instead, we use previous observations from a single variable (or set of variables) to predict future observations of that same variable (or set). The `y` parameter on `Keras.fit()` contains the same variable as the `x` parameter, but only the predicted sequences.

# Evaluating the Bitcoin Model

We created a test set during our activities in *Chapter 4, Introduction to Neural Networks and Deep Learning*. That test set has 19 weeks of Bitcoin daily price observations, which is equivalent to about 20 percent of the original dataset.

We have also trained our neural network using the other 80 percent of data (that is, the train set with 56 weeks of data, minus one for the validation set) in *Chapter 5, Model Architecture*, and stored the trained network on disk (`bitcoin_lstm_v0`). We can now use the `evaluate()` method in each one of the 19 weeks of data from the test set and inspect how that first neural network performs.

In order to do that, though, we have to provide 76 preceding weeks. We have to do this because our network has been trained to predict one week of data using exactly 76 weeks of continuous data (we will deal with this behavior by re-training our network periodically with larger periods in *Chapter 7, Productization,* when we deploy a neural network as a web application):

```
combined_set = np.concatenate((train_data, test_data), axis=1)
    evaluated_weeks = []
    for i in range(0, validation_data.shape[1]):
    input_series = combined_set[0:,i:i+77]

    X_test = input_series[0:,:-1].reshape(1, input_series.shape[1] - 1,)
    Y_test = input_series[0:,-1:][0]

    result = B.model.evaluate(x=X_test, y=Y_test, verbose=0)
    evaluated_weeks.append(result)
```

*Snippet 4*: Snippet that implements the `evaluate()` method to evaluate the performance of our model in a test dataset

In the preceding code, we evaluate each week using Keras' `model.evaluate()`, then store its output in the variable evaluated_weeks. We then plot the resulting MSE for each week in the following figure:

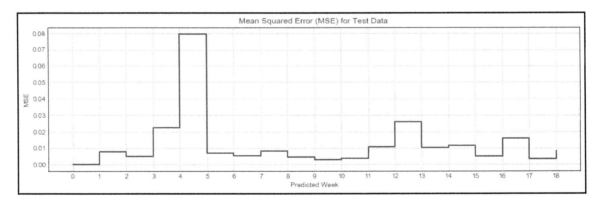

Figure 4: MSE for each week in the test set; notice that in week 5, the model predictions are worse than in any other week

The resulting MSE from our model suggests that our model performs well during most weeks, except for week 5, when its value increases to about $0.08$. Our model seems to be performing well for almost all of the other test weeks

# Overfitting

Our first trained network (`bitcoin_lstm_v0`) may be suffering from a phenomenon known as overfitting. Overfitting is when a model is trained to optimize a validation set, but it does so at the expense of more generalizable patterns from the phenomenon we are interested in predicting. The main issue with overfitting is that a model learns how to predict the validation set, but fails to predict new data.

The loss function used in our model reaches very low levels (about 2.9 * 10-6) at the end of our training process. Not only that, but this happens early: the MSE loss function used to predict the last week in our data decreases to a stable plateau in about epoch 30. This means that our model is predicting the data from week 77 almost perfectly, using the preceding 76 weeks. Could this be the result of overfitting?

Let's look at *Figure 4* again. We know that our LSTM model reaches extremely low values in our validation set (about 2.9 * 10-6), yet it also reaches low values in our test set. The key difference, however, is in the scale. The MSE for each week in our test set is about 4,000 times bigger (on average) than in the test set. This means that the model is performing much worse in our test data than in the validation set. This is worth considering.

The scale, though, hides the power of our LSTM model: even performing much worse in our test set, the predictions' MSE errors are still very, very low. That suggests that our model may be learning patterns from the data.

# Model Predictions

One thing is to measure our model comparing MSE errors, and another is to be able to interpret its results intuitively.

Using the same model, let's now create a series of predictions for the following weeks, using 76 weeks as input. We do that by sliding a window of 76 weeks over the complete series (that is, train plus test sets), and making predictions for each of those windows. Predictions are done using the Keras `model.predict()` method:

```
combined_set = np.concatenate((train_data, test_data), axis=1)

predicted_weeks = []
for i in range(0, validation_data.shape[1] + 1):
input_series = combined_set[0:,i:i+76]
predicted_weeks.append(B.predict(input_series))
```

*Snippet 5*: Snippet that uses the `model.predict()` method for making predictions for all the weeks of the test dataset

In the preceding code, we make predictions using `model.predict()`, then store these predictions in the `predicted_weeks` variable. We then plot the resulting predictions, making the following figure:

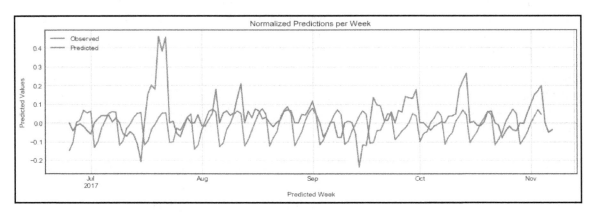

*Figure 5*: MSE for each week in the test set. Notice that in week 5, the model predictions are worse than in any other week.

The results of our model (as shown in *Figure 5*) suggest that its performance isn't all that bad. By observing the pattern from the Predicted line, one can notice that the network has identified a fluctuating pattern happening on a weekly basis, in which the normalized prices go up in the middle of the week, then down by the end of it. With the exception of a few weeks—most notably week 5, the same from our previous MSE analysis—most weeks fall close to the correct values.

Let's now denormalize the predictions so that we can investigate the prediction values using the same scale as the original data (that is, US Dollars). We can do this by implementing a denormalization function that uses the day index from the predicted data to identify the equivalent week on the test data. After that week is identified, the function then takes the first value of that week and uses that value to denormalize the predicted values by using the same point-relative normalization technique, but inverted:

```
def denormalize(reference, series,

normalized_variable='close_point_relative_normalization',
denormalized_variable='close'):
week_values = observed[reference['iso_week']==series['iso_week'].
values[0]]
last_value = week_values[denormalized_variable].values[0]
series[denormalized_variable] =
last_value*(series[normalized_variable]+1)

return series
```

```
predicted_close = predicted.groupby('iso_week').apply
(lambda x: denormalize(observed, x))
```

*Snippet 6*: De-normalization of data using an inverted point-relative normalization technique. The denormalize() function takes the first closing price from the test's first day of an equivalent week.

Our results now compare the predicted values with the test set, using US Dollars. As seen in Figure 5, the bitcoin_lstm_v0 model seems to perform quite well in predicting the Bitcoin prices for the following seven days. But, how can we measure that performance in interpretable terms?

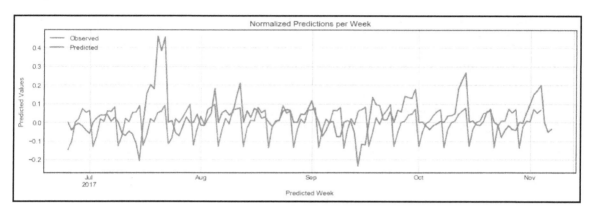

Figure 6: MSE for each week in the test set; notice that in week 5, the model predictions are worse than in any other week

# Interpreting Predictions

Our last step is to add interpretability to our predictions. Figure 6 seems to show that our model prediction matches the test data somewhat closely, but how closely?

Keras' model.evaluate() function is useful for understanding how a model is performing at each evaluation step. However, given that we are typically using normalized datasets to train neural networks, the metrics generated by the model.evaluate() method are also hard to interpret.

In order to solve that problem, we can collect the complete set of predictions from our model and compare it with the test set using two other functions from *Table 1* that are easier to interpret: MAPE and RMSE, implemented as mape() and rmse(), respectively:

```
def mape(A, B):
    return np.mean(np.abs((A - B) / A)) * 100
```

```
def rmse(A, B):
    return np.sqrt(np.square(np.subtract(A, B)).mean())
```

*Snippet 7*: Implementation of the *mape()* and *rmse()* functions

 These functions are implemented using `NumPy`. Original implementations come from `https://stats.stackexchange.com/ questions/58391/mean-absolute-percentage-error-mapein-scikit-learn` (MAPE) and `https:/ /stackoverflow.com/ questions/16774849/mean-squared-error-in-numpy` (RMSE).

After comparing our test set with our predictions using both of those functions, we have the following results:

- Denormalized RMSE: $399.6
- Denormalized MAPE: 8.4 percent

This indicates that our predictions differ, on average, about $399 from real data. That represents a difference of about 8.4 percent from real Bitcoin prices.

These results facilitate the understanding of our predictions. We will continue to use the model.evaluate() method to keep track of how our LSTM model is improving, but will also compute both `rmse()` and `mape()` on the complete series on every version of our model to interpret how close we are to predicting Bitcoin prices.

# Activity:Creating an Active Training Environment

In this activity, we create a training environment for our neural network that facilitates both its training and evaluation. This environment is particularly important to our next chapter, in which we search for an optimal combination of hyperparameters. F

First, we will start both a Jupyter Notebook instance and a TensorBoard instance. Both of these instances can remain open for the remainder of this activity.

1. Using your terminal, navigate to the directory chapter_6/activity_6 and execute the following code to start a Jupyter Notebook instance:

```
$ jupyter notebook
```

2. Open the URL provided by the application in your browser and open the Jupyter Notebook
named `Activity_6_Creating_an_active_training_environment.ipynb`:

Figure 7: Jupyter Notebook highlighting the section Evaluate LSTM Model

3. Also using your terminal, start a TensorBoard instance by executing the following command:

```
$ cd ./chapter_3/activity_6/
$ tensorboard --logdir=logs/
```

4. Open the URL that appears on the screen and leave that browser tab open, as well.

5. Now, load both the training (`train_dataset.csv`) and the test set (`test_dataset. csv`), and also our previously compiled model (`bitcoin_lstm_v0.h5`), into the Notebook.

6. Load the train and test datasets in the Jupyter Notebook instance using:

```
$ train = pd.read_csv('data/train_dataset.csv')
$ test = pd.read_csv('data/test_dataset.csv')
```

7. Also, load our previously compiled model using the following command:

```
$ model = load_model('bitcoin_lstm_v0.h5')
```

Let us now evaluate how our model performed against test data. Our model is trained using 76 weeks to predict a week into the future—that is, the following sequence of seven days. When we built our first model, we divided our original dataset between a training and a test set. We will now take a combined version of both datasets (let's call it combined set) and move a sliding window of 76 weeks. At each window, we execute Keras' `model.evaluate()` method to evaluate how the network performed on that specific week.

8. Execute the cells under the header Evaluate LSTM Model. The key concept of these cells it to call the model.evaluate() method for each of the weeks in the test set. This line is the most important:

```
$ result = model.evaluate(x=X_test, y=Y_test, verbose=0)
```

9. Each evaluation result is now stored in the variable `evaluated_weeks`. That variable is a simple array containing the sequence of MSE predictions for every week in the test set. Go ahead and also plot these results:

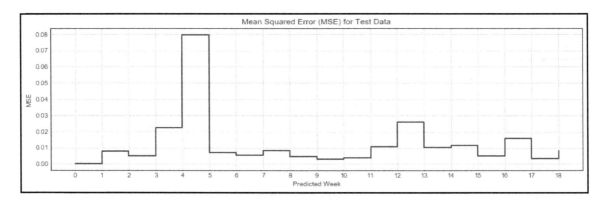

As discussed during our chapter, the MSE loss function is difficult to interpret. To facilitate our understanding of how our model is performing, we also call the method `model.predict()` on each week from the test set and compare its predicted results with the set's values.

10. Navigate to the section **Interpreting Model** Results and execute the code cells under the sub-header **Make Predictions**. Notice that we are calling the method `model.predict()` , but with a slightly different combination of parameters. Instead of using both X and Y values, we only use X:

```
predicted_weeks = []
for i in range(0, test_data.shape[1]):
input_series = combined_set[0:,i:i+76]
predicted_weeks.append(model.predict(input_series))
```

At each window, we will issue predictions for the following week and store the results. We can now plot the normalized results alongside the normalized values from the test set, as shown in the following figure:

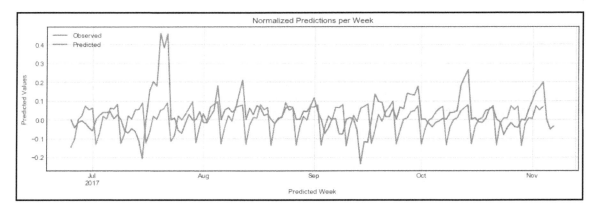

Figure 9: Plotting the normalized values returned from *model.predict()* for each week of the test set

We will also make the same comparisons but using denormalized values. In order to denormalize our data, we must first identify the equivalent week between the test set and the predictions. Then, we take the first price value for that week and use it to reverse the point-relative normalization equation from *Chapter 5, Model Architecture*.

11. Navigate to the header Denormalizing Predictions and execute all cells under that header.

12. In this section, we defiled the function `denormalize()`, which performs the complete de-normalization process. Different than other functions, this function takes in a Pandas DataFrame instead of a NumPy array. We do so for using dates as an index. This is the most relevant cell block from that header:

```
predicted_close = predicted.groupby('iso_week').apply(
    lambda x: denormalize(observed, x))
```

Our denormalized results (as seen in the following figure) show that our model makes predictions that are close to the real Bitcoin prices. But how close?

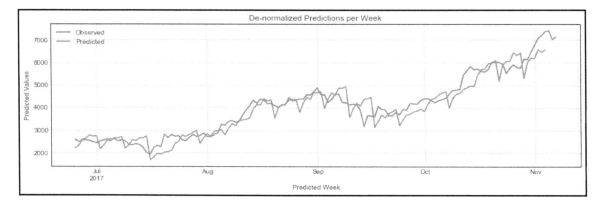

Figure 10: Plotting the denormalized values returned from `model.predict()` for each week of the test set

The LSTM network uses MSE values as its loss function. However, as discussed during the chapter, MSE values are difficult to interpret. To solve that, we implement two functions (loaded from the `script utilities.py`) that implement the functions RMSE and MAPE. Those functions add interpretability to our model by returning a measurement in the same scale that our original data used, and by comparing the difference in scale as a percentage.

13. Navigate to the header Denormalizing Predictions and load two functions from the `utilities.py` script:

```
from scripts.utilities import rmse, mape
```

The functions from the script are actually really simple:

```
def mape(A, B):
    return np.mean(np.abs((A - B) / A)) * 100

def rmse(A, B):
    return np.sqrt(np.square(np.subtract(A, B)).mean())
```

Each function is implemented using NumPy's vector-wise operations. They work well in vectors of the same length. They are designed to be applied on a complete set of results.

Using the `mape()` function, we can now understand that our model predictions are about 8.4 percent away from the prices from the test set. This is equivalent to a root mean squared error (calculated using the `rmse()` function) of about $399.6.

Before moving on to the next section, go back into the Notebook and find the header **Re-train Model with TensorBoard**. You may have noticed that we created a helper function called `train_model()`. This function is a wrapper around our model that trains (using `model.fit()`) our model, storing its respective results under a new directory. Those results are then used by TensorBoard as a discriminator, in order to display statistics for different models.

14. Go ahead and modify some of the values for the parameters passed to the `model.fit()` function (try epochs, for instance). Now, run the cells that load the model into memory from disk (this will replace your trained model):

```
model = load_model('bitcoin_lstm_v0.h5')
```

15. Now, run the `train_model()` function again, but with different parameters, indicating a new run version:

```
train_model(X=X_train, Y=Y_validate, version=0, run_number=0)
```

In this section, we learned how to evaluate a network using loss functions. We learned that loss functions are key elements of neural networks, as they evaluate the performance of a network at each epoch and are the starting point for the propagation of adjustments back into layers and nodes. We also explored why some loss functions can be difficult to interpret (for instance, the MSE) and developed a strategy using two other functions—RMSE and MAPE—to interpret the predicted results from our LSTM model.

Most importantly, this chapter concludes with an active training environment. We now have a system that can train a deep learning model and evaluate its results continuously. This will be key when we move to optimizing our network in the next session.

# Hyperparameter Optimization

We have trained a neural network to predict the next seven days of Bitcoin prices using the preceding 76 weeks of prices. On average, that model issues predictions that are about 8.4 percent distant from real Bitcoin prices.

This section describes common strategies for improving the performance of neural network models:

- Adding or removing layers and changing the number of nodes
- Increasing or decreasing the number of training epochs
- Experimenting with different activation functions
- Using different regularization strategies

We will evaluate each modification using the same active learning environment developed by the end of the *Model Evaluation* section, measuring how each one of these strategies may help us develop a more precise model.

## Layers and Nodes - Adding More Layers

Neural networks with single hidden layers can perform fairly well on many problems. Our first Bitcoin model (`bitcoin_lstm_v0`) is a good example: it can predict the next seven days of Bitcoin prices (from the test set) with error rates of about 8.4 percent using a single LSTM layer. However, not all problems can be modeled with single layers.

The more complex the function that you are working to predict is, the higher the likelihood that you will need to add more layers. A good intuition to determine whether adding new layers is a good idea is to understand what their role in a neural network is.

Each layer creates a model representation of its input data. Earlier layers in the chain create lower-level representations, and later layers, higher-level.

While that description may be difficult to translate into real-world problems, its practical intuition is simple: when working with complex functions that have different levels of representation, you may want to experiment with the addition of layers.

# Adding More Nodes

The number of neurons that your layer requires is related to how both the input and output data are structured.

For instance, if you are working to classify a 4 x 4 pixel image into one of two categories, one can start with a hidden layer that has 12 neurons (one for each available pixel) and an output layer that has only two (one for each predicted class).

It is common to add new neurons alongside the addition of new layers. Then, one can add a layer that has either the same number of neurons as the previous one, or a multiple of the number of neurons from the previous layer. For instance, if your first hidden layer has 12 neurons, you can experiment with adding a second layer that has either 12, 6, or 24.

Adding layers and neurons can have significant performance limitations. Feel free to experiment with adding layers and nodes. It is common to start with a smaller network (that is, a network with a small number of layers and neurons), then grow according to its performance gains.

If the above comes across as imprecise, your intuition is right. To quote Aurélien Géron, YouTube's former lead for video classification, *Finding the perfect amount of neurons is still somewhat of a black art.*

 Hands-on Machine Learning with Scikit-Learn and TensorFlow, by Aurelién Géron, published by O'Reilly, March 2017.

Finally, a word of caution: the more layers you add, the more hyper parameters you have to tune—and the longer your network will take to train. If your model is performing fairly well and not overfitting your data, experiment with the other strategies outlined in this chapter before adding new layers to your network.

# Layers and Nodes - Implementation

We will now modify our original LSTM model by adding more layers. In LSTM models, one typically adds LSTM layers in a sequence, making a chain between LSTM layers. In our case, the new LSTM layer has the same number of neurons as the original layer, so we don't have to configure that parameter.

We will name the modified version of our model `bitcoin_lstm_v1`. It is good practice to name each one of the models in which one is attempting different hyperparameter configurations differently. This helps you to keep track of how each different architecture performs, and also to easily compare model differences in TensorBoard. We will compare all the different modified architectures at the end of this chapter.

 Before adding a new LSTM layer, we need to modify the parameter `return_sequences` to True on the first LSTM layer. We do this because the first layer expects a sequence of data with the same input as that of the first layer. When this parameter is set to `False`, the LSTM layer outputs the predicted parameters in a different, incompatible output.

Consider the following code example:

```
period_length = 7
number_of_periods = 76
batch_size = 1

model = Sequential()
model.add(LSTM(
    units=period_length,
    batch_input_shape=(batch_size, number_of_periods, period_length),
    input_shape=(number_of_periods, period_length),
    return_sequences=True, stateful=False))

model.add(LSTM(
    units=period_length,
    batch_input_shape=(batch_size, number_of_periods, period_length),
    input_shape=(number_of_periods, period_length),
    return_sequences=False, stateful=False))

model.add(Dense(units=period_length))
model.add(Activation("linear"))

model.compile(loss="mse", optimizer="rmsprop")
```

*Snippet 8*: Adding a second LSTM layer to the original `bitcoin_lstm_v0` model, making it `bitcoin_lstm_v1`

# Epochs

Epochs are the number of times the network adjust its weights in response to data passing through and its loss function. Running a model for more epochs can allow it to learn more from data, but you also run the risk of overfitting.

When training a model, prefer to increase the epochs exponentially until the loss function starts to plateau. In the case of the `bitcoin_lstm_v0` model, its loss function plateaus at about 100 epochs.

Our LSTM model uses a small amount of data to train, so increasing the number of epochs does not affect its performance in significant ways. For instance, if one attempts to train it at 103 epochs, the model barely gains any improvements. This will not be the case if the model being trained uses enormous amounts of data. In those cases, a large number of epochs is crucial to achieve good performance.

I suggest you use the following association: the larger the date used to train your model, the more epochs it will need to achieve good performance.

# Epochs - Implementation

Our Bitcoin dataset is rather small, so increasing the epochs that our model trains may have only a marginal effect on its performance. In order to have the model train for more epochs, one only has to change the epochs parameter in `model.fit()`:

```
number_of_epochs = 10**3
model.fit(x=X, y=Y, batch_size=1,
    epochs=number_of_epochs,
    verbose=0,
callbacks=[tensorboard])
```

*Snippet 9*: Changing the number of epochs that our model trains for, making it `bitcoin_lstm_v2`

That change bumps our model to v2, effectively making it `bitcoin_lstm_v2`.

# Activation Functions

Activation functions evaluate how much you need to activate individual neurons. They determine the value that each neuron will pass to the next element of the network, using both the input from the previous layer and the results from the loss function—or if a neuron should pass any values at all.

 Activation functions are a topic of great interest in the scientific community researching neural networks. For an overview of research currently being done on the topic and a more detailed review on how activation functions work, please refer to *Deep Learning* by Ian Goodfellow et. al., MIT Press, 2017.

TensorFlow and Keras provide many activation functions—and new ones are occasionally added. As an introduction, three are important to consider; let's explore each of them.

 This section has been greatly inspired by the article *Understanding Activation Functions in Neural Networks* by Avinash Sharma V, available at: `https://medium.com/the-theory-of-everything/ understanding-activation-functions-in-neural-networks- 9491262884e0.`

## Linear (Identity)

Linear functions only activate a neuron based on a constant value. They are defined by:

$$f(x) = c \ ^* \ (0, x)$$

When c = 1, neurons will pass the values as-is, without modification by the activation function. The issue with using linear functions is that, due to the fact that neurons are activated linearly, chained layers now function as a single large layer. In other words, one loses the ability to construct networks with many layers, in which the output of one influences the other:

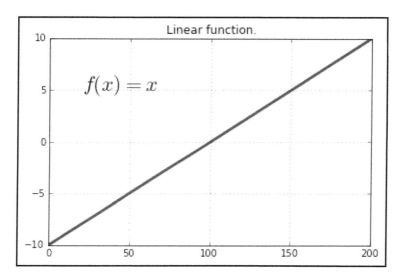

Figure 11: Illustration of a linear function

The use of linear functions is generally considered obsolete for most networks.

# Hyperbolic Tangent (Tanh)

Tanh is a non-linear function, and is represented by the following formula:

$$f(x) = \frac{2}{2 + e^{-2x}} - 1$$

This means that the effect they have on nodes is evaluated continuously. Also, because of its non-linearity, one can use this function to change how one layer influences the next layer in the chain. When using non-linear functions, layers activate neurons in different ways, making it easier to learn different representations from data. However, they have a sigmoid-like pattern which penalizes extreme node values repeatedly, causing a problem called vanishing gradients. Vanishing gradients have negative effects on the ability of a network to learn:

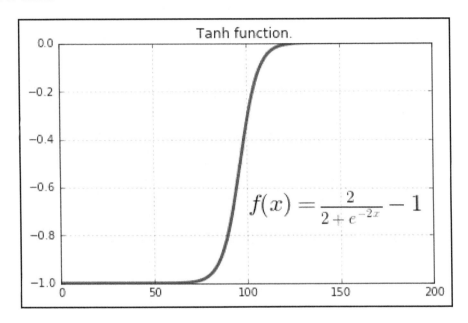

Figure 12: Illustration of a t a n h function

Tanhs are popular choices, but due to fact that they are computationally expensive, ReLUs are often used instead.

# Rectifid Linear Unit

ReLUs have non-linear properties. They are defined by:

$$f(x) = max(0, x)$$

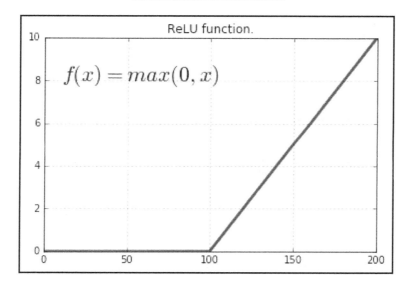

Figure 13: Illustration of a ReLU function

ReLU functions are often recommended as great starting points before trying other functions. ReLUs tend to penalize negative values. So, if the input data (for instance, normalized between -1 and 1) contains negative values, those will now be penalized by ReLUs. That may not be the intended behavior.

We will not be using ReLU functions in our network because our normalization process creates many negative values, yielding a much slower learning model.

# Activation Functions - Implementation

The easiest way to implement activation functions in Keras is by instantiating the Activation() class and adding it to the `Sequential()` model. `Activation()` can be instantiated with any activation function available in Keras (for a complete list, see `https://keras.io/activations/`). In our case, we will use the `tanh` function.

After implementing an activation function, we bump the version of our model to v2, making it `bitcoin_lstm_v3`:

```
model = Sequential()

model.add(LSTM(
    units=period_length,
    batch_input_shape=(batch_size, number_of_periods, period_length),
    input_shape=(number_of_periods, period_length),
    return_sequences=True, stateful=False))

model.add(LSTM(
    units=period_length,
    batch_input_shape=(batch_size, number_of_periods, period_length),
    input_shape=(number_of_periods, period_length),
    return_sequences=False, stateful=False))

model.add(Dense(units=period_length))
model.add(Activation("tanh"))

model.compile(loss="mse", optimizer="rmsprop")
```

*Snippet 10*: Adding the activation function $tanh$ to the `bitcoin_lstm_v2` model, making it `bitcoin_lstm_v3`

There are a number of other activation functions worth experimenting with. Both TensorFlow and Keras provide a list of implemented functions in their respective official documentations. Before implementing your own, start with the ones already implemented in both TensorFlow and Keras.

# Regularization Strategies

Neural networks are particularly prone to overfitting. Overfitting happens when a network learns the patterns of the Neural networks are particularly prone to overfitting. Overfitting happens when a network learns the patterns of the training data but is unable to find generalizable patterns that can also be applied to the test data.he training data but is unable to find generalizable patterns that can also be applied to the test data.

Regularization strategies refer to techniques that deal with the problem of overfitting by adjusting how the network learns. In this book, we discuss two common strategies: L2 and Dropout.

# L2 Regularization

L2 regularization (or weight decay) is a common technique for dealing with overfitting models. In some models, certain parameters vary in great magnitudes. The L2 regularization penalizes such parameters, reducing the effect of these parameters on the network.

L2 regularizations use the $\lambda$ parameter to determine how much to penalize a model neuron. One typically sets that to a very low value (that is, `0.0001`); otherwise, one risks eliminating the input from a given neuron completely.

# Dropout

Dropout is a regularization technique based on a simple question: if one randomly takes away a proportion of nodes from layers, how will the other node adapt? It turns out that the remaining neurons adapt, learning to represent patterns that were previously handled by those neurons that are missing.

The dropout strategy is simple to implement and is typically very effective to avoid overfitting. This will be our preferred regularization.

# Regularization Strategies – Implementation

In order to implement the dropout strategy using Keras, we import the `Dropout()` class and add it to our network immediately after each LSTM layer.

This addition effectively makes our network `bitcoin_lstm_v4`:

```
model = Sequential()
model.add(LSTM(
    units=period_length,
    batch_input_shape=(batch_size, number_of_periods, period_length),
    input_shape=(number_of_periods, period_length),
    return_sequences=True, stateful=False))

model.add(Dropout(0.2))
model.add(LSTM(
    units=period_length,
    batch_input_shape=(batch_size, number_of_periods, period_length),
    input_shape=(number_of_periods, period_length),
    return_sequences=False, stateful=False))

model.add(Dropout(0.2))
```

```
model.add(Dense(units=period_length))
model.add(Activation("tanh"))

model.compile(loss="mse", optimizer="rmsprop")
```

*Snippet 11*: In this snippet, we add the `Dropout ()` step to our model (`bitcoin_lstm_v3`), making it `bitcoin_lstm_v4`

One could have used the L2 regularization instead of Dropout. In order to do that, simply instantiate the `ActivityRegularization()` class with the L2 parameter set to a low value (`0.0001`, for instance). Then, place it in the place where the Dropout() class is added to the network. Feel free to experiment by adding that to the network while keeping both `Dropout()` steps, or simply replace all the `Dropout()` instances with `ActivityRegularization()` instead.

# Optimization Results

All in all, we have created four versions of our model. Three of these versions were created by the application of different optimization techniques outlined in this chapter.

After creating all these versions, we now have to evaluate which model performs best. In order to do that, we use the same metrics used in our first model: MSE, RMSE, and MAPE. MSE is used to compare the error rates of the model on each predicted week. RMSE and MAPE are computed to make the model results easier to interpret.

| Model | MSE (last epoch) | RMSE (whole series) | MAPE (whole series) | Training Time |
|---|---|---|---|---|
| bitcoin_lstm_v0 | - | 399.6 | 8.4 percent | - |
| bitcoin_lstm_v1 | $7.15*10^{-6}$ | 419.3 | 8.8 percent | 49.3 s |
| bitcoin_lstm_v2 | $3.55*10^{-6}$ | 425.4 | 9.0 percent | 1 min 13s |
| bitcoin_lstm_v3 | $2.8*10^{-4}$ | 423.9 | 8.8 percent | 1 min 19s |
| bitcoin_lstm_v4 | $4.8*10^{-7}$ | 442.4 | 8.8 percent | 1 min 20s |

Table 2: Model results for all models

Interestingly, our first model (`bitcoin_lstm_v0`) performed the best in nearly all defiled metrics. We will be using that model to build our web application and continuously predict Bitcoin prices.

# Activity:Optimizing a Deep Learning Model

In this activity, we implement different optimization strategies to the model created in *Chapter 5, Model Architecture* (`bitcoin_lstm_v0`). That model achieves a MAPE performance on the complete denormalization test set of about 8.4 percent. We will try to reduce that gap.

1. Using your terminal, start a TensorBoard instance by executing the following command:

```
$ cd ./chapter_3/activity_7/
$ tensorboard --logdir=logs/
```

2. Open the URL that appears on the screen and leave that browser tab open, as well. Also, start a Jupyter Notebook instance with:

```
$ jupyter notebook
```

Open the URL that appears in a different browser window.

3. Now, open the Jupyter Notebook called `Activity_7_Optimizing_a_deep_learning_model.ipynb` and navigate to the title of the Notebook and import all required libraries. We will load the train and test data like in previous activities. We will also split it into train and test groups using the utility function `split_lstm_input()`.

In each section of this Notebook, we will implement new optimization techniques in our model. Each time we do so, we train a fresh model and store its trained instance in a variable that describes the model version. For instance, our first model, `bitcoin_lstm_v0`, is called`model_v0` in this Notebook. At the very end of the Notebook, we evaluate all models using MSE, RMSE, and MAPE.

4. Now, in the open Jupyter Notebook, navigate to the header **Adding Layers and Nodes**.You will recognize our first model in the next cell. This is the basic LSTM network that we built in *Chapter 5, Model Architecture*. Now, we have to add a new LSTM layer to this network.

Using knowledge from this chapter, go ahead and add a new LSTM layer, compile, and train the model. While training your models, remember to frequently visit the running TensorBoard instance.

You will be able to see each model run and compare the results of their loss functions there:

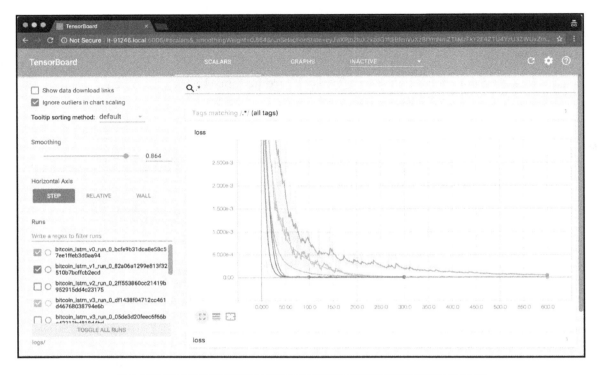

Figure 14: Running the TensorBoard instance, which is displaying many different model runs. TensorBoard is really

useful for tracking model training in real time.

5. Now, navigate to the header Epochs. In this section, we are interested in exploring different magnitudes of **epochs**. Use the utility function `train_model()` to name different model versions and runs:

```
train_model(model=model_v0, X=X_train, Y=Y_validate, epochs=100,
version=0, run_number=0)
```

Train the model with a few different epoch parameters.

At this point, you are interested in making sure the model doesn't overfit the training data. You want to avoid this, because if it does, it will not be able to predict patterns that are represented in the training data but have different representations in the test data.

After you are done experimenting with epochs, move to the next optimization technique: activation functions.

6. Now, navigate to the header **Activation Functions** in the Notebook. In this section, you only need to change the following variable:

```
activation_function = "tanh"
```

We have used the `tanh` function in this section, but feel free to try other activation functions. Review the list available at `https://keras.io/activations/` and try other possibilities.

Our final option is to try different regularization strategies. This is notably more complex and may take a few iterations to notice any gains—especially with so little data. Also, adding regularization strategies typically increases the training time of your network.

7. Now, navigate to the header **Regularization Strategies** in the Notebook. In this section, you need to implement the `Dropout()` regularization strategy. Find the right place to place that step and implement it in our model.

8. You can also try the L2 regularization here, as well (or combine both). Do the same as with `Dropout()`, but now using `ActivityRegularization(l2=0.0001)`.

9. Now, navigate to the header **Evaluate Models** in the Notebook. In this section, we will evaluate the model predictions for the next 19 weeks of data in the test set. Then, we will compute the RMSE and MAPE of the predicted series versus the test series.

We have implemented the same evaluation techniques from Activity 6, all wrapped in utility functions. Simply run all the cells from this section until the end of the notebook to see the results.

Take this opportunity to tweak the values for the preceding optimization techniques and attempt to beat the performance of that model.

# Summary

In this chapter, we learned how to evaluate our model using the metrics mean squared error (MSE), squared mean squared error (RMSE), and mean averaged percentage error (MAPE). We computed the latter two metrics in a series of 19 week predictions made by our first neural network model. We then learned that it was performing well.

We also learned how to optimize a model. We looked at optimization techniques typically used to increase the performance of neural networks. Also, we implemented a number of these techniques and created a few more models to predict Bitcoin prices with different error rates.

In the next chapter, we will be turning our model into a web application that does two things: re-trains our model periodically with new data, and is able to make predictions using an HTTP API interface.

# Productization 7

This chapter focuses on how to *productize* a deep learning model. We use the word *productize* to define the creation of a software product from a deep learning model that can be used by other people and applications.

We are interested in models that use new data when it becomes available, continuously learning patterns from new data and, consequently, making better predictions. We study two strategies to deal with new data: one that re-trains an existing model, and another that creates a completely new model. Then, we implement the latter strategy in our Bitcoin prices prediction model so that it can continuously predict new Bitcoin prices.

This chapter also provides an exercise of how to deploy a model as a web application. By the end of this chapter, we will be able to deploy a working web-application (with a functioning HTTP API) and modify it to our heart's content.

We use a web application as an example of how to deploy deep learning models because of its simplicity and prevalence (after all, web application are quite common), but many other possibilities are available.

By the end of this chapter, you will be able to:

- Handle new data
- Deploy a model as a web application

## Handling New Data

Models can be trained once in a set of data and can then be used to make predictions. Such static models can be very useful, but it is often the case that we want our model to continuously learn from new data—and to continuously get better as it does so.

In this section, we will discuss two strategies on how to re-train a deep learning model and how to implement them in Python.

# Separating Data and Model

When building a deep learning application, the two most important areas are data and model. From an architectural point of view, we suggest that these two areas be separate. We believe that is a good suggestion because each of these areas include functions inherently separated from each other. Data is often required to be collected, cleaned, organized, and normalized; and models need to be trained, evaluated, and able to make predictions. Both of these areas are dependent, but are better dealt with separately.

As a matter of following that suggestion, we will be using two classes to help us build our web application: `CoinMarketCap()` and `Model()`:

- `CoinMarketCap()`: This is a class designed for fetching Bitcoin prices from the following website: `http://www.coinmarketcap.com`. This is the same place where our original Bitcoin data comes from. This class makes it easy to retrieve that data on a regular schedule, returning a Pandas DataFrame with the parsed records and all available historical data. `CoinMarketCap()` is our data component.
- `Model()`: This class implements all the code we have written so far into a single class. That class provides facilities for interacting with our previously trained models, and also allows for the making of predictions using de-normalized data— which is much easier to understand. The `Model()` class is our model component.

These two classes are used extensively throughout our example application and define the data and model components.

## Data Component

The `CoinMarketCap()` class creates methods for retrieving and parsing data. It contains one relevant method, `historic()`, which is detailed in the following code:

```python
@classmethod
def historic(cls, start='2013-04-28', stop=None,
ticker='bitcoin', return_json=False):
    start = start.replace('-', '')
    if not stop:
        stop = datetime.now().strftime('%Y%m%d')
    base_url = 'https://coinmarketcap.com/currencies'
```

```
url = '/{}/historical-10. data/?start={}&end={}'.format(ticker, start,
stop)
r = requests.get(url)
```

*Snippet 1:* historic () method from the CoinMarketCap () class.

This method collects data from the CoinMarketCap website,parses it, and returns a Pandas DataFrame.

The historic() class returns a Pandas DataFrame, ready to be used by the Model() class.

When working in other models, consider creating a program component (for example, a Python class) that fulfils the same functions the CoinMarketCap() class does. That is, create a component that fetches data from wherever it is available, parses that data, and makes it available in a usable format for your modeling component.

The CoinMarketCap() class uses the parameter ticker to determine what cryptocurrency to collect. CoinMarketCap has many other cryptocurrencies available, including very popular ones like Ethereum (ethereum) and Bitcoin Cash (bitcoin-cash). Use the ticker parameter to change the cryptocurrency and train a different model than using the Bitcoin model created in this book.

# Model Component

The Model() class is where we implement the application's model component. That class contains file methods that implement all the different modeling topics from this book. These are:

- build(): Builds an LSTM model using Keras. This function works as a simple wrapper for a manually created model.
- train(): Trains model using data that the class was instantiated with.
- evaluate(): Makes an evaluation of the model using a set of loss functions.
- save(): Saves the model as a file locally.
- predict(): Makes and returns predictions based on an input sequence of weeks ordered observations.

We use these methods throughout this chapter to work, train, evaluate, and issue predictions with our model. The Model() class is an example of how to wrap essential Keras functions into a web application. The preceding methods are implemented almost exactly as in preceded chapters, but with syntactic sugar added for enhancing their interfaces.

For example, the method `train()` is implemented in the following code:

```
def train(self, data=None, epochs=300, verbose=0, batch_size=1):
    self.train_history = self.model.fit(
        x=self.X, y=self.Y,
        batch_size=batch_size, epochs=epochs,
        verbose=verbose, shuffle=False)
    self.last_trained = datetime.now().strftime('%Y-%m-%d %H:%M:%S')
    return self.train_history
```

*Snippet 2:* `train()` method from the `Model()` class. This method trains a model available in `self.model` using data from self.X and self.Y.

In the preceding snippet, you will be able to notice that the `train()` method resembles the solution to *Activities 6* and *7* from *Chapter 6, Model Evaluation and Optimization*. The general idea is that each of the processes from the Keras workflow (build or design, train, evaluate, and predict) can easily be turned into distinct parts of a program. In our case, we made them into methods that can be invoked from the `Model()` class. This organizes our program and provides a series of constraints (such as on the model architecture or certain API parameters) which help us deploy our model in a stable environment.

In the next sections, we explore common strategies for dealing with new data.

# Dealing with New Data

The core idea of machine learning models—neural networks included—is that they can learn patterns from data. Imagine that a model was trained with a certain dataset and it is now issuing predictions. Now, imagine that new data is available. What strategies can we employ so that a model can take advantage of the newly available data to learn new patterns and improve its predictions?

In this section, we discuss two strategies: re-training an old model and training a new model.

# Re-Training an Old Model

With this strategy, we re-train an existing model with new data. Using this strategy, one can continuously adjust the model parameters to adapt to new phenomena. However, data used in later training periods may be significantly different from the earlier data. Such differences may cause significant changes to the model parameters, making it learn new patterns and forget old patterns. This phenomenon is generally referred to as *catastrophic forgetting*.

Catastrophic forgetting is a common phenomenon affecting neural networks. Deep learning researchers have been trying to tackle this problem for many years. DeepMind, a Google-owned deep learning research group from the United Kingdom, has made notable advancements in finding a solution. The article *Overcoming Catastrophic Forgetting in Neural Networks*, by et. al. is a good reference of such work. The paper is available at: https://arxiv. org/pdf/1612.00796.pdf.

The same interface used for training (`model.fit()`) for the first time can be used for training with new data:

```
X_train_new, Y_train_new = load_new_data()

model.fit(x=X_train_new, y=Y_train_new,
batch_size=1, epochs=100,
verbose=0)
```

*Snippet 3*: Snippet that implements a TensorBoard callback in our LSTM model

In Keras, when models are trained, their weight information is kept—this is the model's state. When one uses the `model.save()` method, that state is also saved. And when one invokes the method `model.fit()`, the model is re-trained with the new dataset, using the previous state as a starting point.

In typical Keras models, this technique can be used without further issues. However, when working with LSTM models, this technique has one key limitation: the shape of both train and validation data must be the same. For example, our LSTM model (`bitcoin_lstm_v0`) uses 76 weeks to predict one week into the future. If we attempt to re-train the network with 77 weeks in the coming week, the model raises an exception with information regarding the incorrect shape of data.

One way of dealing with this is to arrange data in the format expected by the model. In our case, we would need to configure our model to predict a future week using 40 weeks. Using this solution, we first train the model with the first 40 weeks of 2017, then continue to re-train it over the following weeks until we reach week 50.

We use the `Model()` class to perform this operation in the following code:

```
M = Model(data=model_data[0*7:7*40 + 7],
    variable='close',
    predicted_period_size=7)
M.build()
6 M.train()
for i in range(1, 10 + 1):
M.train(model_data[i*7:7*(40 + i) + 7])
```

*Snippet 4*: Snippet that implements a re-training technique

This technique tends to be fast to train, and also tends to work well with series that are large. The next technique is easier to implement and works well in smaller series.

# Training a New Model

Another strategy is to create and train a new model every time new data is available. This approach tends to reduce catastrophic forgetting, but training time increases as data increases. Its implementation is quite simple.

Using the Bitcoin model as an example, let's now assume that we have old data for 49 weeks of 2017, and that after a week, new data is available. We represent this with the variables `old_data` and `new_data` in the following quotes:

```
old_data = model_data[0*7:7*48 + 7]
new_data = model_data[0*7:7*49 + 7]

M = Model(data=old_data,
    variable='close',
    predicted_period_size=7)
M.build()
M.train()

M = Model(data=new_data,
    variable='close',
    predicted_period_size=7)
M.build()
M.train()
```

*Snippet 5*: Snippet that implements a strategy for training a new model when new data is available

This approach is very simple to implement and tends to work well for small datasets. This will be the preferred solution for our Bitcoin price-predictions application.

# Activity: Dealing with New Data

In this activity, we re-train our model every time new data is available.

First, we start by importing `cryptonic`. Cryptonic is a simple software application developed for this book that implements all the steps up to this section using Python classes and modules. Consider Cryptonic as a template of how you could develop similar applications.

`cryptonic` is provided as a Python module alongside this activity. First, we will start a Jupyter Notebook instance, and then we will load the `cryptonic` package.

1. Using your terminal, navigate to the directory *Chapter_7/activity_8* and execute the following code to start a Jupyter Notebook instance:

   ```
   $ jupyter notebook
   ```

2. Open the URL provided by the application in your browser and open the Jupyter Notebook named `Activity_8_Re_training_a_model_dynamically.ipynb`.

   Now, we will load both classes from `cryptonic`: `Model()` and`CoinMarketCap()`. These classes facilitate the process of manipulating our model and also the process of getting data from the website CoinMarketCap (`https://coinmarketcap.com/`).

3. In the Jupyter Notebook instance, navigate to the header **Fetching Real-Time Data**. We will now be fetching updated historical data from `CoinMarketCap`. Simply call the method:

   ```
   $ historic_data = CoinMarketCap.historic()
   ```

   The variable `historic_data` is now populated with a Pandas DataFrame that contains data up to today or yesterday. This is great and makes it easier to retrain our model when more data is available.

   The data contains practically the same variables from our earlier dataset. However, much of the data comes from an earlier period. Recent Bitcoin prices have gained a lot of volatility compared to the prices of a few years ago. Before using this data in our model, let's make sure to filter it to dates after January 1, 2017.

4. Using the Pandas API, filter the data for only the dates available in 2017:

```
$ model_data = # filter the dataset using pandas here
```

You should be able to do this by using the date variable as the filtering index. Make sure the data is filtered before you continue.

The class `Model()` compiles all the code we have written so far in all of our activities. We will use that class to build, train, and evaluate our model in this activity.

5. Using the Model() class, we now train a model using the preceding filtered data:

```
M = Model(data=model_data,
    variable='close',
    predicted_period_size=7)
M.build()
M.train()
M.predict(denormalized=True)
```

The preceding steps showcase the complete workflow when using the `Model()` class for training a model.

Next, we'll focus on re-training our model every time more data is available. This re-adjusts the weights of the network to new data.

In order to do this, we have configured our model to predict a week using 40 weeks. We now want to use the remaining 10 full weeks to create overlapping periods of 40 weeks that include one of those 10 weeks at a time, and re-train the model for every one of those periods.

6. Navigate to the header **Re-Train Old Model** in the Jupyter Notebook. Now, complete the range function and the **model_data** filtering parameters, using an index to split the data into overlapping groups of seven days. Then, re-train our model and collect the results:

```
results = []
for i in range(A, B):
    M.train(model_data[C:D])
    results.append(M.evaluate())
```

The variables A, B, C, and D are placeholders. Use integers to create overlapping groups of seven days in which the overlap is of one day.

After you have re-trained your model, go ahead and invoke the `M.predict(denormalized=True)` function and appreciate the results.

Next, we'll focus on creating and training a new model every time new data is available. In order to do this, we now assume that we have old data for 49 weeks of 2017, and after a week, we now have new data. We represent this with the variables `old_data` and `new_data`.

7. Navigate to the header **Training a New Model** and split the data between the variables `old_data` and `new_data`:

```
old_data = model_data[0*7:7*48 + 7]
new_data = model_data[0*7:7*49 + 7]
```

8. Then, train the model with `old_data` first:

```
M = Model(data=old_data,
    variable='close',
    predicted_period_size=7)
M.build()
M.train()
```

This strategy is about building the model from scratch and training it when new data is available. Go ahead and implement that in the following cells.

We now have all the pieces that we need in order to train our model dynamically. In the next section, we will deploy our model as a web application, making its predictions available in the browser via an HTTP API.

In this section, we learned about two strategies for training a model when new data is available:

- Re-training an old model
- Training a new model

The latter creates a new model that is trained with the full set of data, except the observations in the test set. The former trains a model once on available data, then continues to create overlapping batches to re-train that same model every time new data is available.

# Deploying a Model as a Web Application

In this section, we will deploy our model as a web application. We will use an example web application—called "cryptonic"—to deploy our model, exploring its architecture so that we can make modifications in the future. The intention is to have you use this application as a starter for more complex applications; a starter that is fully working and can be expanded as you see fit.

Aside from familiarity with Python, this topic assumes familiarity with creating web applications. Specifically, we assume that you have some knowledge about web servers, routing, the HTTP protocol, and caching. You will be able to locally deploy the demonstrated cryptonic application without extensive knowledge of these topics, but learning these topics will make any future development much easier.

Finally, Docker is used to deploy our web applications, so basic knowledge of that technology is also useful.

# Application Architecture and Technologies

In order to deploy our web applications, we will use the tools and technologies described on Table 1. Flask is key because it helps us create an HTTP interface to our model, allowing us to access an HTTP endpoint (such as /predict) and receive data back in a universal format. The other components are used because they are popular choices when developing web applications:

| Tool or Technology | Description | Role |
|---|---|---|
| Docker | Docker is a technology used for working with applications packaged in the form of containers. Docker is an increasingly popular technology for building web applications. | Packages Python application and UI. |
| Flask | Flask is a micro-framework for building web applications in Python. | Creates application routes |
| Vue.js | JavaScript framework that works by dynamically changing templates on the frontend based on data inputs from the backend. | Renders a user interface. |

| Nginx | Web server easily configurable to route traffic to Dockerized applications and handle SSL certificates for an HTTPS connection. | Routes traffic between user and Flask application. |
|---|---|---|
| Redis | Key-value database. It's a popular choice for implementing caching systems due to its simplicity and speed. | Cache API requests. |

*Table 1*: Tools and technologies used for deploying a deep learning web application

These components fit together, as shown in the following figure:

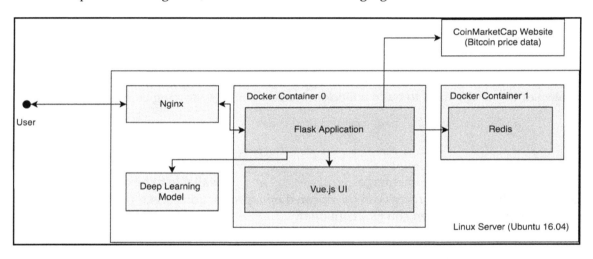

Figure 1: System architecture for the web application built in this project

A user visits the web application using their browser. That traffic is then routed by Nginx to the Docker container containing the Flask application (by default, running on port 5000). The Flask application has instantiated our Bitcoin model at startup. If a model has been given, it uses that model without training; if not, it creates a new model and trains it from scratch using data from CoinMarketCap.

After having a model ready, the application verifies if the request has been cached on Redis—if yes, it returns the cached data. If no cache exists, then it will go ahead and issue predictions which are rendered in the UI.

# Deploying and Using Cryptonic

`cryptonic` is developed as a Dockerized application. In Docker terms, that means that the application can be built as a Docker image and then deployed as a Docker container in either a development or a production environment.

Docker uses files called `Dockerfile` for describing the rules for how to build an image and what happens when that image is deployed as a container. Cryptonic's Dockerfile is available in the following code:

```
FROM python:3.6
COPY . /cryptonic
WORKDIR "/cryptonic"
RUN pip install -r requirements.txt
EXPOSE 5000
CMD ["python", "run.py"]
```

*Snippet 6*: Docker file for the cryptonic image

A Docker file can be used to build a Docker image with the following command:

```
$ docker build --tag cryptonic:latest
```

*Snippet 7*: Docker command for building a Docker image locally

This command will make the image `cryptonic:latest` available to be deployed as a container. The building process can be repeated on a production server, or the image can be directly deployed and then run as a container.

After an image has been built and is available, one can run the cryptonic application by using the command docker run, as shown in the following code:

```
$ docker run --publish 5000:5000 \
      --detach cryptonic:latest
```

*Snippet 8*: Example executing the docker run command in the terminal

The `--publish` flag binds port 5000 on localhost to port 5000 on the Docker container, and `--detach` runs the container as a daemon in the background.

In case you have trained a different model and would like to use that instead of training a new model, you can alter the `MODEL_NAME` environment variable on the docker-compose.yml, as shown in Snippet 9. That variable should contain the filename of the model you have trained and want served (for example, `bitcoin_lstm_v1_trained.h5`)—it should also be a Keras model. If you do that, make sure to also mount a local directory into the / models folder. The directory that you decide to mount must have your model file.

The `cryptonic` application also includes a number of environment variables that you may find useful when deploying your own model:

- `MODEL_NAME`: Allows one to provide a trained model to be used by the application.
- `BITCOIN_START_DATE`: Determines which day to use as the starting day for the Bitcoin series. Bitcoin prices have a lot more variance in recent years than earlier ones. This parameter filters the data to only years of interest. The default is January 1, 2017.
- `PERIOD_SIZE`: Sets the period size in terms of days. The default is 7.
- `EPOCHS`: Configures the number of epochs that the model trains on every run. The default is 300.

These variables can be configured in the `docker-compose.yml` file, as shown in the following code:

```
version: "3"
services:
cache:
image: cryptonic-cache:latest
volumes: - $PWD/cache_data:/data
networks:- cryptonic
ports: - "6379:6379"
    environment:
        - MODEL_NAME=bitcoin_lstm_v0_trained.h5
        - BITCOIN_START_DATE=2017-01-01
        - EPOCH=300
        - PERIOD_SIZE=7
```

*Snippet 9:* `docker-compose.yml` file including environment variables

The easiest way to deploy cryptonic is to use the `docker-compose.yml` file from Snippet 9. This file contains all the specifications necessary for the application to run, including instructions on how to connect with the Redis cache, and what environment variables to use. After navigating to the location of the `docker-compose.yml file`, cryptonic can then be started with the command `docker-compose up`, as shown in the following code:

```
$ docker-compose up -d
```

*Snippet 10*: Starting a Docker application with docker-compose. The flag -d executes the application in the background.

After being deployed, cryptonic can be accessed on port $5000$ via a web browser. The application has a simple user interface with a time-series plot depicting real historical prices (in other words, observed) and predicted future prices from the deep learning model (in other words, predicted). One can also read, in the text, both the RMSE and the MAPE calculated using the `Model().evaluate()` method:

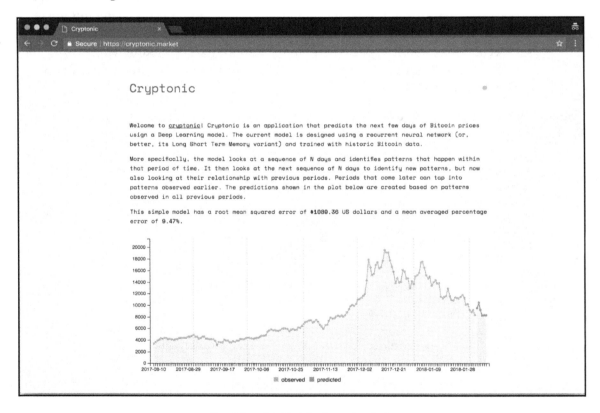

Figure 2: Screenshot of the deployed cryptonic application

Aside from its user interface (developed using `Vue.js`), the application has an HTTP API that makes predictions when invoked.

The API has the endpoint `/predict`, which returns a JSON object containing the de-normalized Bitcoin prices prediction for a week into the future:

```
{
message: "API for making predictions.",
period_length: 7,
result: [
    15847.7,
    15289.36,
    17879.07,
...
    17877.23,
    17773.08
],
    success: true,
    version: 1
}
```

*Snippet 11*: Example JSON output from the /predict endpoint

The application can now be deployed in a remote server and used to continuously predict Bitcoin prices.

# Activity: Deploying a Deep Learning Application

In this activity, we deploy our model as a web application locally. This allows us to connect to the web application using a browser or to use another application through the application's HTTP API. Before we continue, make sure that you have the following applications installed and available in your computer:

- Docker (Community Edition) 17.12.0-ce or later
- Docker Compose (docker-compose) 1.18.0 or later

Both of the components above can be downloaded and installed in all major systems from the website: `http://docker.com/`. These are essential for completing this activity. Make sure these are available in your system before moving forward.

1. Using your terminal, navigate to the cryptonic directory and build the docker images for all the required components:

```
$ docker build --tag cryptonic:latest .
$ docker build --tag cryptonic-cache:latest ./ cryptonic-cache/
```

2. Those two commands build the two images that we will use in this application: cryptonic (containing the Flask application) and cryptonic-cache (containing the Redis cache).

3. After building the images, identify the `docker-compose.yml` file and open it in a text editor. Change the parameter `BITCOIN_START_DATE` to a date other than 2017- 01-01:

```
BITCOIN_START_DATE = # Use other date here
```

4. As a final step, deploy your web application locally using docker-compose, as follows:

```
docker-compose up
```

You should see a log of activity on your terminal, including training epochs from your model.

5. After the model has been trained, you can visit your application on `http://localhost:5000` and make predictions on `http://localhost:5000/predict`:

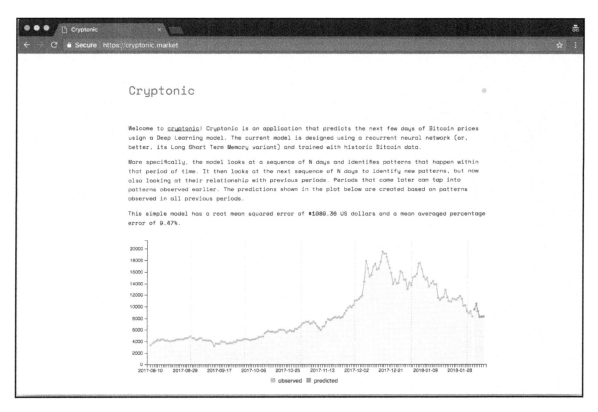

Figure 3: Screenshot of the cryptonic application deployed locally

# Summary

This chapter concludes our journey into creating a deep learning model and deploying it as a web application. Our very last steps included deploying a model that predicts Bitcoin prices built using Keras and using a TensorFlow engine. We finished our work by packaging the application as a Docker container and deploying it so that others can consume the predictions of our model—as well as other applications via its API.

Aside from that work, you have also learned that there is much that can be improved. Our Bitcoin model is only an example of what a model can do (particularly LSTMs). The challenge now is two-fold: how can you make that model perform better as time passes? And, what features can you add to your web application to make your model more accessible? Good luck and keep learning!

# Other Books You May Enjoy

If you enjoyed this book, you may be interested in these other books by Packt:

**Hands-On Data Science and Python Machine Learning**
Frank Kane

ISBN: 978-1-78728-074-8

- Learn how to clean your data and ready it for analysis
- Implement the popular clustering and regression methods in Python
- Train efficient machine learning models using decision trees and random forests
- Visualize the results of your analysis using Python's Matplotlib library
- Use Apache Spark's MLlib package to perform machine learning on large datasets

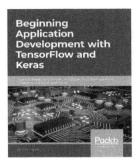

## Beginning Application Development with TensorFlow and Keras
Luis Capelo

ISBN: 978-1-78953-729-1

- Learn how to create an application that generates predictions from deep learning.
- Learn to build a deep learning model with different components together and measuring their performance in prediction.
- Exploring the common components of a neural network and its essential performance.
- Learn how to improve our prediction accuracy.
- Exploring a trained neural network created using TensorFlow.
- Train to deploy TensorFlow and Keras models into real-world applications.

# Leave a review - let other readers know what you think

Please share your thoughts on this book with others by leaving a review on the site that you bought it from. If you purchased the book from Amazon, please leave us an honest review on this book's Amazon page. This is vital so that other potential readers can see and use your unbiased opinion to make purchasing decisions, we can understand what our customers think about our products, and our authors can see your feedback on the title that they have worked with Packt to create. It will only take a few minutes of your time, but is valuable to other potential customers, our authors, and Packt. Thank you!

# Index

two-feature classification models
  training, with scikitlearn  97, 100, 101, 104, 105

# V

validation curves
  about  117
  using, in Python with scikit-learn  120, 122

# W

web scraping
  about  136

HTML, parsing in Jupyter Notebook  143
HTTP requests  136
web page data  136
with Jupyter Notebooks  152, 153, 155, 156

# X

XML (eXtensible Markup Language)  144

# Z

Z-score
  about  220

www.ingramcontent.com/pod-product-compliance
Lightning Source LLC
Chambersburg PA
CBHW080624060326

40690CB00021B/4805